Buckingham Palace

A Complete Guide

Edited by Robin Simon

Published by APOLLO Magazine Ltd

ISBN 0 9522081 0 5

BUCKINGHAM PALACE

A Complete Guide

CONTENTS

1	Introduction: The Royal Collection Trust
2	Buckingham Palace: A tour through history Colin Amery
28	From Buckingham House to Palace: The box within the box within the box John Harris
37	From Blore to Webb: Inventing a sense of tradition Alan Powers
44	'A noble simplicity': Pyne's views of Buckingham House Gervase Jackson-Stops
57	The Nash state rooms: Opulence, ingenuity, and originality John Martin Robinson
63	Royal portraits: Convention and domesticity Brian Allen
73	A place in history: The changing significance of Buckingham Palace Andrew Sanders
80	Imperial splendour: Buckingham Palace in 1913
85	George IV: Furnishing in the French taste - the place of Dominique Daguerre in the Royal Collection John Whitehead
92	Clocks in the Royal Collection: From commissioning to collecting Richard Garnier
96	Dining in state: Towards a greater simplicity Susan Jenkins
102	Fashion in the Gallery: the Picture Gallery's changing hang Charles Noble
108	The Picture Gallery today Christopher Lloyd
115	Zuccarelli in the Royal Collection: George III knew what he liked George Knox
118	A taste for history: Reynolds, West, George III and George IV Martin Postle
124	Forming the taste of a prince: Richard Cosway and George IV's early collecting Stephen Lloyd
127	The Guards and the Palace: Unchanging in splendour Philip Mansel
129	The Arch at Constitution Hill: A new axis for London Dana Arnold
134	The Buckingham Palace Gardens today: A surviving oasis Dana Arnold
136	Contributors

INTRODUCTION

The Royal Collection Trust

The Royal Collection Trust was formally established as a charity with effect from 1 April 1993, and one of its principal objects is to enhance public access to the Collection. The opening of Buckingham Palace is a signal of that determination. It is a curious fact that in 1864 it was suggested that Buckingham Palace should be sold by the Crown and become the home of the National Gallery. In 1898 the opening of the Palace to the public was the subject of earnest debate in Parliament. Neither of these two proposals, of course, took effect, but the spectacular position of the Palace, at the end of the Mall, in the heart of London, makes it a very public symbol of the hopes now being entertained for the future, yet more active, role of the Royal Collection in the cultural life of the nation.

The Royal Collection is quite unlike anything assembled by a group of curators and academics, however distinguished or flexible in their ideas. It is a fascinating, not to say occasionally whimsical, reflection of the taste of successive individuals. Those individuals happened also to be monarchs, with both the will and the resources to indulge their tastes; but they were also conscious of the need, in days before photography, for the scrupulous record of national events; and also to provide a fitting stage for the business of government and the enactment of state ceremony.

This unusual amalgam of interests gives the Collection its unique character, with this one distinguishing overall feature: its exceptionally high quality across the whole range of furniture, paintings, plate, ceramics and sculpture. The Royal Collection is a strange but marvellous creation: privately assembled but, in effect, held in trust by successive monarchs for the nation.

Already the Collection has made determined efforts to become more visible outside London, in the form of loan exhibitions to regional centres. Restoration programmes, in co-operation with Historic Royal Palaces, are being undertaken at Hampton Court, Kensington Palace, the Palace of Holyroodhouse and, of course, Windsor Castle.

All this work means that many more pictures and works of art from this very large collection will be on view than ever before, and all are now subject to careful conservation. Until now, there has never been a complete inventory taken of the objects which the Royal Collection Trust will have in its care, so vast was the proposed task. That record is now in hand and is being created on computer: it will have to cover some ten thousand pictures, enamels and miniatures, twenty thousand drawings, ten thousand watercolours, half a million prints and hundreds upon hundreds of thousands of 'works of art'—a term which covers everything except pictures.

The Royal Collection Trust is financially independent. Its obligations include making a success of the many exhibitions, restoration projects and other activities which it oversees. In time, it will have to review the question of further acquisitions, with an aim to making the Collection as vigorous in the future as it has been in the past, if not quite on the same scale. The Royal Collection recognizes a duty to buying and commissioning works of art from British artists, though not exclusively. It intends to maintain the breadth of vision that inspired such distinguished patrons and collectors as Charles I, George III, George IV, Queen Victoria and Prince Albert.

The Royal Collection will certainly be much more an object of public attention after 1993 than hitherto. The aim of the Royal Collection Trust is to ensure that it continues to embody the nation's historic and artistic heritage.

Acknowledgements

We are particularly indebted to the following for their co-operation during the preparation of this volume: Sir Geoffrey de Bellaigue, Director of the Royal Collections; Mr Hugh Roberts, Surveyor of The Queen's Works of Art; The Hon Jane Roberts, Curator of the Print Room, Windsor; Mr Christopher Lloyd, Surveyor of The Queen's Pictures; Mr Dickie Arbiter, Director of Media Relations, Royal Collection Enterprises; Miss Gwyneth Campling, Head of Photographic Services, Royal Collection Enterprises; Miss Belinda Harley, Assistant Private Secretary to HRH The Prince of Wales; Dr Brian Allen and Miss Elizabeth Powys, The Paul Mellon Centre for Studies in British Art; Dr Andrew Sanders; Mr Paul Collen, The Royal College of Music.

Frontispiece (opposite)
The shipbuilder and his wife (Jan Rijcksen or Harden (1560/1–1637) and Griet Jans) by Rembrandt Harmensz van Rijn (1606–69), signed and dated 1633 (detail). Oil on canvas, 114 × 169 cm. One of the outstanding masterpieces in the Royal Collection on view in the Picture Gallery at Buckingham Palace

Buckingham Palace

A tour through history

COLIN AMERY

For the first time, Buckingham Palace is open to the general public.
Throughout its long history, it has always been both a private dwelling
and a setting for the most splendid state occasions.
It remains the grandest example of a working palace

Palaces are places of power and mystery. Throughout the world from Potala to Versailles great edifices have been built to enshrine ideas of absolutism or to offer a hint of the prospect of heaven on earth. History has encouraged us to believe that behind palace walls life follows elevated and arcane rituals that are somehow both timeless and crucial. Mystery is important in sustaining historical myths of sovereignty and power—palaces have kept secrets of courtly life for centuries, they have sustained cabals and protected privilege. Glory and aggrandisement may not be the style of the late twentieth century but there is no doubt that palaces can still provide a sense of national historical and cultural continuity.

In London the decision to open the sealed doors of Buckingham Palace to the general public has stimulated an interest that lies somewhere between wonder and curiosity. It provides an extraordinary opportunity to view a hitherto invisible pantheon of British royal taste, collecting and architectural achievement. There is an added fascination in the fact that Buckingham Palace is the best known of the few occupied, working royal palaces in the world. Unlike Versailles today, for example, where visitors have to imagine a recreation of court life, at Buckingham Palace you can be confident that a real monarch will still appear on the balcony; that real guards are protecting a real sovereign; and that the courtiers continue to work in their offices to ensure that the duties and rituals of constitutional monarchy continue to be performed with dignity, discipline and dispatch.

Visitors to Buckingham Palace will see eighteen major State Rooms and will absorb the atmosphere of a palace that has grown and changed substantially since the reign of its principal creator, King George IV. For many visitors the palace already holds a potent place in their hearts. Many will remember the photographs of Their Majesties King George VI and Queen Elizabeth looking at the ruins of the chapel which was bombed while they were living at Buckingham Palace in the darkest days of the London Blitz during the Second World War. Many more will recall the moment when Her Majesty Queen Elizabeth II rode in the State Coach to her Coronation in 1953, passing through the great gates of the palace forecourt into a mass of her people greeting her with almost palpable goodwill. That balcony draped in red velvet beneath the ceremonial Royal Standard has so often been the focus of national feeling when the royal family has appeared to symbolize the heart of an ancient and proud kingdom on important national occasions.

But behind the familiar palace façade and the clockwork perfection of the changing of the guard, the great rooms are in regular official and family use. Some 450 people work in the palace and during each year some 40,000 people are entertained there. The Queen meets her ministers there, receives ambassadors, high commissioners and state visitors while maintaining a tradition of palatial hospitality that is both formal and welcoming. The architecture and decoration is not overpowering—indeed there is something very Edwardian and comfortable about the first impression a visitor receives. There is a lot of red and gold about—acres of scarlet carpet and splashes of red liveries and uniforms. The climb up the grand staircase from the low-ceilinged Grand Hall provides something of an architectural tour de force which gives the appropriate sense of anticipation of the riches ahead.

Visitors to the spectacular sequence of rooms now on view enter through the Ambassadors' Entrance (see plan, p. 4). This is where senior diplomats and others who have the entrée traditionally arrive at the palace. In the hall here hang royal portraits of Hanoverian monarchs, George I and George II and Frederick, Prince of Wales. From here we pass into the Quadrangle of the Palace—a great sweep of gravel which looks its best when a State Visit arrives. Then the carriages roll through the central arch of the east front (to the right) and arrive under the porte-cochère of the Grand Entrance (left). The two-storeyed portico of the Grand Entrance is one of Nash's best compositions and the architecture is richly embellished by sculpture. The pediment of the portico contains some rich carvings representing Britannia in her chariot accompanied by tritons and Neptune. Nash had intended the pediment to be seen against the sky and the additional attic storey put on by Blore rather spoils this effect.

The extra storey, however, did provide space for the installation of more sculpture in the form of two large relief panels by Sir Richard Westmacott, to the south *The death of Nelson* and to the north, *Meeting of Blücher and Wellington*, both originally intended for the parapet of the Marble Arch. Standing on the pediment are fine Coade stone figures made in 1827 by William Croggan of *Neptune*, *Commerce* and *Navigation*. Despite all this grandeur, even the State visitor will alight from his carriage on to good oldfashioned white linoleum laid on the steps (very practical with so many horses around).

The Grand Hall is approached via a short flight of steps which leads to a low-ceilinged hall designed ingeniously by Nash to maximize a sense of processional stepped spaces. It is in the Grand Hall (Plate I) that the visitor sees for the first time the cream and gold colour scheme devised in 1902 by C. H. Bessant when he was commissioned to redecorate almost the whole of the palace. Bessant was encouraged by King Edward VII to introduce the fashionable French taste that was then current at the time of the Entente Cordiale. It was at this time that much of the mid-Victorian polychromy that had been so favoured at Buckingham Palace by Queen Victoria and Prince Albert under the influence of Ludwig Grüner was obliterated.

Ludwig Grüner was born in Dresden and had been trained as an artist in Rome. He was an important influence upon the Prince Consort and was really responsible for encouraging the Prince's interest in Raphael. He carried out the decorative painting of the main Nash Staircase at Buckingham Palace, work which was later painted over at the time of the enthusiasm for French *dix-huitième* taste encouraged by Edward VII, and also the internal painting at Queen Victoria's house Osborne on the Isle of Wight. Visitors to the Palace today see virtually nothing of Grüner or of Prince Albert's favoured renaissance cinquecento style of interior decoration, although some of it must survive underneath Bessant's redecoration.

One of the more touching things to observe in the Grand Hall is at the centre of top of the chimney-piece and overmantel that was designed by Joshua Theakston that occupies the raised end of the hall (see Plate I). This rather grandly carved marble is topped by a small bust of King George IV—a modest tribute to the man who really created the Palace (Fig. 1).

Proceeding up the Grand Staircase there is a strong sense here of the very high quality of the craftsmanship that was intended for the early nineteenth-century palace. This is particularly evident in the quality of the remarkable gilt-bronze balustrade. It was made by Samuel Parker in 1828–30 in a design of scrolling acanthus leaves and bands of oak leaves and acorns surmounted by a laurel rope. The balustrade is actually more powerful than the architecture, despite the fact that spatially this is one of the more interesting parts of the palace. The rather muted effect of the staircase hall may be due to the fact that its original multicoloured decoration, visible in Lami's watercolour, is now subdued (compare the illustrations Fig. 2 and Plate II). The hang of pictures here is, however, traditional, and follows an installation devised by Queen Victoria to illustrate her succession via a series of

1 George IV by Sir Thomas Lawrence (1769–1830). Oil on canvas, 91·4 × 71·1 cm. (National Portrait Gallery) George IV was the effective creator of Buckingham Palace, and employed the architect John Nash to realize his vision of a truly palatial residence on the site of his parents sumptuous but essentially domestic residence

portraits of her immediate ancestors each of them framed in fixed gilded and carved frames. The Sir William Beechey (1753–1839) portraits of George III and Queen Charlotte are perhaps the most characterful although the Wilkie of Augustus, Duke of Sussex in a kilt is a memorable Victorianism.

The whole of the Grand Staircase is lit by a fine domed skylight composed of a series of eighty panes etched by Wainwright with classical female figures in the larger panes and showing the Crown in the smaller panes. The small replica of Benvenuto Cellini's bronze *Perseus and Medusa* (the original is in the Loggia dei Lanzi in Florence) which now stands at the head of the staircase (Fig. 2) is a

somewhat unwelcoming presence at the main door to the State apartments. The four Chinese vases with French gilt-bronze mounts came from Carlton House. The Grand Staircase comes most vividly to life when there is a large reception or State banquet or ball at the palace, and Eugène Lami's painting illustrated here of a State Ball held in July 1848 gives an impression of this rather monumental yet sumptuous space enlivened by a crowd of uniformed and be-jewelled guests.

The present route follows that intended to take us towards the Throne Room. If we pause at the top of the stairs, however, and look in the opposite direction, we see that

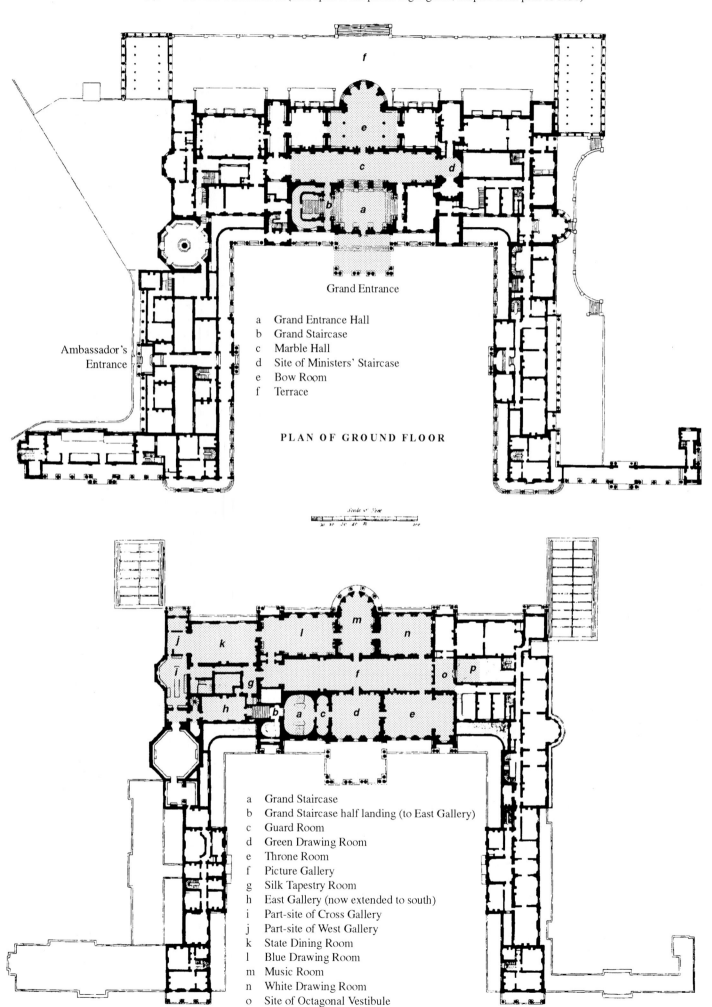

BUCKINGHAM PALACE (area open to the public highlighted, adapted from plan of 1838)

f

Grand Entrance

a   Grand Entrance Hall
b   Grand Staircase
c   Marble Hall
d   Site of Ministers' Staircase
e   Bow Room
f   Terrace

Ambassador's
Entrance

PLAN OF GROUND FLOOR

a   Grand Staircase
b   Grand Staircase half landing (to East Gallery)
c   Guard Room
d   Green Drawing Room
e   Throne Room
f   Picture Gallery
g   Silk Tapestry Room
h   East Gallery (now extended to south)
i   Part-site of Cross Gallery
j   Part-site of West Gallery
k   State Dining Room
l   Blue Drawing Room
m   Music Room
n   White Drawing Room
o   Site of Octagonal Vestibule

PLAN OF THE FIRST FLOOR

I The Grand Hall, looking towards Theakston's chimney piece (at the right of the entrance). The carrara marble columns by Joseph Browne have gilded bronze Corinthian capitals by Samuel Parker. The white and gold Edwardian decoration (1902) by C. H. Bessant was painted over a polychrome decoration of the mid-nineteenth-century by Ludwig Grüner. The fireplace by Theakstone originally cost £1,000, and is the most elaborate of his works in the Palace. It is surmounted by a small bust of George IV

another staircase leads off the half-landing. This directed visitors, on more purely social occasions, towards the East Gallery, the Picture Gallery and the great sequence of Nash state rooms.

Tradition dictates that there is a substantial difference in atmosphere between the relatively public world of the Grand Hall and the Grand Staircase and the apartments closest to the throne. The Guard Room, which we enter first (Plate III) and the Green Drawing Room which follows are places of assembly and calm ordering of guests and official visitors before their arrival at the symbolic heart of the palace—the Throne Room.

Nash was at his most ingenious in the smaller rooms of the palace, such as the Guard Room, for he often used a combination of glass-roof lights and looking-glass doors to create a sense of space and an element of fantasy. The Guard Room is a good example, for it is relatively modest in scale but is much enriched by its gilded ceiling alcoves and the fine Gobelins tapestries

(eighteenth-century, from the series *Les portières des Dieux*) which hang as backdrops to the Victorian marble sculptures of, among others, Queen Victoria and Prince Albert, and the enchanting Mary Thornycroft of the sisters, *The Princesses Victoria and Maud of Wales*. John Gibson's standing figure of Queen Victoria (1847) was originally tinted in lifelike colours.

We now pass into the Green Drawing Room (Plate IV), which is the central room on the west side of the Quadrangle and occupying the site of Queen Charlotte's saloon in the eighteenth-century Buckingham House. Its three windows open onto the loggia above the Grand Entrance. This is the first state apartment that guests enter and from it they usually proceed through one of the mirrored doors on the left into the Picture Gallery which is the great spine of the palace's State apartments. The room is also used as a point of assembly for deputations who may be presenting a loyal address to The Queen. There are certain privileged bodies entitled to present addresses to the

monarch on occasions of special public interest, usually the Sovereign's accession or jubilee. The Secretary of State for the Home Department is normally present and the procedure is gone though with military precision in the Throne Room, where The Queen is likely to deliver a prepared written reply from the steps of the Throne and receive the members of the deputation.

The Green Drawing Room is one of the handsomest apartments in the Palace, with a particularly fine coved white and gold plaster ceiling designed by Nash that rises from a gilded frieze of swagged laurels and wreaths. There are some outstanding examples of cabinet-making in this room. On the far wall to the left of the door is a late eighteenth-century cabinet made by Adam Weisweiler, superbly enriched with *pietre dure* and gilt bronze mounts. To the right on the same wall is an extravagant creation by Martin Carlin, made in about 1775 but using raised *pietre dure* panels dating from the previous century. Throughout the State Apartments are gilt bronze and ormolu

2 Detail of the Grand Staircase today, showing small-scale nineteenth-century replica of Cellini's *Perseus and Medusa* (the original is in Florence). The present decoration hides the polychrome scheme of Grüner (compare Plate III). The relief panels are to designs by Thomas Stothard and the pictures are still as arranged by Queen Victoria. The nineteenth-century sculptures were birthday presents from Queen Victoria to Prince Albert, and the four early-nineteenth-century Chinese porcelain vases with French gilt bronze mounts were probably bought by George IV in 1823

II *The Grand Staircase* (opposite). Watercolour by Eugene Lami (1800–1890) on the occasion of the State Ball in July 1848. Note the elaborate balustrade by Samuel Parker, supplied in 1828–30 at a cost of £3,900, and the polychrome decoration which Grüner was employed to design in 1845. The double arms of the staircase seen here sweep up to the Guard Room, Green Drawing Room and Throne Room, while another ascent (behind the viewer) leads into the East Gallery and thence around the sequence of great state rooms on the garden front for more 'social' events

clocks and candelabra—many by Vulliamy and many of the finest French Empire craftsmanship, and in the Green Drawing Room we have our first glimpse of examples of Sèvres porcelain from what is undoubtedly the greatest collection in existence.

The Throne Room (Plate V) has all the appropriate red and gold panoply for its regal functions. The place for the Throne is beneath a red throne canopy, set behind an arch framed by a pair of winged genii holding suspended garlands in front of the Royal Alcove. The two throne chairs now beneath the canopy were used during the Coronation ceremony by The Queen and the Duke of Edinburgh (they were made by White, Allom and Company in 1953). Of particular interest is the Council chair that stands in the window embrasure to the right, one of a pair made by Tatham and Bailey for George IV at Carlton House. It is of remarkably original neo-classical design, presumably based on Imperial Roman precedents, with winged sphinxes apparently supporting the seat. The other throne chairs on each side of the dais were used by King George VI and Queen Elizabeth. It is well worth observing the sculptural decorations in the frieze, which are in high relief and depict scenes from the Wars of the Roses. They were executed by E. H. Bailey from designs by Thomas Stothard. The ceiling is ornamented on its coved portion with coloured shields bearing coats of arms of England, Scotland, Ireland—and Hanover, for George IV was, of course, a member of the Hanoverian dynasty established with George I, Elector of Hanover, in 1714.

The great room which separates the east and western state apartments is the Picture Gallery (Plate VII), some 155 feet long. It is entirely top lit and was extensively remodelled in 1914. It was designed originally by Nash to house the collection of Dutch and Flemish pictures acquired by George IV. Nash's series of domed skylights was elaborated by Blore (see pp. 37–43) and then the whole roof was replaced by the present curved glass roof in the 1914 redecoration. Queen Mary at that time chose an olive-green damask which was replaced in the present reign by a pink-beige flock wall covering. The four marble chimney pieces were supplied by Joseph Browne in the late 1820s and they honour four artists with portrait busts—Dürer, Rubens, Titian and Michelangelo. Queen Victoria used this room for large State banquets until the State Ballroom and State Supper Room was added in the 1850s by Sir James Pennethorne. Although this room houses many important pieces of furniture, including four armchairs by Georges Jacob, and four marble topped console tables by Adam Weisweiler and some remarkable black Sèvres, it is the quality of the pictures that make it one of the

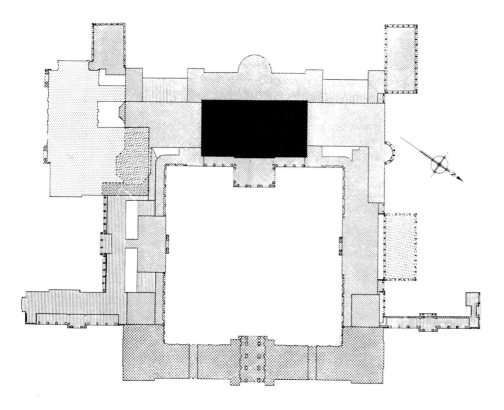

■ The Duke of Buckingham, 1702–5 (William Winde)

▨ King George III, 1762–80 (Sir William Chambers)

▧ King George IV, 1825–30 (John Nash)

▥ King William IV, 1832–7 (Edward Blore)

▨ Queen Victoria, 1847–50 (Edward Blore)

▨ Queen Victoria, 1852–5 (William Cubitt and Sir James Pennethorne)

Demolished Buildings shown in Broken Hatching.

The development of Buckingham Palace, showing the periods of construction

---

III The Guard Room. This small but ornate room provides a transition between the public space of the Grand Staircase and the splendour of the Green Drawing Room and the following Throne Room. Nash characteristically used light effects to add grandeur to a limited space. Nash top-lit the room with a series of oval convex windows made of Wainright's engraved glass, which diffuse a soft light over the relief panel of *Peace and War* by William Pitt, the distinguished nineteenth-century sculptures and the eighteenth-century Gobelins tapestries. By the time of George IV, the Guard Room traditional in royal palaces had taken on a purely symbolic function and, although richly decorated, this one is minute in comparison with those at Hampton Court and Windsor Castle

most remarkable rooms in Europe. Fashions in picture hanging have changed over the years and many may feel that the present hang is rather a spare one. This does not diminish the quality of the masterpieces by Rembrandt (Plate VI), Rubens (Plate VIII) and Van Dyck on view.

The minor linking rooms, the Silk Tapestry Room, East (Fig. 4), West and Cross (Fig. 5) Galleries which follow all contain fine furniture and sculpture and some remarkable paintings (see Plate IX) but they do not have the high style of the suite of state rooms on the garden front which represents the pinnacle of Nash's achievement at the Palace. The State Dining Room, the Blue Drawing Room, the Music Room, and the White Drawing Room are a magnificent enfilade of richly decorated rooms. These are the rooms where the looking-glass doors and the endless reflections of chandeliers look their best at night when they are all in use, as they are at least once a year for the November Diplomatic reception when the Queen entertains over one thousand members of the diplomatic corps.

The State Dining Room (Plate X) is dominated by two things: the complex and almost over-rich gilded ceiling designed by Blore and the splendid row of full-length royal portraits. The dominant central portrait of King George IV in Garter robes, by Sir Thomas Lawrence, is over the chimney piece and the six companion full-lengths demonstrate clearly the development of state portraiture. Visitors during the public opening will not see this room with its dining table and plate. It is principally used for state dinners that are not as large as the banquets held in the ballroom.

Once used as the palace ballroom, the Blue Drawing Room (Plate XII) is one of Nash's most successful rooms. It can be read as an exercise in the Corinthian Order with thirty columns painted in imitation onyx. Apart from the extreme richness of the colouring this room also has remarkable sculptural decoration. Emblematical groups in the ceiling arches designed by William Pitts represent the glories of English literature. Shakespeare, Milton and Spenser are surrounded by fat cherubs—a plaster fantasy executed in 1835. The State portraits of King Edward VII and Queen Alexandra by Sir Luke Fildes seem at home in the imperial richness of this room, and one of the most important pieces of furniture in the entire Royal Collection is here. The 'Table of the Grand Commanders' (Plate XIII) with its Sèvres top was commissioned by Napoleon in 1806 and presented to King George IV by King Louis XVIII in 1817. It is to be seen in the portrait of King George IV in the State Dining Room.

The centre of the garden front is the bow windowed Music Room (Plate XIV)

which is pure Nash and can be said to be one of his tautest designs. Under this ingeniously vaulted and gilded ceiling, royal babies are frequently christened—the Queen's three eldest children were christened here as was Prince William of Wales in water brought specially from the River Jordan. This is also the room where guests having assembled in the Green Drawing Room are presented before a dinner or banquet. The lapis lazuli-coloured columns and the rich marquetry floor demonstrate the richness and craftsmanship that Nash wanted for this room.

The Royal Family assembles in the White Drawing Room (Plate XV) before passing through to the State Dining Room or the Ballroom. They emerge in a dramatic fashion through a secret door to the Royal Closet which is concealed by a looking glass and a pier table. The decoration of this room is substantially of 1831. The twenty-eight pilasters are decorated with the Star and Garter painted in heraldic colours and the sculptural frieze is by William Pitts depicting what the 1831 Report to the Select Committee described as, 'the sports of boys'—more officially described as an allegory of the 'Origins and Progress of Pleasure'. The great Reisener roll-top desk to the left by the window was bought by George IV and made for one of Louis XV's daughters.

To leave the Palace on the summer visits the route will take visitors via the ante room to the White Drawing Room (the 'Octagonal Vestibule', lined with images of Queen Victoria's daughters-in-law), down the Ministers' Stairs and so to the Marble Hall (Plate XVI). At the foot of the stairs is one of George IV's great commissions— *Mars and Venus* by Antonio Canova which the King ordered following Canova's visit to England in 1815. *A Fountain Nymph*, also by Canova, from Carlton House is also to be seen in the Marble Hall. The ground floor room are known as the semi-state apartments which suits their low-ceilinged quality and the fact that they are not used for highly formal occasions. Today the public will leave through the Bow Room (Fig. 7) on to the Terrace and out into the garden. The Bow Room is where the members of the Privy Council are politely mustered before they file in to meet with the Queen, as well as being the route through to the grounds for the summer garden parties.

So far as aesthetic pleasure goes Buckingham Palace offers two particular things. One is the glory of the Nash rooms and the high quality of their immaculate furnishings. The other is the almost incredible quality of the pictures and works of art in the Royal Collection and the pleasure of seeing them in the near-private surroundings of the Palace. Every visitor will sense the highly Edwardian flavour of much of the decoration and also the continuing sense of agreeable Imperial nostalgia which still informs much of the ceremonial and the elaborate nature of the British monarchy. They will also feel, after walking through the State Apartments, a strong presence of the genius of King George IV—the monarch who brought his remarkable taste to the creation of Buckingham Palace, and elevated the quality of the Royal Collection to an unsurpassed degree.

Key to paintings

Green Drawing Room

Guard Room	Picture Gallery		Throne Room
	3	4	5
	2		6
	1		7

1 Studio of Allan Ramsay (1713–84), *Augusta, Princess of Wales*, c. 1764

2 German School, 17th century, *Frederick Henry, Charles Louis and Elizabeth, children of Frederick V and Elizabeth, King and Queen of Bohemia*, c. 1620

3 Nathaniel Dance (1735–1811), *Edward Augustus, Duke of York*, brother of Georege III, 1764

4 John Michael Wright (1617–94), *James, Duke of Cambridge*, 1666–67

5 Francis Cotes (1726–70), *Princesses Louisa Ann and Caroline Matilda* (later Queen of Denmark), sisters of George III, 1767

6 Attributed to Sofonisba Anguissola (1527–1623), *Isabella Clara Eugenia and Catharina, daughters of Philip II, King of Spain*, c. 1569–70

7 Sir Martin Archer Shee (1769–1850), *Richard, Marquess Wellesley*, brother of the 1st Duke of Wellington, when Lord Steward of the Household, c. 1832

IV The Green Drawing Room. Note Carlin cabinet to the right of the Throne Room doors. The room is furnished with fine examples of Regency mahogany and gilt furniture, including a set of seats made by Morel and Seddon for Windsor Castle (1826–8). The green stamped brocade was made at the request of Queen Adelaide, who, as the Earl of Errol wrote, 'expressed a wish to employ the Irish' in its manufacture. The crimson Axminster carpet is decorated with Tudor roses. The left-hand chimney-piece is topped by a French Empire clock with a figure of Apollo bought by George IV in 1803. To the left of the Throne Room doors is a cabinet by Weisweiler with floral pietra dura panels. Above the Carlin cabinet stands a pot-pourri vase in the form of a ship (1758), made of soft-paste Sèvres porcelain, like all the porcelain in this room. The vase probably belonged to Madame de Pompadour and was bought by George IV in 1817. The grand piano by Mott (1817) was bought by George IV in 1820

V The Throne Room, finished after George IV's death in 1830 by Blore, was decorated in 1902. The ceiling and most of the sculptural details follow Nash's design. The throne chairs on the platform were made by White, Allom & Co. and used during the Queen's Coronation ceremony in 1953. They are flanked on the walls by carved wood and gilt trophies by Henry Holland. A secret jib-door near the throne leads into the Octagonal Vestibule at the head of the Minister's Staircase. In the window embrasure is the Council Chair, one of a pair made by Tatham, Bailey & Sanders for George IV at Carlton House (1812). The *Oath of the Horatii* clock by Claude Galle is based on the famous painting by Jacques-Louis David (1784) and was bought by George IV in 1809

VI *Agatha Bas* by Rembrandt Harmensz van Rijn (1606–69) 1641. Oil on canvas, 105·4 × 83·8 cm.
Bought by George IV in 1819 from the sale of Lord Charles Townshend (*Picture Gallery*)

VII The Picture Gallery (looking north). The display (see diagram, p. 16) includes masterpieces by Rembrandt, Rubens and Van Dyck. Nash's original skylight designs were reworked by Blore in the 1830s and then removed in 1914, when the present curved roof was installed. Browne's four chimney pieces commemorate Titian, Dürer, Rubens and Michelangelo. Midway down the Gallery, the four armchairs by Georges Jacob (*c.* 1786) were imported into England by Dominique Daguerre and bear his label. They were originally placed in George IV's bedroom at Carlton House. On the chimney-pieces of the left-hand wall (as the visitor enters) stand two pairs of hard-paste Sèvres porcelain vases painted in platinum and gold on a black ground with *chinoiserie* scenes and fitted with gilt bronze mounts (*c.* 1790–92). Note the four Weisweiler marble-topped console tables (*c.* 1785), and a pair of ebony cabinets with inlays of pewter, tortoise-shell and brass by Pierre Garnier (*c.* 1770), bought for George IV in Paris in 1819. Two pedestals for clocks by Joubert of 1762 are now surmounted by bronze busts of emperors.

From here the visitor passes through the Picture Gallery Lobby, with its sculpture of Mrs Jordan, William IV's mistress, a bequest to Her Majesty The Queen in 1975 from the descendant of that union the Earl of Munster, and into the Silk Tapestry Room, with its furniture by Weisweiler and by Morel and Seddon and eighteenth-century French clocks, and so into the East Gallery

VIII Detail of *The Farm at Laeken* by Peter Paul Rubens (1577–1640), *c.* 1617–18 (*Picture Gallery*)

Key to paintings

Picture Gallery – north wall

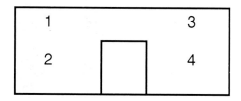

1 Guido Reni (1575–1642), *Cleopatra, c. 1630*

2 Gonzales Coques (1614 or 1618–84), *Family of Jan-Baptista Anthoine*. Copper, 1664

3 Guercino (1591–1666), *The Libyan Sibyl, c. 1651*

4 Barent Graat (1628–1709), *A Family Group*, 1658

Picture Gallery – east wall – on left, to central door

```
5        8        11        14
   7        10        13
6        9        12        15
```

5 David Teniers (1610–90), *The Stolen Kiss, c. 1640*

6 Jan Steen (1626–79), *Interior of a Tavern with Cardplayers and a Viola Player, c. 1665*

7 Aelbert Cuyp (1620–91), *The Passage Boat, c. 1650*

8 Nicolaes Berchem (1620–83), *A mountainous Landscape with Herdsmen driving Cattle down a Road*, 1673

9 Rembrandt van Rijn (1606–69), *Christ and the Magdalen at the Tomb: 'Noli Me Tangere'*. Panel, 1638 (*or* Jan Vermeer (1632–75) *A lady at the virginals, c. 1660–70*)

10 Francesco Zuccarelli (1702–88), *Landscape with two seated Women embracing*, 1743

11 David Teniers, *Fishermen on the Seashore, c. 1660*

12 Frans Hals (1580?–1666), *Portrait of a Man*, 1630

13 Rembrandt van Rijn, *The Shipbuilder and his Wife*, 1633

14 Aelbert Cuyp, *Cows in a Pasture beside a River, before the Ruins of the Abbey of Rijnsburg, 1640–50*

15 Rembrandt van Rijn, *Agatha Bas*, 1641

Picture Gallery – west wall – on right, to central door

```
29  27  25  22  20  18        16
            24
30  28  26  23  21  19        17
```

16 Nicholas Maes (1634–93), *The Listening Housewife*, 1655

17 Gabriel Metsu (1629–67), *The Cello Player, c. 1665*

18 Philips Wouwermans (1619–68), *The Hayfield, c. 1660*

19 Sir Peter Paul Rubens (1577–1640), *The Assumption of the Virgin, c. 1611*

20 Sir Anthony van Dyck (1549–1641), *The Mystic Marriage of St Catherine, c. 1630*

21 Sir Peter Paul Rubens, *Milkmaids with Cattle in a Landscape: 'The Farm at Laeken'*. Panel, c. 1617–18

22 Philips Wouwermans, *A Horse Fair in front of a Town, c. 1660*

23 Pieter de Hooch (1629–84), *A Courtyard in Delft at Evening: a Woman spinning, c. 1657*

24 Francesco Zuccarelli, *Landscape with two young Children offering Fruit to a Woman, c. 1743*

25 Spanish School, *Don Luis de Haro, c. 1650*

26 William van de Velde (1633–1707), *A Calm: a States Yacht under Sail, close to the Shore, and many other Vessels*. Panel, c. 1655

27 Sir Anthony van Dyck, *Christ healing the Paralytic, c. 1619*

28 David Teniers, *Peasants dancing outside a Country House*. Panel, 1645

29 Sir Anthony Van Dyck, *Virgin and Child, c. 1630–2*

30 William van de Velde, *'The Golden Leeuw' at Sea in heavy weather, c. 1671*

Picture gallery – east wall – on left, beyond central door

```
              33        36
31  32            35
              34        37
```

31 Sir Anthony Van Dyck, *Charles I and Henrietta Maria with their two Eldest Children, 'The Greate Peece', c. 1632*

32 Melchior Hondecoeter (1636–95), *Birds and a Spaniel, c. 1665*

33 Luca Carlevaris (1665–1731), *A Caprice Landscape with a Fountain and an Artist sketching, c. 1710*

34 Gaspar Poussin (1615–75), *Jonah and the Whale, c. 1653–4*

35 Sir Peter Paul Rubens, *Landscape with St George and the Dragon, c. 1630*

36 Luca Carlevaris, *A Caprice View of a Seaport, c. 1710*

37 Claude Lorrain (1600–82), *The Rape of Europa*, 1667

Picture Gallery – west wall – on right, beyond central door

```
43        40
     42            39    38
44        41
```

38 Sir Anthony Van Dyck, *Charles I with M. de St Antoine*, 1633

39 Aelbert Cuyp, *A Cavalry Trooper decorating his dappled grey Horse, with a reclining Spaniel at his Feet, c. 1650*

40 Luca Carlevaris, *A Caprice View with a Shipyard, c. 1710*

41 Gaspar Poussin, *Landscape with a Waterfall, c. 1653–4*

42 Aelbert Cuyp, *Landscape with a Negro Page, c. 1655*

43 Luca Carlevaris, *A Caprice View of a Harbour, c. 1710*

44 Gaspar Poussin, *Landscape with Figures by a Pool, c. 1665*

Silk Tapestry Room

It contains: Francesco Zuccarelli (1702–88), *River Landscape with the Finding of Moses*, 1768; Allan Ramsay (1713–84), *Queen Charlotte with her two eldest Children*, 1764; Benjamin West (1728–1820), *The Apotheosis of Prince Octavius*, 1783; and an important large clock by de la Croix (c. 1770–75)

3 *The Family of Queen Victoria* by Franz Xaver Winterhalter (1805–73), 1846 (*East Gallery*)

4 The East Gallery in a photograph of 1913 (*courtesy of Marlborough Rare Books*). Today it contains some notable paintings (see diagram)

Key to paintings

East gallery – to the left

1	2	3	4

1 Sir Peter Paul Rubens (1577–1640), *The Family of Balthasar Gerbier, c.* 1630

2 John Russell (1745–1806), *George IV, when Prince of Wales*, in the uniform of the Royal Kentish Bowmen, 1791

3 Franz Xaver Winterhalter (1805–73), *The Family of Queen Victoria*, 1846

4 John Hoppner (1758?–1810), *George IV when Prince of Wales*, 1796

East gallery – to the right

11	10	9	8	7	6	5

5 Benjamin West (1728–1820), *Queen Charlotte*, 1782

6 Benjamin West, *Prince Adolphus, later Duke of Cambridge, with Princess Mary and Princess Sophia*, 1778

7 Benjamin West, *George III*, 1779

8 John Hoppner, *Francis, 5th Duke of Bedford, c.* 1797

9 Sir George Hayter (1792–1871), *The Coronation of Queen Victoria*, 1838

10 John Hoppner, *Francis, 5th Earl of Moira and 1st Marquess of Hastings, c.* 1793

11 Sir Joshua Reynolds (1723–92), *Frederick, Duke of York*, 1787–88

IX Detail of *Queen Victoria's Coronation* by Sir George Hayter (1792–1871), 1838 (*East Gallery*). The moment is that when, after the Crowning, the people 'with loud and repeated shouts' cry 'God Save The Queen', whereupon the peers and peeresses immediately put on their coronets. The Queen described it as 'a most beautiful impressive moment'. She is seated on the Coronation Chair, wearing the Imperial State Crown and holding in her right hand the Sceptre with the Cross and in her left hand the Sceptre with the Dove

5 The Cross Gallery (below) in a photograph of 1913 (*courtesy of Marlborough Rare Books*). Today it shows two paintings by Benjamin West, *The departure of Regulus* (1769) and *The oath of Hannibal* (1770), both commissioned by George III who especially favoured West

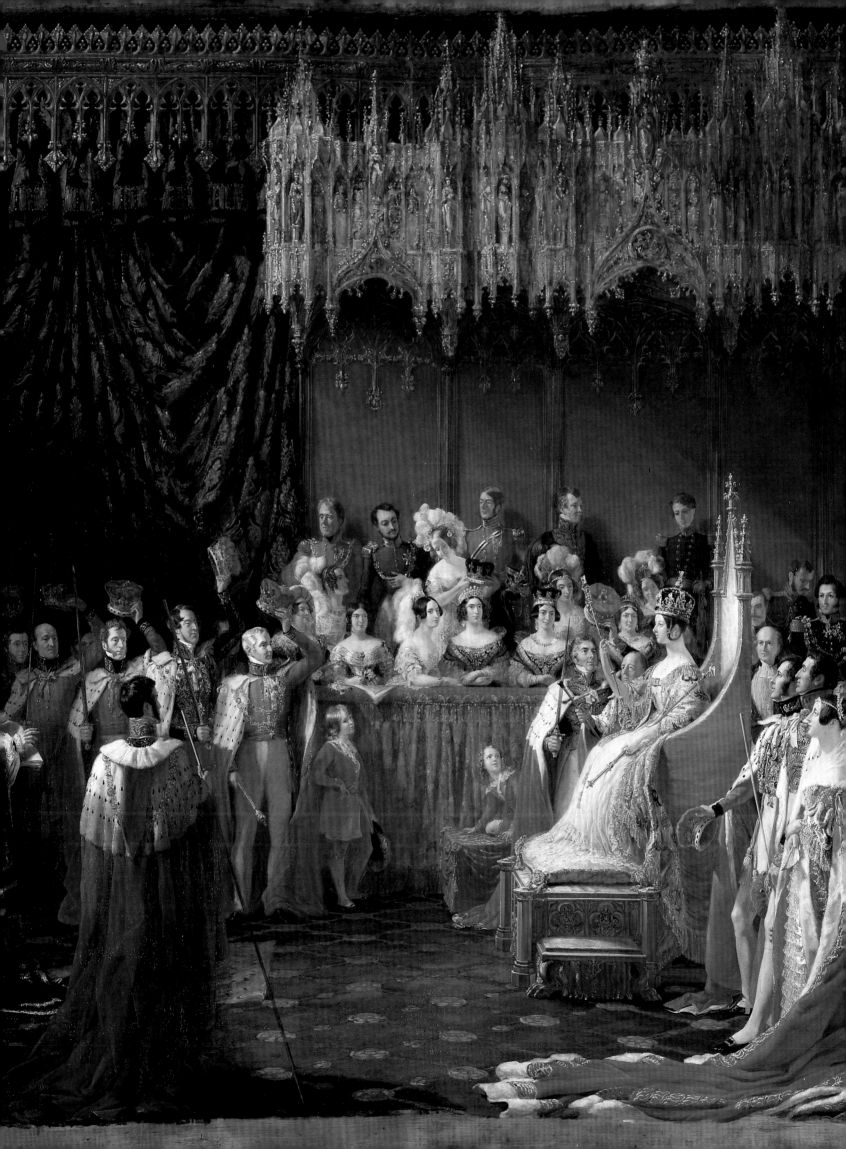

State Dining Room

1	2	3	4	5	6	7

1 Studio of John Shackleton (d. 1767), *George II*, 1755–67

2 Jean-Baptiste Van Loo (1684–1745), *Augusta, Princess of Wales*, wife of Frederick, Prince of Wales, 1742

3 Allan Ramsay (1713–84), *George III*, c. 1763

4 Studio of Sir Thomas Lawrence, *George IV*, c. 1820

5 Allan Ramsay, *Queen Charlotte*, wife of George III, c. 1763

6 Jean-Baptiste Van Loo, *Frederick, Prince of Wales*, 1742

7 Sir Godfrey Kneller (1646?–1723), *Queen Caroline*, wife of George II, when Princess of Wales, 1716

X The State Dining Room designed by Nash and completed by Blore. Here state banquets and smaller private royal dinners are held. This was the last of the State Rooms to be completed. In many medallions of the ornate, coved ceiling, Queen Victoria's cipher appears, which suggests that the room was completed during her reign, even though Nash had fallen from grace as early as 1830. The furniture includes ten gilded mahogany sideboards (*c.* 1835), on top of which stand Chinese celadon vases (from George IV's Carlton House), mounted in ormolu. The Spanish mahogany dining table can extend to seventy feet and accomodate sixty guests. The gilt chairs (1813) were purchased by the Prince Regent for Carlton House. On either side of the entry stand malachite and gilt bronze candelabra by Thomire & Cie (*c.* 1828). The set of four five-light gilt bronze candelabra on red marble bases by Rémond were made originally for the *salon à la Turque* of the comte d'Artois's apartments at Versailles (1783). Vulliamy designed the marble and gilt bronze clock with Derby biscuit figures for the Prince of Wales (later George IV) in 1788, the other clock is French by Thomire, bought in 1810

XI *Her Majesty Queen Elizabeth II in the Blue Drawing Room*, 1955, photographed by Cecil Beaton. This classic picture demonstrates clearly the manipulation of the print by a modern master of the studio image. Note the alterations to the torchère and vase at the right. *Camera Press Ltd*

6 The Blue Drawing Room in a photograph of 1913 (*courtesy of Marlborough Rare Books*)

XII The Blue Drawing Room. It served as the ball room before Sir James Pennethorne built the new Ball Room. The Nash ceiling contains sculpted memorials in the over-arches to the poets Shakespeare, Spenser and Milton by Pitts, which contrast with the sculptor's earlier neo-classical style elsewhere in the Palace. The thirty columns are painted in imitation onyx. The four side-tables of marble and gilt by A.-L. Bellange (1823) were bought by George IV for Windsor Castle; settees and armchairs are from a set by Tatham, Bailey and Sanders; a pair of gilt-bronze candelabra are by Rémond (*c.* 1787). The most spectacular piece on view is the 'Table of the Grand Commanders' (see Plate XIII). The astronomical clock on the mantelpiece is by J.-A. Lepine of about 1790 in which year it was bought by George IV who put it in the Royal Closet at Carlton House. The Sèvres porcelain vases, all with dark blue ground, include some rare models (second half of the eighteenth century)

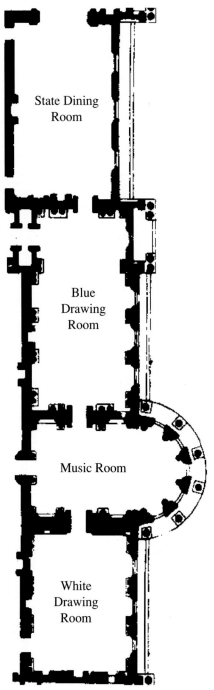

The Garden Front
state rooms
by John Nash

State Dining
Room

Blue
Drawing
Room

Music Room

White
Drawing
Room

Plan of enfilade

XIII *Table of the Grand Commanders* (1806) presented to King George IV by King Louis XVIII in 1817. It is of hard-paste Sèvres porcelain with gilt-bronze mounts. The top is painted with the head of Alexander the Great surrounded by twelve commanders of antiquity in the form of imitation cameo reliefs. It was commissioned by Napoleon in 1806 and finished six years later (it is seen in the Lawrence portrait of George IV in the State Dining Room). The circular top, which revolves, is supported by a column of green and gold porcelain, composed of Roman fasces, and a porcelain plinth in the form of a shield surrounded by a band of oak leaves in ormolu

XIV The Music Room by Nash (finished in 1831) continues the great enfilade of apartments added when he widened Buckingham house on the garden side (see plan on facing page). The vaulted ceiling, full of invention and originality, recalls Nash's work at Brighton Pavilion. A Savonnerie carpet covers the magnificent inlaid marquetry floor by George Seddon which cost £2,400. The two throne chairs (1902) were used by George V and Queen Mary, when Prince and Princess of Wales, during the coronation ceremony of King Edward VII. The small armchairs and settees are by George Jacob (*c.* 1786) and were originally used in Carlton House. The room is still used for royal christenings. The chandeliers in the Empire style are the most spectacular in the Palace and were apparently in the Throne Room in 1841. A fine ornamental gilt bronze vase by Thomire is in the window bow. A display of soft-paste Sèvres porcelain vases includes a *garniture* dated 1764 on the left-hand chimneypiece

XV White Drawing Room. This is the most gilded of the state apartments. On grand occasions, members of the Royal Family appear to their guests by the operation of a hidden door which swings back one of the pair of massive pier glasses (complete with table). The roll-top desk by Riesener (*c.* 1775) is veneered with fret marquetry and inlaid with trophies and flowers. It may have been made for one of Louis XV's daughters, and at the time of its purchase by George IV in 1825, it was thought to have belonged to Louis XVI. All of the vases are of Sèvres porcelain. A pair of gilt-bronze candelabra with bugle-shaped candle arms was bought by George IV in 1813 (by Thomire) and the set of French mid-eighteenth-century cabrioli-legged armchairs is by J.-B. Gourdin

7 The Bow Room in 1913 (*opposite*) (*Courtesy of Marlborough Rare Books*). It had been decorated in the usual white and gold of C. H. Bessant in 1902. Garden-party visitors pass through this room directly from the Grand Entrance Hall and so out on to the Terrace. It contains magnificent Chelsea porcelain, the Mecklenburg-Strehlitz service. The pair of black marble chimney-pieces with gilt bronze mounts (1810) by Vulliamy were commissioned by the Earl of Bridgewater. The portraits were set into the panelling at the wish of Queen Victoria in 1853

XVI The Marble Hall (*above*) with a view towards the Ministers' Staircase, originally by Nash but redecorated in 1902. It was originally a Sculpture Hall. The sculpture of *Mars and Venus* (*c.* 1815–1817) at the foot of the staircase by Antonio Canova (1757–1822) was commissioned by the Prince Regent for Carlton House. Canova's *Fountain nymph with putto* (*c.* 1817–1818) was commissioned by Lord Cawdor, a friend of the Prince Regent. The paintings are of relations of Queen Victoria and Prince Albert and culminate in their official portraits by Winterhalter of 1859. Immediately preceding them is a Winterhaler portrait of Queen Victoria's mother, Victoria, Duchess of Kent, widow of the rather unsatisfactory Duke of Kent, son of George III, (whose portrait Queen Victoria piously placed on the Grand Staircase, where it still hangs)

From Buckingham House to Palace

The box within the box within the box

JOHN HARRIS

Repeated alterations to the buildings on the site of Buckingham Palace explain many of the quirks of the present structure, some of them dating back to the late seventeenth century when the first great house appeared on this key position at the end of St James's Park

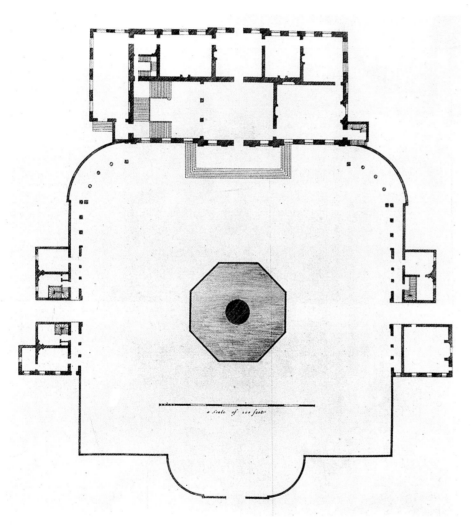

1 Measured plan of Buckingham House by Colen Campbell (1676–1729), 1715. From the first volume of *Vitruvius Britannicus* (compare the view in Fig. 2)

As visitors pass through Buckingham Palace, some might wonder at the unusually low ceiling of the Grand Hall (p. 5, Plate I), for after all this functions as the main entrance hall from the portico in the courtyard. In such a huge royal palace this seems unnecessarily cramped, although there is certainly some spatial excitement in passing from the darker confined space into the bright one of the Grand Staircase (p. 6, Plate II). In fact, this is a mark of adaptation, a telling reminder that this palace contains a house within a house within a house, like Chinese boxes. It

may all have begun in 1674. That year John Evelyn rushed to view the fire-blackened ruins of Goring House, 'consum'd to the ground' on 23 September. Henry Bennet, 1st Earl of Arlington, rebuilt it immediately, and this is the handsome house shown in a view dated 1677 (Royal Library). It was obviously by a leading London architect, perhaps Hugh May; yet this grand house

was to last barely twenty years, for in 1702 John Sheffield, Marquess of Normanby, acquired it and inexplicably pulled it down. His new house, to be called Buckingham House after his dukedom of 23 March 1723, was complete by 1705.

The reason for demolishing what became Arlington House may be explained by examining the early painted view whose attribution is still uncertain (Plate I), a picture now in the Royal Collection, but with a recent provenance of the Sheffield family. We can observe the felicity of site, quite the best near Westminster. The artist is standing in Green Park with coach and riders passing along what is now Constitution Hill, but was then known as the road to Hyde Park Corner. So we are given the garden aspect of Buckingham House, and can see how it resembled a huge country house, not only with thirty acres of garden, but commanding St James's Park and The Mall. Indeed, the Duke of Buckingham was keenly aware of this, and the four bold inscriptions around the frieze included *Sic siti Laectantur Lares* (The Household Gods delight in such a situation) (see Fig. 2) and *Rus in Urbe* (Country within the City). Edward Hatton commented in 1708 in his *New View of London* that this was a seat 'not to be contemned by the greatest Monarch'. Arlington House was reputedly rich inside, and it is difficult to believe that all was demolished. The foundations may have been utilized, and perhaps the five bays of the side walls are those of Arlington's fronts, although Buckingham's was a much taller house. This, however, can only be speculation.

According to Colen Campbell in the first volume of his *Vitruvius Britannicus*, 1715,

I *Buckingham House*, detail of a late seventeenth-century oil painting recently acquired for the Royal Collection and hitherto unpublished. This house replaced Arlington House which was bought by John Sheffield, Marquess of Normanby, in 1702 and demolished by him. This building was complete by 1705 and later took its name from his dukedom of 1723. The artist is standing in Green Park, and coaches are passing along what is now Constitution Hill

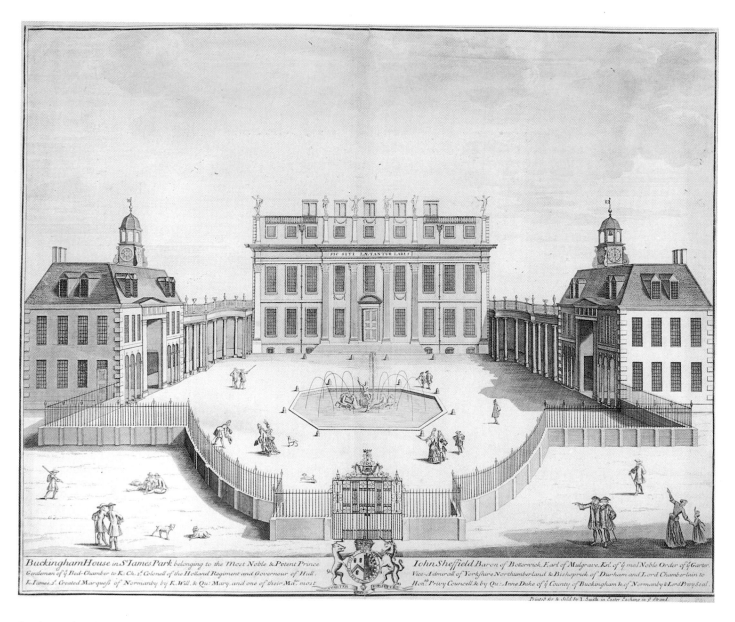

2 Buckingham House illustrated in the *Nouveau Théâtre de la Grande Bretagne, c. 1725*

the 'learned and ingenious' William Winde 'conducted' the work, implying that the design was supplied by another, who may be William Talman, accused by Sir John Vanbrugh in 1703 of causing 'vexation and disappointment' to Lord Normanby. Anyway, the plan and elevation of Buckingham House were innovative and its prominent position and publication made it a popular model. This can be judged not only by Campbell's measured plan and elevation, but by the perspective view of the entrance court from the *Nouveau Théâtre de la Grande Bretagne* (Fig. 2). How this house survived through generations of adaptation can be seen by passing in time to Pyne's view of 1819 (Fig. 3), then to John Nash's design (Fig. 4) of 1825.

If we then turn to Campbell's plan again, and consult those of a later date (Figs. 5, 6 and 7) the house within the house becomes more explicit. The present Grand Staircase and Grand Hall occupy just the height and width of Buckingham's, where a Talmanic effect was passing from the low hall up into a high painted space. Pyne's

views (pp. 44–56), melancholy because all the rich decoration was soon to be scrubbed out, show the colourful story of Dido and Aeneas by Louis Laguerre (although Tijou's ironwork may have survived), and the wall to the landing is a neo-classical trompe l'oeil grisaille of a huge niche that replaced one of Laguerre's murals when it was necessary to make a grand entrance from this landing to the suite of state rooms beyond. But this is the time of the tenure of George III and his consort Queen Charlotte.

The Duke of Buckingham died in 1721, and although his widow thought the house 'too good for any private body to live in', no royal prince or princess would take it on, and so she lingered here until her death in 1742. Sir Charles Sheffield, her husband's illegitimate son, discovered that the house had been partly built upon land belonging to the

old royal Mulberry Garden. This led to all sorts of complicated legal wrangles, and eventually George III acquired it for £28,000, technically as a dower house for his Queen (Fig. 8). In fact, both lived there and brought up their large family, preferring its domestic scale and simplicity to the strict formalities of the Court at St James's Palace.

The new residence of a sovereign required the superintendence of the Office of Works, and this began in July 1762. A musical entertainment in the gardens to celebrate the King's birthday in June 1763 not only marked the beginning of royal occupation, but exposed the rivalries of the two Architects to the King, created in 1761. One was Robert Adam, the designer of the entertainment, the other was William Chambers. There was jockeying for supremacy, and Chambers won, although he was forced to concede some elements of design to Adam and even to James Stuart.

In 1756–7 Chambers had secured the recommendation of John, 3rd Earl of Bute, to be tutor in architecture to George, Prince of Wales, an appointment concurrent with the commission from the Prince's mother, Augusta, Dowager Princess of Wales, to model Kew Gardens anew. Royal favour was now assured, and Chambers's first task as Architect to the King was to supervise the remodelling of Buckingham House.

The problem of using this modest house as a royal palace, with the latter's requirements of state, was that the site was contained by the roads to Chelsea and Hyde Park Corner, preventing extensive enlargement in those directions. At the same time Chambers was trying to interest the King in a new palace in Richmond Gardens. But the attraction for the King was Buckingham House's domestic scale, sympathetic to his simplicity of style. The decision was taken to divide the house horizontally, with the Queen upstairs on the first floor occupying the grand rooms (for after all this was her house), and the King living humbly in the ground floor rooms to the garden. What mattered more for the King was his bibliophile interests, and his libraries first occupied a lateral extension to the south-east with the Great or West Library being built in 1762–4 (Fig. 5); then the South Library was built to turn at right angles with a canted bay to the garden and the south end opening into the Octagon Library (Figs. 5, 9) of 1766–7, a majestic space lit by huge lunette windows. The last library was the East one, really an infill of 1772–3 built back-to-back with the Great Library, and raised by one storey in 1774 to form the Marine Gallery for the display of the King's models of ships and seaports. The King insisted on having his bedroom against the Great Library, where the 1855 Room now is, on the site of the Duke of Buckingham's Greenhouse that faced a 'little wilderness of blackbirds and nightingales'.

On the other side of the house, the matching lateral extension was achieved between 1766 and 1768, mostly for lodgings. In 1776 it was turned at right angles for a wing for the Prince of Wales (or 'Prinny' as he was to be called) with his own private entrance from the garden leading into an octagonal hall. This survives, but remodelled today as the Queen's Garden Entrance.

Not enough is known about the contribution of Adam, who was clearly kept at bay. His is the chimneypiece in the new Saloon (now in the Queen's Presence Chamber at Windsor Castle), and he was allowed to design the Japanned Room ceiling which he published in his *Works in Architecture*. The role of the King is also unclear. He was an enthusiastic amateur architect, who designed doors in his own apartments of a type that appear elsewhere in the house. Most of Chambers's attention was concentrated upon the King's libraries and the Queen's state rooms, notably the Saloon, where Horace Walpole observed that 'the Poets and Sheffield Duke of Buckingham'

3 View of the forecourt front of Buckingham House in 1819. Watercolour for W. H. Pyne's *History of the Royal Residences*

(by Laguerre), had been 'effaced and newly painted in the antique taste by Cipriani'. The whole new ensemble, with neo-Antique grisailles around the walls, a gallic pilaster division, and exceptionally large gilt oval mirrors has been seen as Chambers's answer to the more fashionable Adam style, although in fact it is far more complicated, for George III may have deliberately chosen Chambers, Adam and James Stuart (for the ceiling) as representatives of the new style. In any case the wall system was redecorated after the removal of the Raphael cartoons in 1787.

The Buckingham box, extended for the royal family, was now nearly complete. In 1782 John Yenn became Clerk of Works here. As a pupil of Chambers, he presided over a continuation of the Chambersian style, although the alterations were mostly minor. The exception was in 1799 when James Wyatt, Chambers's successor as Surveyor General, rebuilt the old Duke's Tijou stair, substituting for the flights around a square well, a neo-classical Imperial one where the return flights rest upon huge Palladian openings. Chambers seems to have initiated this change years before. This was the last major alteration to the old reign, and little was done for Queen Charlotte who died in 1818. This was the moment to contemplate a larger box by aggrandizing the Queen's Dower House into a palatial palace.

Although Chambers was an officer of the Board of Works, there is evidence that he enjoyed a personal relationship with the

King, having been the latter's tutor in architecture. This type of relationship was also shared by the new King, George IV, with John Nash. Alas for Nash it was to lead to his downfall, via a House of Commons Select Committee in 1828 and a damning 1831 Report enquiring into the mismanagement involved in attempting to make a proper palace out of a moderate-sized country house. The problem was how to provide for all the varied departments of Court, and at the same time deal with a monarch who insisted on scrutinizing and altering the designs on whim. Already the government was smarting from his extravagance at the Brighton Pavilion and Carlton House while he was Prince of Wales, and the debate is encapsulated by Wellington's irritated retort, 'If you expect me to put my hand to any additional expense, I'll be damned if I will'.

Perhaps Nash has been unfairly criticized, for the difficulties of adaptation and expansion were intractable. As a comparison of plans will show (e.g. Figs. 1 and 6), the dimension of the rooms on the court side remained as in the Queen's House; but now the King's Garden Front rooms were gutted to provide a lateral spine corridor (the Sculpture Room and Gallery), and a new suite of rooms was added on the garden side. Today these are marked by the broad columned bow in the centre (Music Room and so on) and the four strong columned projections, the inner pair marking the extent of the old house, the outer the garden terminations of the South Library range and the Prince of Wales's wing. Both outer angles were linked to single-storey Ionic conservatories, with a balancing third behind the present Doric colonnade to the north-east.

As A. C. Pugin shows (Fig. 4) in his view of Nash's first design, before the building of the Marble Arch as a triumphal prelude to the forecourt, Nash was employing here those same picturesque principles as

4 View of John Nash's 'New Palace' by A. C. Pugin, based on first design of 1825

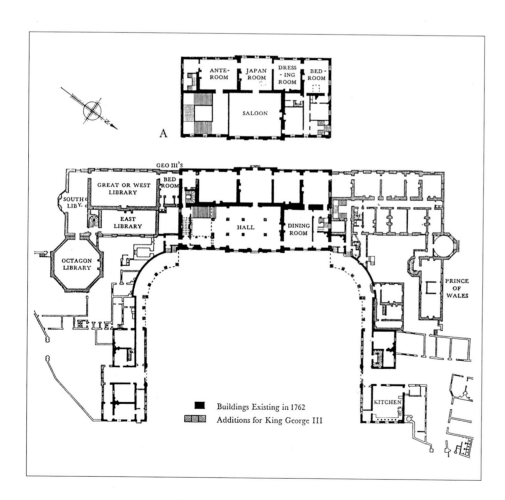

5 The Queen's House, 1762. Modern plan

The adaptation by Nash (compare, e.g., Fig. 6) was to see the gutting of the King's Garden Front rooms to provide a lateral 'spine'

in Regent's Park, with ample columnar articulation and a composition both scenic and yet disparate in the relationship of parts to the whole. This was particularly so on the Garden Front (Fig. 10), once marked by a dome that came in for a great deal of mirth and derision ('a common slop pail turned upside down') because its proportions did not accord with the view from the Court Front (but then, nor did Chambers's one at Somerset House). Nevertheless, not only was it a brilliant adaptation, but it was built of a beautiful honey-coloured Bath stone. The decorative sculptural attachments owe much to Parisian neo-classicism, or rather Revolutionary and post-Revolutionary France, or the Tuileries of Percier and Fontaine, which had been well studied by Nash on his visits to Paris in 1814 and 1818. Like Somerset House, the sculptures by Bailey, Carew, Croggan, Pitt, Rossi and Westmacott form a showpiece of British achievement. The interiors could stand comparison with those in the Tuileries: the richness of the Grand Staircase and its adjacent Guard Room; the brilliant overlay that converted Queen Charlotte's Saloon into the Green Drawing Room; the White Drawing Room; or the Music Room with its lapis-lazuli-blue scagliola columns and its inlaid wood floor, the triumph of George Seddon in 1831 (see p. 25). All of these, too, had remarkably complex ceilings.

Despite the ructions with a parsimonious government, the heart gives a

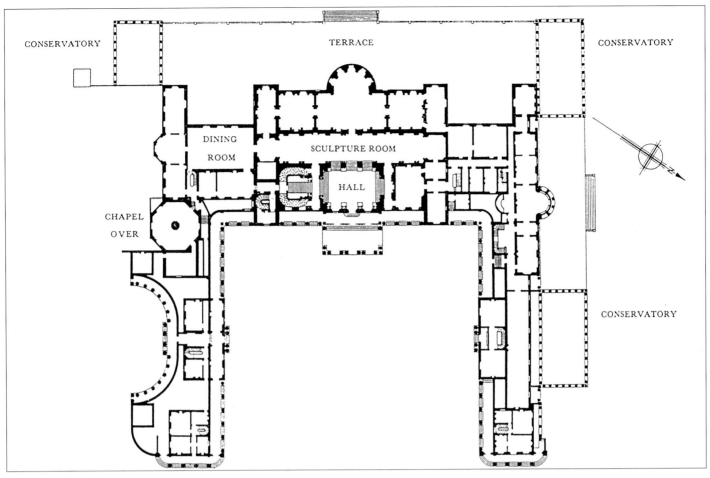

6 Buckingham Palace, 1838. Modern plan

7 Buckingham Palace, 1851. Modern plan

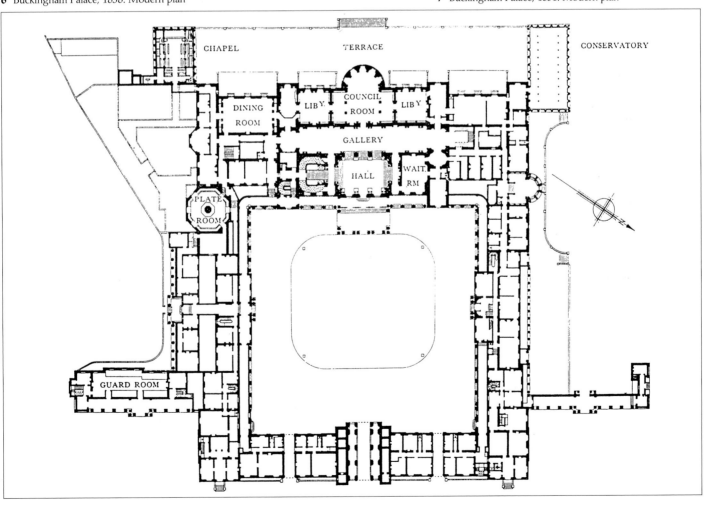

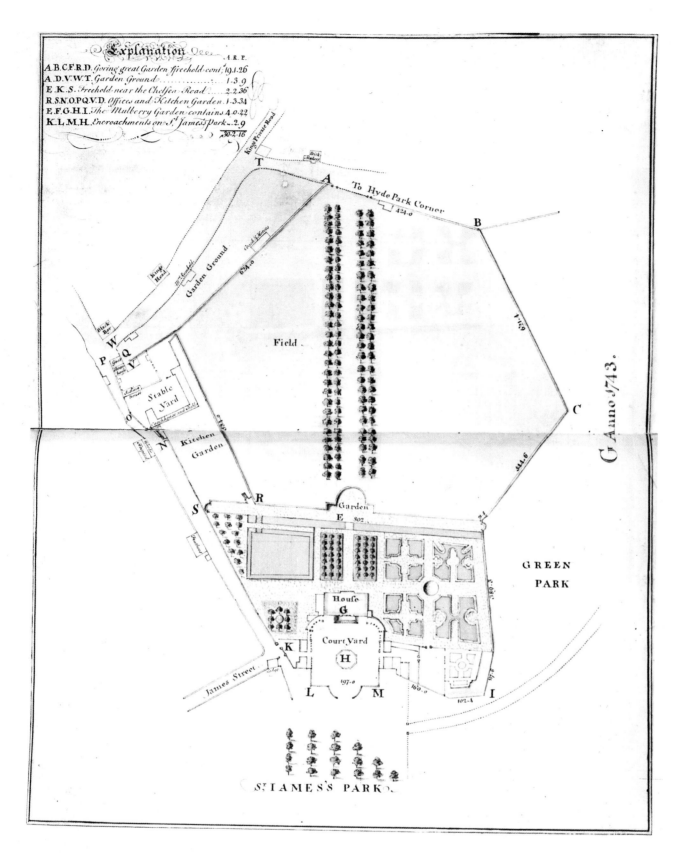

8 The Duke of Buckingham's garden from a survey of 1760

jump when one sees Nash's palace in Joseph Nash's evocation of 1848 (Fig. 11). The splendid Versailles-style *aile Gabriel* porticoes raised at the extremity of the wings visually connect to the Marble Arch, itself a reflection of the Arc du Carrousel, and the whole shimmers beyond the landscaped water of the park. This was our Tuileries, and it spelt out the King's taste for French opulence.

Nash had served him well, and damn the government! But alas, this watercolour was a *memento mori*, for the King had died in 1830, followed by Nash in 1835, mortified by his unfair disgrace. The succeeding King, William IV, had died in 1837, and Queen Victoria was on the throne.

Once George IV died, the personal relationship between monarch and architect

was naturally severed, and the government moved in to gain control. Their man was Edward Blore (so tedious that he was known as 'Blore the bore'), who was summoned to 'finish and ornament' Nash's rooms and to provide additions to a palace that lacked the necessary logistic support for royal and state occasions. The result can be dramatically seen by a comparison of the 1838 and 1851 plans (Figs. 7, 8). The final result is inarticulate in its utter lack of clarity, and its jostling of small room with small room. The story of a courtier lost for three days is too well known for quotation. In fact the demands made upon Blore would have tested the greatest architect. The nadir of this alteration was surely the building of a new Park Front across the forecourt, destroying Nash's lovely porticoes, and removing the Marble Arch.

A modern historian has called Blore's elevation (Fig. 12) a 'monument to architectural incompetence'; and *The Builder* of the day criticized it as 'little more than an ordinary piece of street architecture'. The most that could be said of it was that it looked banal and tired, and it is perhaps fortunate that it was built of Caen stone, and so was condemned to progressive decay, for the effects of pollution in an industrial city had not been tested upon this type of material. Inevitably, the front was destined for rebuilding, the Palace for more and more enlargements. When Sir Aston Webb erased Blore in 1912, we might reflect that, with the King-Emperor, George V, on the throne and with the echoes of an impending war, a decay was at work far more insidious than the pollution of London's air.

The documents quoted are to be found in H. Clifford Smith, *Buckingham Palace*, London 1931; John Harris, Geoffrey de Bellaigue and Oliver Millar, *Buckingham Palace*, London 1968; but particularly in H. M. Colvin (ed.) *The History of the King's Works*, vol. V, 1976 and vol. VI, 1973.

9 Watercolour view of Chambers's Octagon Library by Francis Stephanoff (1788–1860), 1766–7, for Pyne's *Royal Residences*. This was the most majestic of George III's libraries, lit by huge lunette windows. All the libraries were accessible only through the King's bedchamber, which was against the Great Library

10 Garden Front of Buckingham Palace by John Nash (1752–1835), 1831

[35]

11 Watercolour view of Buckingham Palace in 1848 by Joseph Nash

12 Edward Blore's East Front of Buckingham Palace, which closes Nash's courtyard, in a photograph of 1913 (*Courtesy Marlborough Rare Books*)

From Blore to Webb

Inventing a sense of tradition

ALAN POWERS

1 James Pennethorne's Buckingham Palace Ballroom by an unknown artist

The visitor to Buckingham Palace in 1993 sees much that dates from the time of Nash, but little that has not been modified to a greater or lesser extent by redecoration or re-arrangement.

The hands not only of Edward Blore but also of James Pennethorne and Thomas Cubitt were involved in completing the Palace to suit the requirements of Queen Victoria and Prince Albert, although none of the principal rooms conveys an accurate impression of the Palace in Victorian times, owing to later modifications. In its many layers, the Palace resembles the majority of English country houses, and lends itself to the current orthodoxy that every period is of interest if not of equal aesthetic value.

Touches of Blore's work are found in nearly all the State Rooms, in the looking-glass frames in the White Drawing Room, for example, and in other details which tend to be of a coarser baroque or neo-Jacobean character than Nash. His first major alteration to Nash's design was the reconstruction of the upper level of the Garden Front, carried out in 1832, removing the much-criticized Nash dome and substituting a square attic and including some of the sculpture executed for the Marble Arch but which had not yet installed (some also placed on the Grand Portico).

The history of the Palace could be written as a history of developing professionalism in architecture and contracting, starting from the improvised methods of Nash and proceeding to the military discipline with which Sir Aston Webb's refacing of the East Front was carried out in 1913. From the professional point of view, Blore's task was far from easy, given not only the confusion inherited from Nash, but also William IV's lack of interest in using the building.

The accession of Queen Victoria stimulated an accelerated programme of works, notably Blore's East Wing of 1850, the closing of Nash's open courtyard, and the Ballroom Wing added in 1855 by Penne-

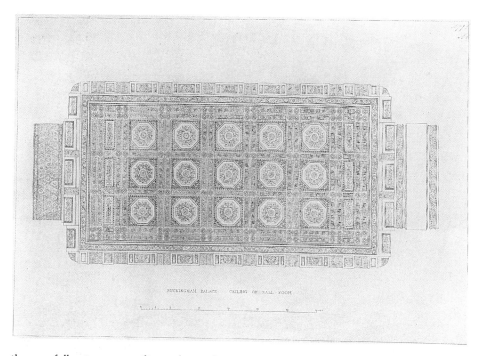

thorne, following an outline scheme by Blore. As Blore's replacement, Pennethorne would certainly have made a more competent job of the East Wing. The Ballroom Wing would probably have been left to Thomas Cubitt to design, since he stood in high favour with the Queen and the Prince Consort following the construction of Osborne, but Cubitt was only a builder, and Lord John Manners, the most benign of Victorian First Commissioners of Works, insisted on the employment of an architect. While the salvaged fittings from the sale of the Brighton Pavilion in 1850 went into the East Wing, the actual proceeds of the sale helped in the construction of the Ballroom with its associated Promenade Gallery and Banqueting Room.

For these rooms, Ludwig (alias Lewis) Grüner of Dresden, who, as Pennethorne wrote in 1854, 'is in the constant employ of the Prince hitherto and has directed all the ornamental painting at Buckingham Palace and Osborne', devised his most extensive decorative scheme. Grüner had been employed initially at the Palace to design the decoration of the Grand Staircase in 1845, seen in the watercolour by Lami of 1848, with its panels and bands of Siena marble and pale grey uniting the scheme of picture hanging and the sculptural reliefs and enhancing Nash's masterstroke of theatrical design.

For Blore's Swiss cottage in the Palace grounds, sadly decayed and demolished in 1926, Grüner devised an elaborate scheme of painted decorations, which may be seen as a more playful counterpart of the contemporaneous attempt by the Prince to inspire a grand school of mural painting in England in the new Palace of Westminster. While Buckingham Palace had nothing as grandiose as William Dyce's fresco at Osborne, it conformed to the polychromatic tendency

which united royal residences from St Petersburg to Potsdam and Paris in the 1840s and 1850s, but is, alas, now hardly recogizable in the Palace of today, apart from the few surviving decorative panels by Nicola Consoni in the Promenade Gallery. The rest of the decorative painting designed by Grüner in a richly-coloured Raphaelesque manner, was carried out by the firm of Charles Moxon (Figs. 1 and 2).

The result was a triumphant demonstration of Albertian taste, fulsomely commended on its opening by Lady Eastlake on its opening in 1856:

I was full of anticipations about the new ballroom and other rooms, but they far exceeded my expectations. The decorations of the ball-room are exquisite, the lighting most original and the raised crimson seats .. all that can be desired to look at, when filled with gorgeously dressed figures .. We were enchanted with the taste of the room .[2]

The effect can be enjoyed in the watercolour by Louis Haghe of 1856, but the achievement of this splendour was not without anxiety for the architect, who like Nash before him was required to be tight-fisted by the Treasury, but open-handed by his royal clients, although Pennethorne was assisted by Cubitt's meticulous contract management. Nonetheless, expensive alterations were made to works only just completed when in 1856 a lighting and ventilating system was installed.

With the completion of the Ballroom, and the Chapel in a converted conservatory on the west front, the Victorian history of building development in the palace comes

virtually to a close. From the Ballroom's triumphant opening, one can move fifty years to its remodelling at the instruction of King Edward VII, which left it in its present state.

The exact dates and responsibilities for the wave of white and gold which effaced the Victorian polychromy in the Palace are confusing. As Queen Mary was to remark in 1915, 'many things were changed here and at Windsor much too quickly by our predecessors'.[3] H. Clifford Smith mentions C. H. Bessant of the decorating firm of Bertram and Son, in connection with the remodelling of the Grand Hall, Marble Hall and Grand Staircase in 1903 and 1902 respectively. To Bessant are attributable the additional reeded moulding and swags on the staircase, which attempt to fill the emptiness left when Grüner's colours were overpainted. In the Marble Hall he also added carved decorations to arches and doorways.

Bessant was not solely responsible for the transformations prior to the renewed royal occupation of the Palace in 1903 ('a duty and a necessity' as the King said twice over to the Grand Duchess of Mecklenburgh-Strelitz in February 1901, the month following his mother's death).[4] Although not mentioned by Clifford Smith, the architect Frank T. Verity played a part in the white and gold regime, as he was well fitted to do, being one of the leading advocates in London of the French taste which the King favoured. Verity may have come to the King's attention as architect of the short-lived Imperial Theatre on the site of the Methodist Central Hall, built for Lily Langtry in 1901. Trained under J.-L. Pascal at the Ecole des Beaux-Arts, Verity had a sense of *mise-en-scène*, if a rather impersonal one. Simon Houfe, in his biography of his grandfather, Sir Albert Richardson, PRA, describes how, early in his career, Richardson, as Verity's assistant, was dispatched to the Palace to measure the Ballroom in 1904, 'making his way through piles of discarded furniture that had belonged to Queen Victoria and which the King was anxious to throw out'.[5] Verity's scheme (Fig. 3) is in the severe 'Neo-Grec' style which certain younger Edwardian architects, Richardson among them, recommended as a cleansing medicine for English eclecticism which would assist a return to the point in the development of classical architecture where Nash left off. The results, seen in Verity's blocks of flats like Cleveland House opposite St James's Palace, have urbanity but little charm.

This may have been the Royal opinion, for the transformation of the Ballroom appears not to have been carried out until 1907 (although Clifford Smith attributes it to 1902), after a new 'powerful and elastic system' for heating and ventilating had been installed. In September, a contract was agreed with the decorators White Allom for

3 Buckingham Palace Ballroom by Frank T. Verity (1864–1937), c. 1904. Formerly in the office of Verity and Beverly, present location unknown

£8,145.4.5. of work undoing what Pennethorne and Grüner had done in the 1850s, removing the finer detail of the Ballroom, and converting it with pilasters from a space divided into two horizontal bands into a single order.[6] In these respects, the executed scheme follows the Verity design, but in others it adopts a more fluid Louis XVI decorative style, more festive in character than Verity even if it is cold compared to Pennethorne and Grüner. Gobelins tapestries of 1776 are architectually framed on the side walls (Fig. 4). The musicians' gallery and throne canopy remained essentially as Pennethorne designed them, and later the gold-embroidered domed canopy was created from the Imperial *shamiana* used to shelter the royal couple at the Delhi Durbar of 1911. This provided a suitably opulent background for the elaborate thrones executed in Paris for the coronation of 1902 under the direction of Sir Joseph Duveen. White Allom continued to work in the Palace for many years afterwards.

The confusion of roles between architect and decorator was typical of the Edwardian period, when much similar reconstruction was in progress in London houses, with a generally loose understanding of period style. Painting out Victorian polychromy was to become a national pastime of the 1920s, as seen for example in Sir Reginald

4 View of the Ballroom in 1913 showing the throne dais and on the left, the doorway to the Annexe Gallery and on the right, the doorway to the West Gallery (courtesy Marlborough Rare Books)

[39]

Blomfield's redecoration of the Locarno Suite at the Foreign Office in 1924, and the progressive de-Victorianizing of the Victoria and Albert Museum. Only a few architects, such as H. S. Goodhart-Rendel, possessed of greater historical awareness, understood the interest and value of painted decoration. Much of the world has yet to learn from their example.

In the reign of George V, the major architectural transformation to the interior of the palace was the redecoration of the Picture Gallery in 1914. The motive was the unsatisfactoriness of the previous system of rooflighting, but not only were Nash's pendant arches removed in the creation of a segmental arched glazed ceiling, but the

doorcases were redesigned, as well as the columnar screen to the 'Sculpture Court' at the south end. The architect for the Picture Gallery was Frank Baines, Chief Architect to the Board of Works (1877–1933), whose artistic claim to fame is the Eltham Well Hall Estate, built for munition workers during World War I. In style, the Picture Gallery more closely resembles the ICI Headquarters and Thames House, Millbank, by Baines (1928), with its rather lightweight version of seventeenth-century ornament. In spite of the solid marble columns forming the screen, with Corinthian capitals cast in bronze, the effect is one of subdued and rather fussy tastefulness strangely at odds with Nash's adjoining State Rooms. The walls were

5 Model of Victoria Memorial by Sir Aston Webb (1849–1930), 1901–4. Royal Institute of British Architects

6 Design for Admiralty Arch by Sir Aston Webb (1849–1930). Webb linked the Mall to the Strand with the two concave faces of Admiralty Arch, which conceal the change of axis. Its accommodation was designed partly as offices and partly as a residence for the First Sea Lord. Since it was impossible to remove the recently-built Drummond's Bank (seen here on the left) a matching building was designed to create a formal approach to the arch. Webb wrote that the Arch 'has the additional advantage of closing the vista both from the Mall and the Strand with an important building, and screening the change of axis of the two roads, while it also shuts out the view of the commercial buildings and advertisements at present seen from the Mall.' (*The Builder*, LXXXVIII, 1905, p. 468)

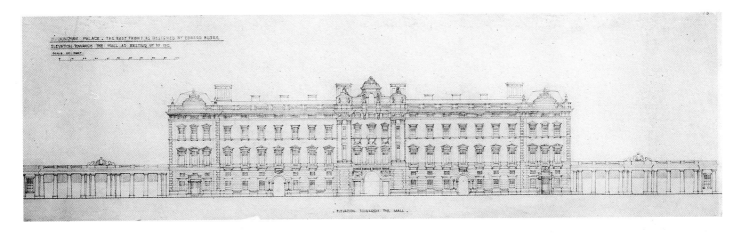

7 The façade of Buckingham Palace as existing up to 1912. Drawing by Sir Aston Webb (1849–1930),
pencil, 19·5 × 57 cm. Royal Institute of British Architecture

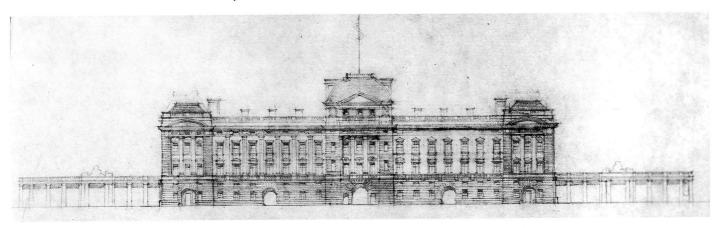

8 Design for the façade of Buckingham Palace by Sir Aston Webb (1849–1930), June 1912. Pencil,
19·5 × 57·5 cm. Royal Institute of British Architects

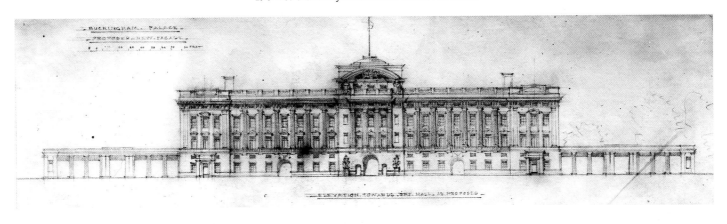

9 Design for the façade of Buckingham Palace by Sir Aston Webb (1849–1930), 1912. Pencil,
18·5 × 55·5 cm. Royal Institute of British Architects

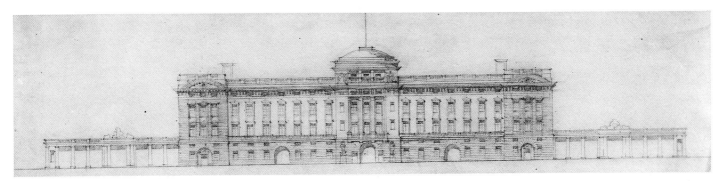

10 Design of the façade of Buckingham Palace by Sir Aston Webb (1849–1930), 1912. Pencil,
17 × 55·5 cm. Royal Institute of British Architects

[41]

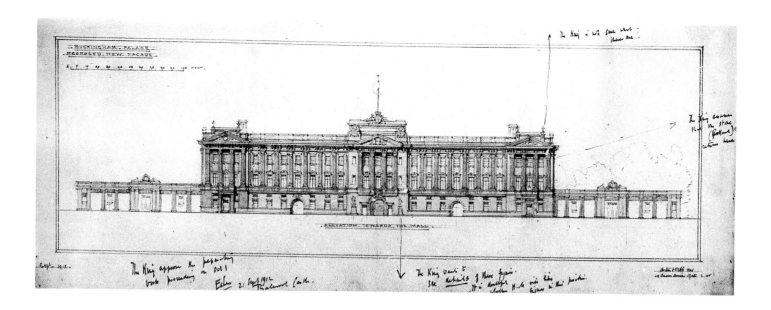

originally hung with green silk by Warners, since, as the Master of the Household Sir Derek Keppel reported to Sir Lionel Earle, the Permanent Secretary to the Office of Works, 'The King expressed his dislike of gold walls and favours green'.[7] Work was on the point of proceeding early in August 1914, when Earle wrote to Lord Stamford-ham on the fatal fourth of the month, 'I feel that, in a moment of crisis such as we are experiencing at present, the more we can go on with, the better from the point of view of alleviating distress among the working classes'.[8]

When one looks at the Picture Gallery, one may be glad that the much more difficult task of refacing the East Front of the Palace was not consigned to the Office of Works. The reasons for this were as much administrative as aesthetic. Blore's East Front had been an embarrassment from its completion, and the Caen stone had started to shed dangerous fragments in 1853. Painted over (as the inner courtyard face of Blore's wing still is), the façade had been patched and kept together, and even in the Edwardian period companies like 'Farnham Limited', stone cleaners with tempting new technologies for sand-blasting and wax treatment, were touting for custom to rescue the remains.

The manner of the refacing involves the history of the Queen Victoria Memorial, which was the subject of a public appeal and limited architectural competition in November 1901 (Fig. 5). The memorial was to include the rearrangement of the space in front of the Palace, hitherto a featureless rectangular yard, its direct axis extended by close-set lines of small trees towards Trafalgar Square, but blocked by a huddle of undistinguished buildings at Spring Gardens. Out of Sir Aston Webb's winning design, in collaboration with the sculptor Thomas Brock, who was knighted by George V in a spontaneous outburst of enthusiasm on its

11 Design for the façade of Buckingham Palace by Sir Aston Webb (1849–1930), 1912, with comments by Lord Esher (recording George V's observations), 21 September 1912. Pencil, pen and buff wash, 23 × 58 cm. Royal Institute of British Architects

completion in 1911, came the project for the Admiralty Arch, also completed in 1911, with the Mall laid out between in its present form (Fig. 6).

Among the original competitors, Sir Thomas Deane of Dublin had proposed a refacing of the Palace, while Webb had more modestly shown a heightened centre-piece. His large axial memorial backed by a colonnade rather than a main gate, served to distract attention from Blore's inadequate centre-piece. The compulsion finally to tackle the East Front arose partly from its deteriorating condition, but also from the new standard of public architecture being set all over London, associated with classical buildings in Portland stone. In July 1910, in response to a parliamentary question from Horatio Bottomley suggesting, as many had done since Nash's earliest days, the rebuilding of Buckingham Palace or removal from it, Lewis Harcourt as First Commissioner of Works replied that 'Buckingham Palace is not internally unsuited for its purpose, but I should be glad if I had the opportunity and the money to reface it in stone on its Eastern front in place of the present covering of stucco and paint'.[9]

A surplus in the Queen Victoria Memorial Fund was deemed sufficient to permit a refacing in 1912, and Aston Webb commissioned to continue the work he had begun. Webb's drawings were prepared in some haste for the King's approval, although he must have given the problem some thought since 1901. Six sketch projects by Webb survive in the Royal Institute of

British Architects Drawings Collection (see Figs. 7, 8, 9 and 10), showing how he modified his original French Second Empire-style dome and moved towards the horizontality of the final design. The sequence is almost a speeded-up film of classicism in the first years of the century, beginning with astylar wings of linked first and second floor windows, resembling Webb's Imperial College of Science in South Kensington, completed in 1911, and gradually moving from a plain Doric to fluted Corinthian detail, carried in pilasters and columns the whole length of the façade. Aston Webb used Roman doric columns in antis for the Royal College of Science and Government Offices, Upper Merrion Street, Dublin, 1905–06 (with Sir T. M. Deane), echoing James Gandon's Customs House, which may therefore be cited as a remote source for Buckingham Palace.

There was little room for manoeuvre, since no alterations to Blore's plans could be made within the budget of £60,000. Even Webb's penultimate design, returned by Lord Esher from Balmoral in September with royal comments in the margin, indicates how George V's fondness for straightforward architecture trimmed Webb's tendency to ornament (Fig. 11). The subsequent alterations to the design, some made during the following winter while the stonework was being prepared, produced the unrelieved squareness of the central and pavilion attics, extended the rustication throughout the basement level, and broadened the central pediment to embrace the whole of the projecting bay, with a wider balcony beneath. Blore's irritating narrow windows on this bay, lighting nothing more than bathrooms, were at the last minute switched from the front to the sides.

In Webb's design the balcony was interrupted by the column bases, but the King requested that it 'should not be curtailed as it is used from time to time on occasions when the King and other members of the Royal Family wish to show themselves to the people'[10] and it was consequently projected on scrolled brackets. The evolution of the design reflected the propaganda for 'monumental Classic' typical of the last years before World War I. This movement criticized the classical designs of Norman Shaw and Aston Webb for their unscholarly and picturesque freedom, yet it was Webb's presidency of the RIBA from 1902 to 1904 which had been crucial in healing the professional breaches of the 1890s and re-establishing the Institute as a learned society controlling the education of architects in the 'Grand Manner'. An early intimation of the trend was the selection of the French-trained J. J. Burnet for the King Edward VII Galleries of the British Museum. By 1912, Webb and his fellow Royal Academician, Reginald Blomfield, were riding this wave, and the scheme for New Delhi by Edwin Lutyens could be seen as its peak.

1912 was the year in which the scholarships in architecture, painting and sculpture were established at the British School at Rome as part of a hoped-for English equivalent of the Ecole des Beaux-Arts, a project which Webb attempted to foster further as President of the RA after the war. Large-scale public works, involving roads, *rondpoints* axial façades and public sculpture were the kind of products it was thought the training in Rome would help to stimulate. The sequence of works created by Webb in the Mall responded to this new impulse, although, as Goodhart-Rendel wrote of Webb in the Dictionary of National Biography, 'in ornament he would always prefer the piquant to the suave'. The metalwork of the forecourt gates, executed by the Bromsgrove Guild (W. Gilbert and L. Weingartner) (Figs. 12 and 13), with its lively foliage and heraldry, is perhaps the most successful decorative aspect of the design, although the pediment sculpture by Thomas Brock is also of high quality.

The East Front refacing can thus be seen as a transitional work, retaining some of the mannerist detailing of the 1890s in the pediments over the windows, with their heavy keystones, but more indicative of a new generation's thinking in its French uniformity. It is tempting to associate the refacing of the Palace with the 'reinvention of tradition' relating to the British monarchy which has been traced to the Edwardian period, particularly in Lord Esher's reconstruction of the Coronation Ceremonial in 1902. Perhaps, like other aspects of newly-realized royal tradition, it is the sense of distance and reserve of Webb's front that characterizes it most strongly. Anything more expressive of 'pomp and circumstance' would have seemed out of place. Also, like other aspects of royal ceremonial, it was thrifty in making use of what already

12 Buckingham Palace gates by Bromsgrove Guild (signed by Gilbert and Weingartner), 1913. Photo by Alan Powers

existed, like the horse-drawn vehicles of the Royal Mews which suddenly became symbolic when on the point of obsolescence in the age of the motor car. While Blore's proportions grin through the refacing to the detriment of its architectural effect, they conveyed the necessary sense of continuity. The palace that Lutyens and his generation would have liked to have built from scratch might best be found in the Queen's Dolls' House of 1924.

Economically, there was hardly an alternative to refacing Blore's façade. The correspondence reveals the political impossibility of asking Parliament for any contribution to the work, had the Queen Victoria Memorial funds proved insufficient. These were invested in Transvaal stock held by the Lord Mayor of London which was depreciating in value during 1913 and created some anxiety about covering the cost. It was fortunate, therefore, that Webb and his contrac-

tors, Leslie & Co., brought the job through on budget, and ahead of time in a period of thirteen weeks during the King's absence. All the stone had been pre-cut and stored in a yard off Lupus Street. The men worked day and night shifts with acetylene lighting cutting back the Blore face as Webb's stonework rose from the ground. In contrast to the traditional style of the design, it was only by use of the most modern American technology, including Waygood electric lifts, that the job was possible.

The devotion of the workforce was recognized when a dinner was given for them at the Holborn Restaurant at the King's expense. As Aston Webb put it, 'The men undoubtedly have all worked like beavers, and loyally resisted attempts made on more than one occasion by the Trades Unions to draw them out during the recent strikes.'[11]

The efficiency of the building process must have appealed to the King's orderly mind. the ghost of Nash was laid, even if more of his animating spirit might have been desirable. The Palace was prepared for the period of the monarchy's greatest popularity.

The first part of this article draws generally on the following printed sources: *History of the King's Works*, vol. VI, 1973; Hermione Hobhouse, *Thomas Cubitt, master builder*, 1971, and *Prince Albert, his life and work*, 1983.
[1] PRO WORK 19/9 ff. 3500
[2] C. Eastlake Smith (ed.), *Journals and Correspondence of Lady Eastlake*, 1895, vol. III, p. 85, quoted in Geoffrey Tyack, *Sir James Pennethorne and the Making of Victorian London*, 1993.
[3] Royal Archives, Queen Mary to Grand Duchess of Mecklenburgh-Strelitz, 29 October 1915, quoted in James Pope-Hennessy, *Queen Mary*, 1959, p. 357.
[4] Royal Archives, Grand Duchess of Mecklenburgh-Strelitz to Duke of Cambridge, 19 February 1901, ibid, p. 355.
[5] Simon Houfe, *Sir Albert Richardson, the professor*, Luton, 1980, p. 21.
[6] PRO WORK 19 64.
[7] Keppel to Earle, 17 March 1914, PRO WORK 19 59
[8] Ibid.
[9] PRO WORK 19 52.
[10] Stamfordham to Earle, 10 November 1912, PRO WORK 19 52.
[11] Aston Webb, quoted in letter from Earle to Stamfordham, 17 October 1913, PRO WORK 19 408.

13 Detail of locks on Palace gates by Bromsgrove Guild

'A noble simplicity'

Pyne's views of Buckingham House

GERVASE JACKSON-STOPS

Few visitors managed to see the interiors of Buckingham House before
it was remodelled as a Palace by Nash, but a remarkable series of
watercolours recorded the appearance of the rooms just a year or two
before they vanished for ever. Some are published here for the first time

Buckingham Palace today fulfils every
visitor's expectation as to what a
palace should be, and for that we have
to thank George IV. But the building in
which he had spent most of his childhood
was a very different place: a country house in
the middle of London, 'not meant for a
Palace, but a retreat', as his father George III
wrote to Lord Bute when acquiring it in
1762.[1]

The fact that St James's Palace continued to be used for official functions meant
that the Queen's House (it was officially
Queen Charlotte's residence) was seldom
visited by outsiders. In March 1767 Mrs
Lybbe Powys 'went to see what is rather a
difficulty to see at all, the Queen's Palace';[2]
and in June 1783 Horace Walpole 'had a
slight view of the Queen's apartment, as I
had of the King's last year'.[3] But few other
diarists managed to penetrate these essentially private and domestic interiors, apart
from one of the Queen's compatriots, the
German Sophie von la Roche, who was in
London in 1786, and who thought 'the noble
simplicity of the furnishings, the order and
neatness, were marks of the character of the
owner—marks of the wise humility upon
the throne'.[4]

A series of anonymous diagrams of the
rooms was made about 1774 in order to
show the arrangement of the pictures,[5] but
there is otherwise very little visual evidence
as to how the interior of the Queen's House
appeared in George III's reign. So it is fortunate indeed that eleven of the hundred plates
in W. H. Pyne's History of the Royal Residences
were devoted to the building, only a year or
two before it was completely remodelled by
Nash. These coloured aquatints correspond
with a series of original watercolours now in
the Royal Library at Windsor, and it has been
suggested that the latter (which are of
exactly the same size) may have been
intended as guides for those who were paid
to add colour (by hand) to the monochrome
printed plates.[6]

Pyne's venture was not the financial
success he had expected, and in the

'Advertisement' at the start of the first
volume (published in 1819) he regretted that
'an expence of some thousand pounds above
the estimate [had] been incurred'. There is
no evidence as to when the watercolours
entered the Royal Library, but it is likely that
he sold them to George IV. When Pyne
finally died in 1843, his obituarist in the
Literary Gazette wrote that 'fortune did not
reward his efforts so liberally as to bless his
closing days with the independence his genius
so richly deserved': which was a polite way
of saying that he spent his last years in the
King's Bench Debtors' Prison.

As might be expected, there is a wealth
of detail in the watercolours of Buckingham
House that makes them still more valuable
than the aquatints in illustrating the 'noble
simplicity' of Queen Charlotte's taste. Some
have been published before,[7] but the opening
of the palace to the public seems a good
opportunity to reproduce most of the series,
with colour illustrations of those not
published in that form until now.

Pyne was himself an artist, responsible
for 'above a thousand groups of small figures
for the embellishment of landscape', published as the Microcosm . . . of the Arts,
Agriculture and Manufactures of Great Britain
in 1803–6. For the Royal Residences, however, and for several other books published
by Pyne's collaborator, the bookseller
Rudolph Ackermann, Pyne acted as author
of the text rather than artist. 'The pains he
bestowed on his anecdotal inquiries were
extraordinary,' according to his obituarist,
and if his commentaries now seem somewhat chatty and diffuse, he established quite
a reputation among London literati of the
time, both under his own name and under
the pseudonym Ephraim Hardcastle.[8]

On the title page of Royal Residences,
Pyne claimed that the illustrations were
'Fac-Similes of original drawings by the most
eminent artists', and four of these were
involved with the Buckingham House series.
Apart from William Westall, who was
responsible for the exterior view from the
Mall (see page 31), Richard Cattermole con-

tributed the view of the lower flight of the
great staircase (Plate II), and Charles Wild,
the Blue Velvet Room (Plate X). All the rest
of the watercolours were made by James
Stephanoff, who later assisted with Nash's
Views of the Royal Pavilion, Brighton (1826),
adding the figures to A. C. Pugin's watercolours of the Music and Banqueting Rooms.[9]

Stephanoff's delight in the human
element is evident in his masterly watercolour of the great staircase (Plate I), with a
guardsman and his lady friend on one of the
upper flights, and a footman approaching on
the lower. None of these was included in
the final aquatint. Laguerre's painted decoration[10] was the one major survival from old
Buckingham House. But it is interesting to
note the doorcase within a feigned niche on
the upper landing, introduced during William
Chambers' alterations of the 1760s so as to
give direct access to the saloon on the first
floor. The new trompe l'oeil painting on this
wall was probably the work of William
Oram, who held the post of Master Car-
penter in the Board of Works, and who also
restored Verrio's Kings Staircase at Hampton
Court.[11]

The original stone staircase was a more
conventional affair, climbing round the four
walls, and the grander 'imperial' stair shown
by Stephanoff was inserted by James Wyatt
in 1799, apparently following a proposal
Chambers had made as early as 1776.[12] The
ironwork balusters look very much like
Tijou's originals, and may simply have been
re-used. Cattermole's view of the staircase
from the Grand Hall (see Plate II) gives an
idea of the monumental effect Wyatt
achieved, with open arches like Venetian
windows either side of the lower flight,
lighting the passages. The Venetian theme
was particularly appropriate since the hall
itself was hung with Canalettos and
Zuccarellis from Consul Smith's collection,
acquired by George III in 1763.[13] Two of
these can just be seen on the right of Cattermole's view.

It is a little surprising to find that none
of the King's apartments on the ground floor

is illustrated in Pyne's *Royal Residences*, apart from two of the four libraries which Chambers added to the south of George III's bedchamber (Plate XI). Three of the rooms are described, with lists of their paintings, in Pyne's text—the King's Breakfast Room (probably the room formerly known as his dining room, on the east front next to the entrance hall); West's Gallery (formerly known as the Warm Room, and hung with seven pictures by Benjamin West, specially commissioned by the King between 1769 and 1773); and the King's Dining Room (probably the room next to it on the west front, formerly known as the Passage Room).

One of the reasons why these rooms were not depicted may have been their extreme austerity. Early on, Mrs Lybbe Powys had found them 'fitted up rather neatly elegant than profusely ornamental';[14] and Pyne himself comments that this

suite of apartments, although sufficiently spacious to admit of splendid decoration, are remarkable for their plainness, being in character with those habits of simplicity which some great men have affected, but which in his Majesty . . . were the offspring of a genuine love for domestic quiet in the bosom of his family.[15]

Another good reason for not illustrating the rooms may have been that they were no longer used, and were under dust covers: since finally succumbing to madness in 1812, the King had been kept in the strictest privacy at Windsor; but even before that date, in 1804–5, he had had many of his best pictures and books brought from Buckingham House to Windsor Castle, following the remodelling of the Upper Ward by James Wyatt.[16]

The Queen's apartments, which had always occupied the first floor, were, by contrast, still very much in use. Pyne's *Royal Residences* illustrates the rooms more or less in the order visitors would have seen them, starting with the great two-storey saloon at the head of the staircase, which occupied the central three bays of the entrance front (Plate III). In 1763, when the King and Queen first moved in to Buckingham House, this room was hung with the seven great Raphael tapestry cartoons (now on loan to the Victoria and Albert Museum). The decision to bring these huge paintings from the Cartoon Gallery at Hampton Court may have been made on sentimental grounds, for Queen Charlotte had admired the series of Mortlake tapestries based on them, which hung in the Chapel Royal at St James's on the occasion of her wedding.[17] The cartoons were arranged literally edge to edge, on all but the window wall, with 'light green Damask' below, as described by Horace Walpole in 1783.[18]

By this time, Laguerre's ceiling, painted for the Duke of Buckingham, had been 'effaced' (again in Walpole's words) '& newly

Unless otherwise stated, all the watercolours of Buckingham House illustrated in this article are of the same size, and were made in connection with W. H. Pyne's *History of the Royal Residences*, published in three volumes in 1819. The watercolours are now in the Royal Library at Windsor, and are reproduced by gracious permission of Her Majesty the Queen

I *The Great Staircase at Buckingham House*, by James Stephanoff (*c.* 1786–1874). Watercolour, 20·1 × 24·8 cm

painted in the antique taste by Cipriani, as are two more cielings'. It has recently been suggested that this new ceiling in the Saloon could have been designed by James 'Athenian' Stuart: the *trompe l'oeil* coffering is virtually identical with one at Holderness House, where he was employed in 1760–5; and Stuart is also known to have designed a throne for Queen Charlotte at St James's Palace in 1761.[19] As we shall see, the two other ceilings mentioned by Walpole were designed by Robert Adam and William Chambers respectively. If Stuart was also involved at Buckingham House, we can perhaps imagine George III employing the three great neo-classical architects of the day in a spirit of fairness, and as a way of encouraging friendly competition.

Four years after Horace Walpole's visit, in 1787, the Raphael cartoons were moved to

Windsor, and it was presumably only at this moment that Chambers designed the wall decorations of the Saloon seen in Stephanoff's view. Two drawings for these decorations, thought to be by his draughtsman, John Yenn, survive in the library of the Royal Academy: one for the window wall in monochrome, and one for the south wall in colour (Plate IV). In the past, these painted pilasters and bas-reliefs have been variously attributed to William Oram[20] and Giovanni-Battista Cipriani.[21] By 1787, however, both artists were dead. Further research in the Lord Chamberlain's papers may reveal who was responsible, but a likely candidate would be Michelangelo Pergolesi, who had worked for William Chambers at Gower House and for Robert Adam in the Long Gallery at Syon[22]—on both occasions adopting the arabesque pilaster as a decorative

II *The Staircase from the Hall*, by Richard Cattermole (1795–1858). This gives a good idea of the monumental effect achieved here, with open arches like Venetian windows either side of the lower flight lighting the passages

device. Pyne describes the *trompe l'oeil* bas-reliefs as 'allegorical of some subject of the arts and sciences, or the useful occupations of life'.

Rather surprisingly, in this refined and francophile interior, probably part Stuart and part Chambers, the white marble chimneypiece turns out to have been designed by Robert Adam in 1761, and is engraved in his *Works in Architecture*.[23] The great rivals shared the post of Architect of the Works from 1761 to 1769, and although Chambers managed to secure most of the work at Buckingham House, through the influence of George III's old tutor, Lord Bute, it was Adam who designed Queen Charlotte's surprise *fête champêtre* for the king's birthday in the garden in June 1761.[24] His chimneypiece is now in the Queen's Presence Chamber at Windsor Castle, still surmounted by the same white marble clock,

with its figures of Vigilance and Patience, carved by John Bacon the elder in 1789.[25]

Ten years later, in 1799, the carver and gilder William Adair supplied six large and 'three small sofas to go between the windows of the Great Saloon',[26] and these are presumably the pieces shown in Stephanoff's watercolour reproduced in Plate III—though one of the small sofas was evidently removed later on, when the throne and canopy were introduced, blocking the central window. This seat furniture (now in the Picture Gallery at Buckingham Palace) was originally covered with white cotton velvet painted with flowers by Princess Elizabeth, the most artistic of Queen Charlotte's offspring.[27] They must have been re-upholstered later to match the crimson velvet canopy and window curtains. The latter have not yet been identified in the Lord Chamberlain's accounts, but the likelihood is that they were introduced in 1812, when the

restrictions on the Regency finally expired and the Royal Household was put on a new footing. Queen Charlotte was then given an additional £10,000 a year for the upkeep of Buckingham House, and began to hold her 'public drawing rooms' and receptions here instead of at St James's. As a contemporary wrote, it was 'proper for the Queen and Princesses to appear again, they having been shut up so long that have lived a most melancholy life'.[28] In February 1817, only a year before her death, the United States Minister, Richard Rush, presented his letters of credence to the Queen in this room, and two months later, her daughter Princess Elizabeth married the Landgrave of Hesse-Homburg here.[29] In 1824 the canopy and throne were sent to Holyrood by George IV, and re-used for his famous visit to Scotland in that year. Miraculously, parts of the canopy still survive in the National Museum of Scotland's stores, and it is hoped that they

III *The Saloon*, by James Stephanoff. This great two-storey room occupied three bays of the entrance front and at first was lined with the Raphael cartoons now at the Victoria and Albert Museum. It seems that the wall designs were by Chambers (see Plate IV), the ceiling possibly by Stuart and the chimneypiece by Adam. The doors to the left led into the Crimson Drawing Room (Plate VI, Fig. 1). Parts of the original throne canopy survive in the National Museum of Scotland stores. It is possible that George III employed the three great neo-classical architects of the day in a spirit of fairness and by way of encouraging friendly competition. Stuart is known to have designed a throne for Queen Charlotte at St James's Palace in 1761 and the *trompe l'oeil* coffering is virtually identical with an example at Holderness House where he was employed in 1760–5

IV *Design for the decoration of the south wall of The Saloon at Buckingham House*, attributed to John Yenn (1750–1821) after a design by Sir William Chambers. Pen and ink and watercolour, 35·7 × 56 cm (Royal Academy)

V *The Queen's Breakfast Room*, by James Stephanoff. It is decorated with black and gold 'japanned' lacquer panels, repositioned here in 1763 after their removal from what became the Crimson Drawing Room (Plate VI, Fig. 1)

1 *The Crimson Drawing Room* by James Stephanoff, see detail in Plate VI. The Saloon can by seen through the doors (see Plate III). Van Dyck's *St Martin dividing his cloak* is to the left of the door. On the other side of the door is a Rubens studio equestrian portrait of Philip II of Spain. To the left of the chimneypiece is the great Domenichino *St Agnes* in a splendid Kentian frame surmounted by a crown. Immediately to the left of Van Dyck's *St Martin* is *The family of Balthasar Gerbier* by Rubens which today hangs in the East Gallery (see colour detail, Plate VI opposite). The ceiling was designed by Robert Adam and executed by Cipriani

VI *The Crimson Drawing Room* (opposite) by James Stephanoff (detail of Fig. 1). The throne is clearly visible through the door leading to the Saloon. The armchairs survive, some of them now in the Blue Drawing Room

[48]

VII *The Second Drawing Room*, by James Stephanoff, compare with Plate VIII, a painting set in the same room, and showing Van Dyck's portrait *The Villiers Boys* still hanging in the same position to the right of the door. Van Dyck's *Three Eldest Children of Charles I* can also be seen still in place above the chimneypiece

can be restored in the not-too-distant future.

The double doors opposite the throne in Stephanoff's view led through to the Crimson Drawing Room, as it was described by Pyne (Plate VI, Fig. 1), occupying the centre of the garden front. In the Duke of Buckingham's day, this was the Japanned Room, called after the black and gold lacquer panels apparently used to wainscot the whole room.[30] This type of decoration was usually reserved for smaller dressing rooms and closets in the early eighteenth century, and it was distinctly unusual to find it in a room of this size and importance. Queen Charlotte obviously valued the panels, for in 1763 she had William Vile repair and re-assemble them in the adjoining room on the south which was to become her breakfast room (Plate V).[31]

This charming room, reminiscent of some of Queen Charlotte's later decoration at Frogmore, was, strange to say, hung with

pictures in the 1770s and '80s, among them, the two gigantic Van Dycks of 'Charles 1st on the white horse, and He & his Queen and Children sitting',[32] which flanked the door on the left leading to the great staircase. These were among the pictures removed by the King to Windsor about 1804 (they are now in the Picture Gallery at Buckingham Palace).

Vile's bill, which amounted to £572 12s, included making new panels, and decorating the doorcases and the earlier Kentian pier glasses and tables in the same manner. The mirrors, which may originally have been made by Benjamin Goodison for St James's, still survive at Buckingham Palace though they have lost their pediments.[33] A visitor in 1802 described the floor as carpetless and the curtains as being brown and maroon, painted in imitation of cut velvet by Princess Elizabeth.[34] The 'continuous drapery' shown here, probably in red broadcloth or

felt, trimmed with black borders and fringes, is in a more advanced Regency taste and can be identified with the '3 Prs of Scarlet emboss'd Cloth Curtains Cornice &c' supplied for this room by Elliott Son & Francis, upholsterers, on 5 January 1810.[35] They also supplied '2 Elbows & 1 Stool & 6 Single Chairs, with Covers of Embossed Cloth' for a further £38 13s. The carpet, probably of Brussels weave (made either at Wilton or Kidderminster) and with a pattern of gold neo-classical urns in a trellis pattern, must have been laid about the same time.

The white marble chimneypiece was evidently designed by Chambers, and the garnitures of brightly coloured ceramics on the mantelpiece, on the shelf above it, and on the doorcases, are reminiscent of much earlier porcelain 'cabinets'. Walpole commented on 'some modern jars of Chinese porcelaine, many of Chelsea porcelaine, & a few of Seve' in the Queen's apartments,[36]

VIII *George, Prince of Wales, and Frederick, later Duke of York*, by Johan Zoffany (*c.* 1733–1810),
Oil on canvas, 111·8 × 127·9 cm (Windsor Castle). See Plate VII

anticipating some of her son's great passions as a collector. One piece that is clearly recognizable is the pink and white Chelsea porcelain clock above the chimneypiece, one of a pair known to have belonged to Queen Charlotte, and still in the Royal Collection.[37]

Another important feature of the room was the organ, in a mahogany case supplied by John Bradburn in 1766.[38] This may originally have stood on the south wall opposite the chimneypiece. It is seen here crowned by Roubiliac's bust of Handel, evidently the Queen's own choice, as Pyne calls her 'a good performer on the piano-forte, [who] delighted to play the concertos of Handel'.[39] According to Sophie von la Roche, it was also used for family prayers.[40]

Returning now to the Crimson Drawing Room, in the centre of the garden front,

Stephanoff's watercolour (Plate VI, Fig. 1) gives an excellent idea of the painted ceiling: Robert Adam's only other contribution to the decoration of Buckingham House. An engraving of it appears in the *Works of Architecture* (1778), and it is presumably one of the two ceilings described by Walpole in 1783 as 'newly painted in the antique taste by Cipriani'. Just how 'newly painted' is open to question, however: it can scarcely have been after 1769, when Adam resigned his position as 'Architect of the Works'. The doorcases and cornice are of a typical Chambers pattern, and also of the 1760s.

Walpole describes the drawing room and the three rooms to the north of it—the Queen's dressing room, bedchamber and closet—as one suite, all 'hung with red Damask and pictures'.[41] By Pyne's day, the walls of this room had been re-covered in

'crimson satin, and the gilt chairs and sofas are covered with the same rich material'.[42] Again, the likeliest date for the introduction of both furniture and wall-hangings is around 1812. The armchairs survive, some of them now in the Blue Drawing Room at Buckingham Palace,[43] though their maker has yet to be identified.

The pictures shown here also represent a change of heart. The diagrams of *c.* 1774 indicate a large pair of canvases by Guido Reni (now in the National Gallery) flanking the door to the Saloon,[44] but these have been replaced by the early Van Dyck *St Martin* on the left, and the equestrian portrait of Philip II of Spain from Rubens' studio on the right. Until about 1804, these had hung as a pair (despite their very different frames) in the same position in the King's drawing room, immediately below. The beautiful Domenichino *St Agnes*, formerly isolated on the north wall, is shown by Stephanoff in a less conspicuous position to the left of the chimneypiece, but still retains its splendid Kentian frame surmounted by a crown. The *Mystic Marriage of St Catherine*, after Veronese, remains in place above the chimneypiece, together with the three overdoors, including a Titian copy of a *Magdalen* and a Ribera *St John with a Lamb*.

The Second Drawing Room, immediately to the north (Plate VII), began life as the Queen's dressing room, with her bedchamber beyond. But by 1768, a new bedchamber had been made, and the old one was used as a dressing room. By about 1774 the Second Drawing Room was called the Warm Room, like the room immediately below in the King's apartments. Mrs Lybbe Powys, in 1767, had been 'amazed to find so large a house so warm, but fires, it seems, are kept the whole day, even in the closets'.[45] Their names certainly imply that this was the case in these two rooms, which were probably intended for informal everyday use.

Zoffany's portrait of Queen Charlotte's two eldest children, George, Prince of Wales, and Frederick, later Duke of York (Plate VIII), was painted in 1764 in this same room (then still the Queen's dressing room), and clearly shows William Chambers' white marble chimneypiece with its ram's head masks (now in the King's Bedchamber at Windsor), one of the doorcases reflected in the overmantel mirror, and the walls hung with crimson damask supplied by the mercer Robert Carr.[46] This location was undoubtedly chosen because of the two Van Dyck paintings of children, which Stephanoff shows still in the same position over fifty years later: the *Villiers Boys* on the left (children of the 1st Duke of Buckingham, and thus appropriate for Buckingham House), and the *Three Eldest Children of Charles I* above the chimneypiece. Zoffany took liberties with the other pictures, however, introducing an *Infant Christ* by a follower of Maratta, and portraits of the King and Queen immediately above the little princes.

Zoffany's yet more celebrated portrait of the Queen with her two children (Plate IX) shows her seated at her dressing table, and historians have thus assumed that it was also painted in her dressing room.[47] Yet there is no sign of crimson damask on the walls (always a feature of that room), the doorcase is of an altogether simpler type than those in the rest of the Queen's apartment, and above all, the view of the garden through the open window is clearly at ground-floor, not first-floor, level. The inescapable conclusion seems to be that this is one of the King's apartments on the floor below, which the artist has dressed up for the occasion with some of the Queen's most treasured possessions. That would explain the 'drab' or grey-green paintwork, the simple panelled

walls of the room beyond (either the King's 'Warm Room' or his dressing room to judge by the number of windows), and finally the pier table in that room, in the style of William Kent, which features prominently in Zoffany's 1771 portrait of the King.[48]

Returning to the Second Drawing Room and comparing Zoffany (Plate VIII) with Pyne (Plate VII), the main difference is the replacement of the pretty rococo 'landskip glass' with a much larger overmantel mirror (as also happened in the Crimson Drawing Room). The set of seat furniture has also changed and is more formally arranged, but the armchairs, with lion's masks on the arms and sharply raked back legs, are evidently of the 1760s, and not a Regency addition.

At first sight, the ceiling here looks very similar to Adam's in the Crimson Drawing Room. However, William Chambers' design for it exists, apparently coloured by

The anonymous writer describing the house in the *Gentleman's Magazine* in 1802 particularly commented on the absence of carpeting: 'A luxury of which his Majesty deprives himself in almost every apartment, from the opinion that carpets and other means of great warmth are injurious to health.' Presumably the Queen did not share these scruples.

Cipriani, who executed all the figures.[49] The drawing, done as if it were an antique fragment (and thereby omitting much repetitious detail) is one of the architect's most charming conceits. An inscription on the back reveals that Cipriani's '17 pictures & 4 Genii' cost £225, and that Charles Cotton was paid £120 for 'painting in Gold & colour all the ornaments' cost £120; while the upholsterer Samuel Norman charged £12.12.0 'for pasting up the work'.

The walls are described by Pyne as 'hung with crimson of a deeper colour' than the preceding room,[50] and the arrangement of the pictures is virtually identical with the diagram of *c*. 1774[51]—only lacking the decorative bows and ropes from which they were suspended. Flanking the *Villiers Boys* are the two 'Andrea del Sartos, holy Families' so much admired by Walpole, who called one of them 'equal to Raphael',[52] while the large canvases either side of the chimneypiece are a Maratta *Virgin and Child with St*

Francis and Cagnacci's *Jacob, Rachel and Leah*. The theme of family, parenthood and childhood, is continued by Guido Reni's *St Joseph and the Infant Jesus* on the south wall, and we can surely detect Queen Charlotte's personal, somewhat sentimental, taste here.

Beyond the Second Drawing Room lay the Blue Velvet Room (Plate X), originally the Queen's bedchamber, and after 1768 her dressing room. In this latter state, it had an upper register of pictures consisting almost entirely of seventeenth-century portraits, hung from still more prominent bows and ropes, while six large frames were suspended below them, divided into hexagonal compartments.[53] According to Walpole, these held 'a vast quantity of enamelled pictures, miniatures and Cameos, amongst which six or eight at least of Charles 1st'.[54] They were glazed, and backed with red damask, presumably to match the wall-hangings. This arrangement survived until at least 1796,[55] but the room was entirely redecorated and re-arranged at some later date. About 1812 again seems likely, to judge by the up-to-date Regency curtains, reminiscent of the designs of Percier and Fontaine, and the massive chairs and settees, identical to those in the Crimson Drawing Room, but covered in blue velvet to complement the light blue silk wall-hangings. The heavy gilt borders to the silk, and the ornaments applied in the corners, are very much in the Carlton House taste.

Despite its formality, the Blue Velvet Room was still evidently used as the Queen's dressing room. The dressing table between the windows is draped in the Empire style with heavily-fringed silk; another Kentian pier glass, like those in the Breakfast Room, serves as a toilet mirror; and Matthew Boulton's blue-john candelabra (two from a set of four 'King's vases' designed by Chambers in 1771, and still in the Royal Collection)[56] would have cast plenty of light on the royal complexion—raised as they are on tall Empire-style torchères. The window drapery, surmounted by a royal crown in the centre, in effect acts as a canopy of state, framing this ensemble, and stressing its ceremonial use. The Boulle 'marriage coffer' in the corner by the door would probably have been used to store some of the Queen's jewels. It could have been supplied by a dealer like Robert Fogg, 'chinaman to His Majesty', who sold Boulle furniture to the Prince Regent for Carlton House in 1812–13.[57] As the only piece of its kind shown in Pyne's views of Buckingham House, it may not be too fanciful to imagine it as a gift to the Queen from her son.

Unlike many of the more public rooms, where bare floor boards were more suitable for the entertainment of large numbers, the Blue Velvet has a magnificent carpet, again probably Brussels weave (manufactured at

IX *Queen Charlotte with her two eldest sons*, by Johan Zoffany. Oil on canvas, 112·4 × 129·2 cm (Windsor Castle).
It has always been assumed that the scene is the Queen's dressing room, yet it seems clear that it is one of the
King's apartments on the ground floor, furnished for the occasion with some of the Queen's treasured possessions

either Wilton or Kidderminster),[58] with a hearth rug featuring the royal arms in the foreground. The anonymous writer describing the house in the *Gentleman's Magazine* in 1802 particularly commented on the absence of carpeting: 'A luxury of which his Majesty deprives himself in almost every apartment, from the opinion that carpets and other means of great warmth are injurious to health.' Presumably the Queen did not share these scruples.

Charles Wild's view shows some of the original seventeenth-century portraits surviving as overdoors, but the room has otherwise been rehung with landscapes. These include works by Claude, Poussin, Rubens and Gaspar Dughet, all previously hung in the King's dressing room immediately below.

The last of the Queen's apartments illustrated in Pyne's views is the Green Closet. The 'New North Wing', which was being furnished late in 1767 is said to have included 'Their Majesties' new bedchamber

and closet',[59] but this can never have been the case. A recently-discovered watercolour of the garden front of Buckingham House, made in 1770, clearly shows the upper storey of Chambers' wing as a series of low attic rooms, and not a continuation of the state apartments. The diagram of the pictures in the Queen's bedchamber, of *c.* 1774, and later plans in Westminster Public Library, prove that it was not in the new wing at all, but the room above the King's dining room, overlooking the forecourt (now the Throne Room).[60] The Green Closet was the adjoining room on the north, with the Blue Velvet (the Queen's original bedchamber) also adjoining it on the west. There is known to have been a water closet here in 1762 when Vile made a secret door through to it from the bedchamber, disguised in one side of his great mahogany bookcase. The closet unfortunately does not feature among the picture hanging diagrams of *c.* 1774. However, Sophie von la Roche describes it as 'a small

cabinet off the bedroom', hung with 'portraits of the fourteen royal children—thus the first waking moments are dedicated to this sight and the emotions of true motherhood'.[61] These portraits were of course Gainsborough's famous ovals, painted at Windsor in 1782.[62] Pyne calls the Green Closet a 'plain apartment', and it may well have been hung with paper rather than silk. On the other hand its up-to-date Regency furniture includes a set of 'klismos' chairs of a type made fashionable by Thomas Hope, a little writing desk in the French style next to the window, and a chiffonier on the left-hand wall, matching a cabinet set in the window embrasure opposite. These cabinets, with brass-inlaid doors, still survive at Windsor Castle. All this furniture, and the elaborate drapery of the window curtains, suggests a fairly recent redecoration, again around 1812. For some reason, the footstool placed immediately in front of the chiffonier in Pyne's aquatint is missing from Stephanoff's

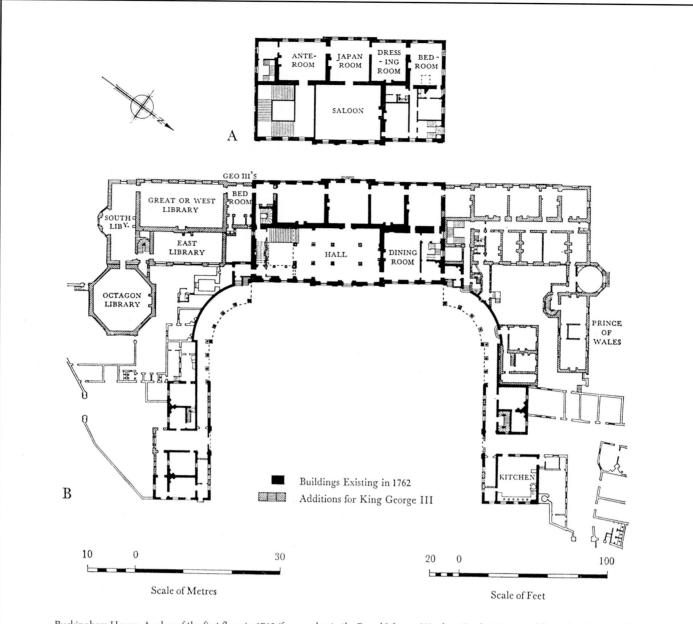

A

BED-
ROOM

ANTE-
ROOM

JAPAN
ROOM

DRESS-
ING
ROOM

SALOON

GEO III'S

GREAT OR WEST
LIBRARY

BED
ROOM

SOUTH
LIB Y.

EAST
LIBRARY

HALL

DINING
ROOM

OCTAGON
LIBRARY

PRINCE
OF
WALES

B

■ Buildings Existing in 1762

▨ Additions for King George III

KITCHEN

10   0   30

Scale of Metres

20   0   100

Scale of Feet

Buckingham House. A: plan of the first floor in 1762 (from a plan in the Royal Library, Windsor Castle). B: ground floor plan showing the
additions made by George III (based on plans in Westminster City Library)

watercolour. The pleated silk screen on a
hinge at the window shows that the room
overlooked a more public area than those
already described: i.e. the service court on
the north side of the house.

The last two views of Buckingham House
published by Pyne illustrate two of the
four large libraries which Chambers added
on the south side of the building to house
George III's ever-growing collections of
books and manuscripts. As can be seen
from the plan of the house made in 1762 (see
above), these rooms could be approached
only through the King's bedchamber at
ground-floor level, and they remained very
much part of his personal domain. The im-
petus for the first of them, the Great or West
Library (Plate XI), was his purchase of Consul
Smith's collection in 1762. When com-

pleted, in 1764, the room seems to have been
fitted with a series of bookcases from St
James's Palace, adapted with 'many Additions and Alterations' by William Vile.[63]
The more utilitarian shelves seen in Stephanoff's watercolour were probably installed at
a slightly later date.

The elaborate wind-dial seen above the
chimneypiece was demonstrated to Sophie
von la Roche in 1786 by the royal clockmaker Justin Vulliamy, who

showed us one of his eldest son's [i.e. Benjamin
Vulliamy's] inventions . . . on a large semi-sphere
set in the wall, he [the King] can follow what parts
of the world are affected if a heavy gale is sweep-
ing England; while the weather-vane on this
house, with its eminent situation, calculates and
records so accurately on this sphere that the King
can conjecture how his fleet is faring.[64]

This vane, on a tall mast supported by wires

like a yard-arm, can be seen rising above the
roofs of the library buildings in Pyne's exterior view of Buckingham House (see page 31).
The two large library tables have the oval
panelled doors usually associated with
William Vile, but they could equally be by
John Bradburn, who started in Vile's work-
shop and succeeded him in the royal
accounts from 1764.

The austerity of Chambers' design, reflecting the simplicity of the King's taste,
applied equally to the South and Octagon
Libraries, added in 1766–7, and the East
Library of 1772–3. The Octagon (see p. 53)
was certainly the most impressive spatially
with its great 'therm' windows and central
dome. Stephanoff's view shows the door
through to the South Library on the far
wall, and, through one of the windows, a
glimpse of the Marine Gallery, added above

X *The Blue Velvet Room*, by Charles Wild (1781–1835). The luxurious carpet (either Wilton or Kidderminster), in what was the Queen's dressing room, did not accord with the views of the King who thought such sources of warmth bad for health

the East Library in 1774 to house John Chamberlain's models of ships, ports and fortifications.

The vast octagonal library table in the centre must have been made for the room by Bradburn, and in the centre, on a stepped plinth, is the celebrated astronomical clock made for the King by Eardley Norton in 1765.[65] With its silver mounts and incredibly complex mechanism, it cost the huge sum of £1,042. The clock is still in the Royal Collection, and the table also survives, though hardly recognizable in its present form—for in 1836 it was entirely re-veneered in ebony (with ivory inlay) for William IV's library at Windsor.[66]

In 1823, George IV gave his father's collection of books and manuscripts to the British Museum, and the great libraries in which they had been housed were almost entirely demolished as part of Nash's re-modelling of the Palace. It was fortunate for posterity that Pyne and his team of artists had recorded their appearance in such detail only a few years earlier.

The author is greatly indebted to Mr Hugh and the Hon Mrs Roberts, respectively Surveyor of the Queen's Works of Art, and Curator of the Print Room in the Royal Library, without whose help this article could not have been written.

[1] Bute MSS Central Library, Cardiff 336/1; quoted by Olwen Hedley, *Queen Charlotte*, 1975, p. 71.
[2] E. J. Climenson, ed., *Passages from the Diaries of Mrs Philip Lybbe Powys*, 1899, p. 116.
[3] Paget Toynbee, ed., 'Horace Walpole's Journals of Visits to Country Seats, &c', *Walpole Society*, vol. 16, 1928, p. 78.
[4] Clare Williams, ed., *Sophie in London 1786 (being the Diary of Sophie v. la Roche*, 1933, p. 145.
[5] Francis Russell, 'King George III's picture hang at Buckingham House', *Burlington Magazine*, CXXIX, 1987, pp. 524–31.
[6] Typescript 'Introduction to Pyne's *Royal Residences*' by Jane Roberts, Royal Library, Windsor; also in the Royal Collection are six much larger watercolours of Windsor and Carlton House by Charles Wild (about 40 × 50 cm) with incised lines and rulings for the architecture, implying that these were the artist's finished working drawings for the plates.
[7] David Watkin, *The Royal Interiors of Regency England*, 1984, pp. 74–87, where eight of the eleven watercolours are reproduced, but only five in colour.
[8] 'Ephraim Hardcastle's' best known work, *Wine and Walnuts*, was published in 1823, and is a valuable source of information on contemporary writers and artists.
[9] Gervase Jackson-Stops, ed., *John Nash's Views of the Royal Pavilion*, 1991, p. 11.
[10] For a full account of the subject matter of Laguerre's paintings, see the manuscript 'Account of the Paintings and Pictures at Buckingham House' in the British Museum, Harl. 6344.
[11] H. M. Colvin, ed., *The History of the King's Works*, vol. 5, 1660–1782, p. 136, where Laguerre's paintings are mistakenly given to Verrio.
[12] John Harris, *Sir William Chambers*, 1970, p. 84.
[13] *A King's Purchase: King George III and the collection of Consul Smith*, exh. cat. (The Queen's Gallery, Buckingham Palace), 1993, pp. 16, 62.
[14] E. J. Climenson, ed., op. cit., p. 116.
[15] W. H. Pyne, *The History of the Royal Residences*, 1819, vol. 2, 'Buckingham House' p. 8.
[16] H. M. Colvin, ed., op. cit., vol. 6, pp. 375–9.
[17] Olwen Hedley, op. cit., p. 45.
[18] Francis Russell, op. cit., fig. 55; Paget Toynbee, ed., op. cit., p. 78.
[19] Giles Worsley, 'Out from Adam's Shadow', *Country Life*, 14 May, pp. 101-2; Gervase Jackson-Stops and Victoria Percy, 'The Travel Journals of the 1st Duchess of Northumberland—II', *Country Life*, 7 Feb. 1974, p. 251.
[20] Edward Croft-Murray, *Decorative Painting in England 1537–1837*, vol. 2, 190, p. 251; this seems to give Pyne as a source for the attribution, although the latter nowhere mentions Oram (who died in 1777) in his text.
[21] David Watkin, op. cit., p. 82; Cipriani died in 1785.
[22] Croft-Murray, op. cit., pp. 256–7.
[23] The drawing for the engravings is in Sir John Soane's Museum, vol. XXII, p. 57 (with variants on pp. 56 and 58), all dated 1761.

XI *The Great or West Library*, by James Stephanoff. George III's four libraries could only be entered through his bedchamber. Above the chimneypiece is a wind-dial which, together with a weather-vane outside, enabled the King to conjecture how his fleet might be faring

[24] A. T. Bolton, *The Architecture of Robert & James Adam*, vol. 1, 1922, pp. 48–9.
[25] Rupert Gunnis, *Dictionary of British Sculptors 1660–1851*, n.d., p. 27
[26] H. Clifford Smith, *Buckingham Palace*, 1931, p. 92.
[27] Watkin, op. cit., p. 83.
[28] Diary of Lucy Kennedy, quoted by Hedley, op. cit., p. 257; the Queen's last 'drawing room' at St James's was held on 18 June 1812, and her first at Buckingham House on 2 June 1814, which helps to date the canopy and curtains (Public Record Office, Lord Chamberlain's papers, LC6/1).
[29] Hedley, op. cit., p. 288.
[30] Colvin, op. cit., p. 136 and fig. 1 on p. 135.
[31] John Harris, Geoffrey de Bellaigue and Oliver Millar, *Buckingham Palace and its Treasures*, 1968, p. 118.
[32] Paget Toynbee, ed., op. cit., p. 78.
[33] Harris, Bellaigue and Millar, op. cit., p. 118 (illustrated).
[34] An anonymous writer (signing himself *H.B.*) in the *Gentleman's Magazine*, vol. 72 (2), 1802, p. 1184.
[35] Public Record Office, Lord Chamberlain's papers, LC9 368, p. 200.
[36] Paget Toynbee, ed., op. cit., p. 78.
[37] *Treasures of the Royal Collection*, Queen's Gallery, Buckingham Palace, 1988–9, exh. cat., no. 113.
[38] Geoffrey Beard and Christopher Gilbert, eds., *Dictionary of English Furniture Makers 1660–1840*, 1986, p. 96.

[39] Pyne, op. cit., p. 21.
[40] Clare Williams, ed., op. cit., p. 146.
[41] Paget Toynbee, ed., op cit., p. 78; the 'crimson Genoa damask' was supplied by the mercer William Hinchcliffe (H. Clifford Smith, op. cit., p. 77).
[42] Pyne, op. cit., p. 14.
[43] Illustrated in Harris, Bellaigue and Millar, op. cit., p. 67.
[44] Russell, op. cit., fig. 59.
[45] E. J. Climenson, ed., op. cit., pp. 116–7.
[46] Gervase Jackson-Stops, 'Johan Zoffany and the Eighteenth-Century Interior', *Antiques Magazine*, June 1987, p. 1266; H. Clifford Smith., op. cit., p. 77.
[47] Mary Webster, *Johan Zoffany 1733–1810*, National Portrait Gallery, 1976, p. 34, exh. cat., no. 25.
[48] Oliver Millar, *The Later Georgian Pictures in the Collection of Her Majesty the Queen*, 1969, no. 1195, was the first to suggest that this might be a ground-floor room; he also identifies some of the pictures hanging in the room beyond as part of Consul Smith's collection, on the basis of their frames.
[49] Harris, op. cit., 217; the drawing is in the RIBA Drawings Collection, G3/1.
[50] Pyne, op. cit., p. 15.
[51] Russell, op. cit., fig. 58.
[52] Paget Toynbee, ed., op. cit., p. 78.
[53] Russell, op. cit., fig. 57.

[54] Paget Toynbee, ed., op. cit., p. 79.
[55] The date of an inventory of the pictures now in the British Library, see Russell, op. cit., footnote 4.
[56] Nicholas Goodison, *Ormolu: The Work of Matthew Boulton*, 1974, fig. 78.
[57] *Carlton House: The Past Glories of George IV's Palace*, Queen's Gallery, Buckingham Palace (exhibition) 1991–2, cat. nos. 21, 32.
[58] Christopher Gilbert et al., *Country House Floors 1660–1850*, Temple Newsam (exhibition) 1987, pp. 61–3.
[59] Tradesmen's bills quoted by Olwen Hedley, op. cit., p. 102.
[60] The watercolour, by Anthony Wilson, is reproduced in David J. Griffin and Simon Lincoln, *Drawings from the Irish Architectural Archive*, London 1993, cat. no. 5; see also Russell, op. cit., fig. 56.
[61] Clare Williams, ed., op. cit., p. 145.
[62] There were in fact only thirteen, Princess Amelia having not yet been born—the series was completed by ovals of the King and Queen; see Harris, de Bellaigue and Millar, op. cit., p. 231.
[63] Hugh Roberts, 'Metaphorphoses in Wood: Royal Library Furniture in the Eighteenth and Nineteenth Centuries,' APOLLO, June 1990, p. 383.
[64] Clare Williams, ed., op. cit., p. 146.
[65] Harris, de Bellaigue and Millar, op. cit., p. 158.
[66] Roberts, op. cit., fig. 9 (to which caption no. 1 refers).

The Nash state rooms

Opulence, ingenuity and originality

JOHN MARTIN ROBINSON

The sequence of state rooms designed by John Nash
remains largely as he created it, and forms one of the greatest
'hidden' treasures of European architecture

The Nash state rooms at Buckingham Palace are the principal feature of the building and one of the great unknown architectural experiences of London. The richness of their fittings and fixtures distinguishes them from any comparable set of rooms in England, while the originality of their architecture marks them out from contemporary palace rooms on the Continent. Despite some unfortunate later modification of their decorations, they are still largely as created by Nash. In their design, they stretch the eighteenth-century classical tradition to its limits in order to create an aura of extreme opulence. Even contemporaries, who were rather scathing about the exterior of the Palace—more for political than aesthetic reasons—were enthusiastic about the interior and praised the 'number, magnificence and excellent arrangement of the principal apartments' though some found the brightness of colouring and richness of detail a bit indigestible.

Designed by John Nash (Fig. 1), and dutifully completed after his downfall by Edward Blore (Fig. 2), the state rooms represent the taste of George IV himself in its final and most developed francophile mode, together with that of the King's principal artistic advisor Charles Long, Lord Farnborough, who was the *éminence grise* behind all the Palace projects of the 1820s including the reconstruction of the state rooms at St James's and the massive transformation of Windsor Castle, as well as Buckingham Palace itself. Even before construction work began, Charles Long attended on the King in May 1825 to decide the future disposition of the furniture and pictures between Windsor Castle and the other palaces.

Charles Long (whose immediate ancestors were prosperous Jamaica merchants) was successively MP for Rye, Midhurst, Wendover and Haslemere before being created a peer in 1826. His principal interests, however, were artistic. He was a recognized judge of pictures and architecture, and formed a famous collection at his own house at Bromley Hill, Kent. He also

1 *John Nash (1752–1835)* by Sir Thomas Lawrence (1769–1830), begun 1824, exhibited RA 1827. Oil on canvas, 138 × 110 cm. Jesus College, Oxford. Nash was the brilliantly inventive architect whom George IV, first as Prince Regent and then as King, employed for his spectacular schemes. They included the Brighton Pavilion, Regent's Park and Regent's Street, Carlton House Terrace on the Mall and the unrivalled sequence of staterooms in Buckingham Palace. When his patron died in 1830, Nash's career came to an abrupt end

G. Koberwein 1868.

2 *Edward Blore* (1787–1879) by George Koberwein, 1868. Chalk, 66 × 54 cm. National Portrait Gallery. Blore completed Nash's work after the death of George IV in 1830

largely completed and *in situ* while most of the rich architectural decorations such as marble chimneypieces, gilt bronzework, scagliola columns and doorcases, parquetry floors and mirrored doors were ready for assembly on site. The only question mark hangs over the final choices for the decorations such as the watered satins and figured silk damasks on the walls, as well as the lavish gilding. It seems likely that this was the responsibility of Viscount Duncannon, the Head of the Office of Works at that time.

The basic layout of the state rooms formed part of Nash's original design for the Palace, prepared in 1825. The plan of the principal floor was arranged so as to permit an axial approach to the Throne Room for ceremonial functions, as well as a full circuit of the state rooms for more social occasions.

> To the casual gaze the frieze in the Throne Room looks like a Grecian cast; it is only the gothic armour on the figures which gives the game away—that the decoration actually depicts the Wars of the Roses

shared George IV's love of things French, and had had the opportunity to study Napoleon's new state rooms by Percier & Fontaine at the Tuileries when he was dispatched by the British Treasury to Paris in 1817 as a commissioner to settle the accounts of the allied army of occupation. It was the Tuileries that formed the main inspiration for George IV's Buckingham Palace.

Charles Long re-visited Paris on several subsequent occasions, and some of these trips were on behalf of George IV. In 1824, for instance, he purchased the Gobelins tapestries and some Louis XV *boiseries* for the Grand Reception Room at Windsor Castle, an apartment which was largely his own conception. Long was responsible for several of the distinctive features of Buckingham Palace, notably the extensive use of marbling and scagliola which repeated the treatment at his own house where the hall and staircase were marbled. The concept of

a sculpture gallery on the ground floor with a picture gallery above also seems to have been Long's; it differed entirely from the mode of display in George IV's previous London palace at Carlton House, although there was a similar arrangement at Bromley Hill.

Though George IV died in 1830, and Nash was then dismissed in disgrace by the Treasury before the state rooms were finished, there can be little doubt that they were completed largely as originally designed. William IV had no interest in them whatsoever and so changed little, while Blore, the completing architect, who was chosen by the government on the strength of his dreary competence at Lambeth Palace, stuck largely to what had already been designed by Nash and created by a team of brilliant, albeit expensive, craftsmen. By 1830, when nemesis struck, the elaborate plaster ceilings (Plate II) were

The key to this arrangement is the staircase (Fig. 3) which, in addition to having two return-arms leading to the Throne Room sequence also has a third arm continuing straight upwards into the East Gallery (later doubled in length by Pennethorne when Queen Victoria's huge Ballroom was added) whence the drawing rooms along the Garden Front of the Palace could be approached.

The latter rooms were a completely new addition by Nash, on the other side of the spinal top-lit Picture Gallery formed in the shell of old Buckingham House. The Throne Room sequence along the east side is a truncated version of the traditional court *enfilade* with a vestigial Guard Room and Green Drawing Room making an overture to the Throne Room itself. It is in these three spaces that the intentions of George IV, Nash and Long can still best be appreciated. The Picture Gallery on the other hand has been almost entirely remodelled and the drawing rooms redecorated, while Nash's

intended Music Room was reconstructed by Blore to create a State Dining Room on the *piano nobile* (Plate I). The only Nash to survive in the latter is the pair of handsome white marble chimneypieces which had already been carved and which indicate the intended function of the room in their flanking female figures playing musical instruments. It is possible, too, that the bed of the ceiling may be Nash as it shows a greater refinement than the somewhat coarse coving of Blore's surround.

Wʜᴇɴ he embarked on the remodelling of Buckingham Palace George IV intended it to be a private residence for use in conjunction with the refurbished state rooms at St James's. But as work progressed he changed his mind and as late as December 1826, when the shell had been roofed in, decided that it should be a state palace after all and that he would hold his courts there. This had no impact on the number and disposition of the state rooms, which had already been fixed, but did lead to a dramatic increase in the enrichment of their decorations. It was at this stage that many of the most distinctive features were introduced such as the lavish scagliola, the sculptured

I *The Banqueting or State Dining Room*, by Douglas Morison (1810–47), 1843. Watercolour. This was originally Nash's intended Music Room but was reconstructed by Blore to form a State Dining Room. The surviving pair of white marble chimneypieces shows flanking female figures playing musical instruments. It is also possible that the bed of the ceiling may be Nash as it is more refined than the coving in Blore's surround

panels in high places, and the extraordinary designs for the ceilings with their concave and convex coving. These ceilings were hailed at the time as something out of the ordinary. *Fraser's Magazine* in 1830 wrote: 'It is indeed, not easy to conceive anything more splendid than the designs for the ceilings which are to be finished in a style new in this country, partaking very much of the boldest style in the Italian taste of the fifteenth century... They will present the effect of embossed gold ornaments, raised on a ground of colour suitable to the character and other decorations of the room.'

Though the detail and motifs are derived from a wide range of sources includ-

ing the Italian Renaissance as well as classical Greece and Rome, the architectural forms are *sui-generis* but prefigured in earlier works by Nash, notably at Brighton Pavilion where billowing and tent-like ceilings were developed as appropriately 'Mogul'. The ceilings in the Music Room and Dining Room at Brighton were the immediate precursors of those in the drawing rooms at Buckingham Palace. The concept of a domed ceiling over a square or rectangular room is a Brighton feature but can also be traced back to earlier Nash buildings such as the Library at Caledon in Ireland which has a domed ceiling with diminishing coffers.

Another particularly distinctive feature of the rooms is the incorporation of a wide range of architectural sculpture in plaster. This reflected the contemporary enthusiasm for British art, as manifested in the forest of white marble monuments to national heroes in St Paul's Cathedral and the myriad proposals for memorials to the victories of Trafalgar and Waterloo. The idea of internal sculptured friezes in high relief may also have been directly inspired by Percier & Fontaine's palace interiors for Napoleon, such as Thorvaldsen's Alexander Frieze installed in the Quirinal in Rome (for a visit

3 The Grand Staircase, in a photograph of 1913 (*courtesy Marlborough Rare Books*). The view shows the stair from the East Gallery (to the back of the viewer) to the half-landing where the two curved arms of the other side of the staircase took visitors to the Throne Room and Green Drawing Room. This straight stair led to the East Gallery and a more 'social' circuit of the splendours of the Palace and so through the Nash rooms in the Garden Front

much of the moulded plaster sculpture, the marble work was put in the hands of Joseph Browne by Nash who sent him to Carrara to obtain suitable white marble and to oversee all that part of the contract. Brown was paid £6,000 between 1827 and 1830 for the chimneypieces in the Drawing Rooms and the Picture Gallery. Those in the latter were designed by Nash and comprise a set of five (one now in the East Gallery) with medallion portraits of famous artists which were almost certainly carved by Italian craftsmen. The other chimneypieces were the work of a cross-section of English talent: Matthew Cotes Wyatt, Joseph Theakstone, Thomas Denman (Flaxman's brother-in-law), R. W. Siever, Richard Westmacott (Junior) and J. E. Carew. Browne also supplied much of the scagliola, and the inlaid marble paving of the Entrance Hall and Sculpture Gallery (where the Marble Hall now is) on the ground floor.

From these latter deliberately low-proportioned and (originally) relatively austere spaces, the Grand Staircase (Fig. 3, and see p. 7) provides a dramatic transition to the state rooms on the first floor. Brilliantly

> ## The architectural forms are *sui-generis* but prefigured in earlier works by Nash, notably at Brighton Pavilion where billowing and tent-like ceilings were developed as appropriately 'Mogul'

top-lit from engraved glass skylights (reminiscent of the patterns in white damask table cloths) Nash's clever manipulation of space was once matched by the richness of the finishes: polychrome scagliola wall panels (now, alas, painted white) and Samuel Parker's sumptuous gilt bronze balustrade, the rich Grecian foliage pattern of which is reflected in the design of the plaster stringcourse. Parker also provided the gilt metal mounts for the unique mahogany-framed, mirror-plated doors designed by Nash and used throughout the state rooms,

---

of Napoleon's which in the event never took place). John Flaxman, the greatest of English neo-classical sculptors, was first approached to design the carved and moulded decorations for the Palace. But he died in 1826 after making sketches only for some of the external sculpture and the Marble Arch. So it was left to various other sculptors to design and execute the internal work. The key figure was William Pitts (1790–1840) who designed and modelled most of the high relief plasterwork, notably the tympana depicting the apotheosis of Spenser, Shakespeare and Milton in the South (now Blue) Drawing Room.

Pitts started out as a silver chaser and modeller and had, for instance, executed the famous silver-gilt 'Achilles Shield' to Flaxman's design. His work in the state rooms at Buckingham Palace has considerable grace and charm but it is too small in scale to be fully appreciated in its lofty situation though

it does contribute, as was intended, to the opulence of the decoration.

More interesting is the frieze in the Throne Room designed by the painter Thomas Stothard RA (who was also responsible for the design of the relief panels on the staircase) executed by Edward Hodges Baily. It depicts scenes from the Wars of the Roses—including the Battle of Tewkesbury and marriage of Henry VII and Elizabeth of York—and is fascinating for its attempt to treat a medieval subject as if it were the Parthenon frieze (Fig. 4). To the casual gaze it looks like a Grecian cast; it is only the gothic armour on the figures which gives the game away. The same brave attempt to assimilate medieval ideas in classical dress imbues the bold display of heraldry in the shields of the four kingdoms of England, Scotland, Ireland and Hanover on the plaster cove of the ceiling in the Throne Room.

While William Pitts was responsible for

II Ceiling of Green Drawing Room showing one of the most lavish of all Nash's extravagant ceilings for George IV's state rooms in his remodelled Buckingham Palace. These spectacular creations were the successors of Nash's inventions at the Brighton Pavilion and reveal his fascination with the forming of domes and elaborate covings over square or rectangular spaces. This particular example would have been finished by the time of Nash's downfall in 1830

adding enormously to their glittery spaciousness. The Guard Room (see p. 9) at the top of the stairs is pure Nash, with its apsidal ends and engraved glass ceiling lights by Wainwright & Brothers. It is, in fact, too small for the Guards of Honour which on state occasions were deployed in the subsequent Drawing Room and the Throne Room itself. The latter, too, retain to a large extent the original character of their Nash architecture with restored silk wall hangings: green in the former and red in the latter,

perpetuating the 1830s treatment and contrasting with the white and gold of the elaborate plasterwork which is partly by Bernasconi and partly by Bullock & Carter. The original gilding, as well as carved cornice work, was done by Edward Wyatt (Junior). Bernasconi's masterpiece is the pair of lively winged genii holding gilded garlands and flanking the 'proscenium' in front of the throne. These almost baroque mouldings are an amazing intervention in a neo-classical interior, but one matched by

William Croggon's doorcase (actually of scagliola but now painted white) which was identical to those designed by Nash for the Picture Gallery which were removed when that space was remodelled earlier this century. (One wonders if they are in store somewhere?) The most interesting Nash feature of the Picture Gallery was the elaborate classical 'hammerbeam' roof with seventeen glazed lanterns. It leaked (as well as failing to light the pictures properly) and so was replaced by the present bland glazed ceiling.

[61]

The *ne plus ultra* of Georgian sumptuousness in architectural decoration is reached in the suite of three drawing rooms in the centre of the West Front of the Palace. These are even more splendid than the Throne Room sequence, but unfortunately have lost their neo-classical colouring and wall finishes. Originally called the North Drawing Room, Bow Drawing Room and South Drawing Room, they are now the White Drawing Room, Music Room and Blue Drawing Room. The first has been altered the most (see p. 26). It was originally hung with gold and white figured damask, while the pilasters were of Siena scagliola, their capitals being a very novel design incorporating the Garter star. Nash's brilliant, billowing, coved ceiling combines a swagger composition with delicate moulded plaster detail by Bernasconi. William Pitts' twelve frieze panels depict the Origin and Progress of Pleasure or the 'sports of boys'.

The Bow Drawing Room (Music Room) originally presented the most dramatic *coup*

4 The Throne Room in a photograph of 1913 (*courtesy Marlborough Rare Books*) which brings out the frieze, remarkable for its attempt to treat a medieval subject—the Wars of the Roses—as if it were the Parthenon frieze. The winged genii holding garlands, flanking the arch before the thrones, are by Bernasconi: an extraordinary baroque detail in a neo-classical interior

d'oeil with lapis lazuli scagliola Corinthian columns contrasting with bright yellow silk on the walls. The beautiful domed ceiling and Pitts' three graceful relief panels of Eloquence, Pleasure and Harmony were always white and gold. The parquetry floor made of satinwood, holly, rosewood and tulipwood is the finest of its type in England and was considered a masterpiece of 'recherché costliness' by contemporaries. The South Drawing Room (Blue Drawing Room), which now has blue flock paper and painted onyx columns was originally a symphony in red with *Porfido rosso* porphyry scagliola columns, crimson velvet curtains and figured

silk wall hangings, forming a superb climax to the Nash circuit.

The original opulent silk wall coverings have disappeared from all three of the western drawing rooms which is a great pity as they helped to give a sense of unity to all the Nash state rooms. Perhaps one day they will be restored (as they have been already in the Green Drawing Room and Throne Room). The over-painting of Browne's scagliola has also dimmed the intended brilliance of effect, though this was made necessary by defects in the composition which became apparent soon after completion. Perhaps with the recent revival of the scagliola technique in England it might prove possible to restore the columns and pilasters to their original finishes and to remove the Edwardian overpainting? If this were to prove possible it would re-create the full splendour of Nash's last and most opulent architectural masterpiece.

I am most grateful to Hugh Roberts for his assistance.

Royal portraits

Convention and domesticity

BRIAN ALLEN

Buckingham Palace contains some magnificent baroque portraits by Van Dyck, but the display currently on view essentially tells the story of the state portrait from the eighteenth century until the period of the First World War

The visitor who goes to Buckingham Palace expecting to see a full panoply of the British monarchy in portraiture may be disappointed to discover that, with the exception of the two great Van Dycks in the Picture Gallery, the story really begins there with the Hanoverian succession: indeed, quite appropriately, with the portrayal of the family of King George III who purchased Buckingham House in 1762. Nevertheless, the rooms of the Palace seen by the public do provide the viewer with a remarkable display of the art of the state portrait from its zenith in the eighteenth century to the terminal decline of the genre in the early years of the present century.[1] Of course the formality of those rooms open to the public inevitably means that the visitor will search in vain for the often more appealing but less regal aspects of royal portraiture as epitomized by the conversation pieces of one of George III's favourite painters, Johan Zoffany (but see pp. 44–56). In this context even Gainsborough, the 'Apollo of the Palace',[2] who came to royal portraiture rather late in his career, is a much lamented absentee.

Until the reign of James I, royal portraits appear to have been made primarily to be given away and it is only with Charles I, the greatest art collector of all our kings, that a number of the finest portraits were painted specifically for the royal palaces. So far as we know, only one portrait of Henry VIII was specifically made for the Palace of Whitehall—the splendid fresco of Henry and Jane Seymour with the King's parents, painted on the wall of the Privy Chamber. This, however, was tragically lost in the Whitehall fire of 1698 and is now only known through the fragment of the cartoon in the National Portrait Gallery and from a small early copy and the engraving made

I *Queen Charlotte and her two eldest children* by Allan Ramsay (1713–84), begun 1764.
Oil on canvas, 248·9 × 161·9 cm *(Silk Tapestry Room)*. The child with the bow is the future George IV
(to be seen as a grown-up archer in the adjoining East Gallery, in a full-length portrait by John Russell).
The younger is Prince Frederick

[63]

2

3

from it.[3] It is perhaps not entirely insignificant that some of the most interesting portraits of kings have been of those whose hold on the throne has been the most tenuous—like Charles I and George IV—or of those heirs whose position was at least ambiguous, like James II when Duke of York, or Frederick, Prince of Wales.

Our story begins with George I, arguably the least interested in portraiture of all our sovereigns. For some time after his arrival in Britain he refused to be painted and it is therefore less surprising that surviving portraits of him should be so remarkably

unrevealing of his character. One of the first images confronting the visitor to Buckingham Palace in the Ambassadors' Entrance is George Wilhelm Fountaine's undistinguished three-quarter length of him (Fig. 2).[4] Probably painted towards the end of the King's life, it is only marginally more vivacious than the other image seen here, John Shackleton's portrait of his son and heir George II (Fig. 3); this version (there are many) appears to have been originally painted in 1757 for Thomas Pownall, Governor of Massachusetts, and was bought for the Royal Collection in the 1830s by William IV.[5] Paradoxically, since it

1 *Frederick, Prince of Wales* by Jean-Baptiste van Loo (1684–1745), 1742. Oil on canvas, 240 × 156·2 cm. *(State Dining Room)*

2 *George I* by George Wilhelm Fountaine (*c.* 1680–1745), 1720–7. Oil on canvas *(Ambassadors' Entrance)*

3 *George II* by John Shackleton (*fl.* 1742–67), 1750–60. Oil on canvas *(Ambassadors' Entrance)*. It says little for the artistic taste of either of the first two Georges that they chose such boring painters to portray them. Both could have done with some flattery but neither received it. George II's son, Frederick, Prince of Wales (father of George III), in contrast, was a man of taste and discernment (Fig. 1), a patron both of art and of early cricket and a collector of distinction. His father detested him. George II is remembered for his observation (in a thick German accent) 'I hate all boetry and bainting too'. This particular version among many appears to have been painted originally in 1757 for Thomas Pownall, Governor of Massachusetts, and was bought, a little surprisingly, by William IV in the 1830s

was apparently done without sittings, it is to the French sculptor Louis-François Roubiliac that we must look for a superb marble bust of George II now at Windsor Castle and easily the most dynamic image of him.[6]

The most impressive display of state portraits in the Palace is in the State Dining Room where four successive generations of the House of Hanover are arrayed (see p. 20). On entering the room the visitor sees to the right a sequence of seven canvases, the first of which is Kneller's portrait of George II's consort *Caroline of Ansbach when Princess of Wales*, signed and dated 1716.[7] This is flanked at the far end of the wall by an indifferent version of Shackleton's official full-length of George II.[8] His son and daughter-in-law, *Frederick, Prince of Wales* and *Augusta, Princess of Wales* (with both of whom he was on very bad terms) are paired within the sequence but the latter were somewhat more discerning in their choice of J. B. Van Loo as their painter.[9] These are amongst the last works executed in London by that exceedingly fashionable French painter before his return to France owing to ill-health late in 1742 (Fig. 1). But by far the most distinguished of this group are the splendid Allan Ramsay portraits of George III and Queen Charlotte. The portrait of the King (Fig. 4) has been justly hailed by Sir Oliver Millar as the most distinguished state portrait of a British monarch since the time of Van Dyck.[10] Given Ramsay's highly developed awareness of contemporary French painting we detect in his image something of Louis Michel Van Loo's state portrait of Louis XIV. After his appointment in 1761 as 'one of His Majesty's Principal Painters in Ordinary' Ramsay, or at least his studio, was responsible for producing the vast number of copies of these official coronation portraits for which there was evidently continuous demand after the completion of this prime pair by March 1762. Unfortunately, Sir Thomas Lawrence's portrait of the son and heir, *George IV*, in his Garter robes, which forms the centrepiece on this wall in the State Dining Room, is a comparatively pedestrian version of the dazzling portrait presented by the Prince to the Corporation of Dublin in 1818.[11]

Quite appropriately, George III and his family are much in evidence on the walls of the Palace but there can be few more sensitive images of the kind of domesticity which the King and Queen favoured in their portraiture than Ramsay's magnificent *Queen Charlotte and her two eldest children* (Plate I), begun in 1764 and now displayed in the Silk Tapestry Room. With its airing at the highly successful Ramsay exhibition in Edinburgh and London in 1992 this picture may have become a little more familiar to the public.[12] Despite the formality of the grandiose architectural setting, Ramsay imbues the Queen and her two sons (the eldest hold-

4 *George III* by Allan Ramsay (1713–84), completed 1762. Oil on canvas, 248·9 × 163·6 cm *(State Dining Room)*. This magnificent image has been described by Sir Oliver Millar as the most distinguished state portrait of a British monarch since the time of Van Dyck. George III inherited many of his amiable and intelligent characteristics from his father Frederick, Prince of Wales, and the composition of the portrait appears to pay homage to that in Fig. 1

ing the bow is the future George IV, the younger son on the Queen's lap is Prince Frederick, later Duke of York and Prince and Bishop of Osnabrück) with a degree of intimacy and maternal tenderness rare in royal portraits before this date. The presence of a copy of John Locke's influential *Some Thoughts concerning Education* (1693), placed beneath the workbasket atop the harpsichord, enhances the essential domesticity of this remarkable image.

In the 1760s the King and Queen patronized many of the leading painters whose reputations had been enhanced by the public exhibitions of the Society of Artists. Many pictures were bought in the 1760s and early 1770s, including Consul Smith's celebrated collection of mostly Venetian paintings, largely to furnish Buckingham House; and others were borrowed from the older royal residences. Horace Walpole noted that the King and Queen intended to form a series of

5

5 *Princess Louisa and Princess Caroline* by Francis Cotes (*c.* 1725–70), 1767. Oil on canvas, 265·7 × 161·9 cm (*Green Drawing Room*)

family portraits in the Dining Room at Buckingham House: 'The King intended to have portraits in that room of all his Brothers & Sisters, but on the marriages of the Dukes of Cumberland and Gloucester they were stopped'.[13]   Nathaniel Dance's portrait of *Edward, Duke of York* in Garter robes (now in the Green Drawing Room was probably intended as part of that series.   It was joined early in the 1780s by the great full-lengths of the King and Queen by Gainsborough which are now at Windsor Castle.[14]   The King's mother, Augusta, Princess of Wales, was also commissioning portraits of her family at this time, including the only picture in the Royal Collection by Angelica Kauffman (it now hangs in the Throne Room) of her eldest daughter *Augusta, Duchess of Brunswick, with her son Charles George Augustus.*   The latter was born during a visit by the Princess to London in 1766.[15]   The Francis Cotes

Sir Joshua Reynolds, Principal Painter to the King, was heartily detested by both George III and Queen Charlotte

double portrait of two of the King's sisters, *Princess Louisa and Princess Caroline*, was probably also commissioned by Princess Augusta.[16]   Signed and dated 1767 this is as ambitious a portrait as Cotes had undertaken to date (Fig. 5) and it provides evidence for his inflated reputation as a serious rival to Joshua Reynolds in the years immediately before his untimely death in 1770.

Reynolds himself, however, never enjoyed a close relationship with George III and although there are more than twenty paintings by Reynolds in the Royal Collection, most of them were acquired by the Prince Regent (see pp. 118–23).   Although knighted by the King in 1769 and appointed successor to Ramsay as his Principal Painter in 1784, George III and Queen Charlotte apparently 'could not endure the presence of him; he was poison to their sight'.[17]   The

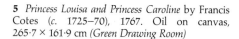

6

6 *Princesses Augusta, Elizabeth and Mary with Princes Ernest, Augustus and Adolphus* by West, 1776. Oil on canvas, 168·2 × 180.3 cm

II *The Royal Family in 1846* (detail) by Franz Xaver Winterhalter (1805–73), 1846. Oil on canvas, 260·2 × 316 cm (*East Gallery*)

shows West at his most torpid. Elsewhere in the Palace is a horizontal group showing the same sitters together with three other siblings (Fig. 6). The former picture must have been completely eclipsed when West's compatriot Copley executed in 1785 a portrait of similar composition: the spectacular *Three youngest daughters of George III* which now hangs at Windsor.[19] The other two portraits by West on view, both in the East Gallery, are full-lengths of the King and Queen Charlotte, the latter a repetition in reverse of the picture now at Windsor (Fig. 7) showing the Queen set against the background of the South Front of Windsor Castle and the Queen's Lodge with all the royal children to date—thirteen in the Windsor version, fourteen by the time the second version was painted in 1782—visible in the background.[20] Sadly, two of the younger royal children died in childhood; Prince Alfred aged two in 1782 and Prince Octavius aged four in 1783. The latter can be seen in

> 'The King intended to have portraits in that room of all his Brothers & Sisters, but on the marriages of the Dukes of Cumberland and Gloucester they were stopped'

the Silk Tapestry Room in one of West's most extraordinary pictures, *The Apotheosis of Prince Octavius* of 1783 (Fig. 8) wherein the Prince is welcomed in Heaven by his brother Alfred under the protective wings of an angel and cherubs, all in a style highly reminiscent of the fashionable German painter Mengs.[21]

Of the later monarchs George IV (as Prince of Wales) can also be seen in the East Gallery in Hoppner's portrait, exhibited at the Royal Academy in 1796, and originally destined for Carlton House; and alongside it in the earlier more languid portrait by John Russell showing the Prince in the green uniform of the Royal Kentish Bowmen.[22]

Soon after entering the Palace the visitor is confronted by the Grand Staircase with its installation of portraits devised by Queen Victoria shortly after her coronation in 1837, showing her immediate ancestors and relatives. Beechey's portraits of *George III* and *Queen Charlotte* were painted in the last years of the eighteenth century when that artist enjoyed considerable royal patronage but later generations of the family are more in evidence here.[23] Queen Victoria's father, the Duke of Kent, is present in George Dawe's portrait, presumably painted to commemorate his years as Governor of Gibraltar, and the Duchess of Kent's portrait by Hayter

7 *Queen Charlotte* by Benjamin West (1738–1820), 1779. Oil on canvas, 226 × 150 cm *(Windsor Castle)*. A replica, with fourteen children rather than thirteen, is in the East Gallery at Buckingham Palace

only Reynolds visible to the public is the full-length of *Frederick, Duke of York*, painted for his brother George IV and exhibited by Reynolds at the Royal Academy in 1788 (Fig. 13). It does not seem to have been noted before that this portrait can be seen very clearly in Martini's engraving after Ramberg's drawing of the Great Room at Somerset House in 1788. It is hanging on the walls of the exhibition room during a private viewing by the royal family, sandwiched between Hoppner's elegant full-length of Mrs Braddyll and Mather Brown's portrait of an unidentified nobleman.

Reynolds' successor as President of the

Royal Academy was Benjamin West. West had been introduced to the King by Robert Drummond, Archbishop of York, as early as 1768 and the two great history paintings now in the Cross Gallery but formerly in the Warm Room of Buckingham House are witness to the King's worthy but nevertheless enlightened taste (see pp. 118–23). A decade later West was at work on a set of portraits of the royal family, some of which were hung in the King's Closet in St James's Palace.[18] Three of these can be seen by the public in the East Gallery; the full-length of *Prince Adolphus, later Duke of Cambridge, with Princess Mary and Princess Sophia* of 1778 was given to Princess Victoria by her mother on her fifteenth birthday in 1834.[24] (Hayter remained a favourite and painted her coronation—see Fig. 12.) To see Lawrence at his best a visit must be made to Windsor Castle but here his portrait of *William IV when Duke of Clarence*, finished in 1827, was only claimed from the artist's studio after the latter's death in 1830.[25] It can be seen in the company of Sir Martin Archer Shee's full-length of his consort *Queen Adelaide*, originally destined for the Goldsmiths' Company but which was so admired by the King that he retained it for himself and ordered another version for the Goldsmiths'.[26] Easily the most striking image in this group is Sir David Wilkie's tempestuous portrait of *Augustus, Duke of Sussex*. Painted in 1833 it was given by the sitter to his niece Queen Victoria in 1838 and although she never warmed to Wilkie's work it was described by Wilkie's biographer Cunningham as 'that first of all modern portraits, for truth of character and harmonious brightness of colour, the Duke of Sussex, as Earl of Inverness, in the costume of a Highland Chief'.[27]

No monarch added more portraits to the Royal Collection or had a more carefully orchestrated iconographic plan than Queen Victoria. Early in her reign she began to arrange family portraits in her rooms at Buckingham Palace. One such room, the 1844 Room as it was known, was later dismantled by George V but an arrangement of family portraits by Winterhalter, de Keyser and other artists dating from 1853 can still be seen by the visitor on leaving the Palace through the Bow Room.[28] Landseer apart, whose work is not seen by the visitor to the Palace, the Queen's favourite artist was the German-born Franz Winterhalter who had been introduced to her by her uncle, Leopold of the Belgians. Of the many works by him in the Royal Collection none was more admired by the Queen that the large group *The Royal Family in 1846*, now in the East Gallery (Plate II).[29] Consciously or not, Winterhalter's antecedents lie with Van Dyck and the contrast with the latter's 'great peece' in the Picture Gallery is instructive. Significantly, it was to Winterhalter that the Queen turned in 1859 when she wanted new official likenesses of herself and Prince Albert. The resulting pair of portraits now hangs in the Marble Hall at Buckingham Palace (together with a portrait of Victoria's mother—see Fig. 11) and it is not difficult to concur with Queen Victoria's own view of them as 'beautiful' and 'truly magnificent' (Figs. 9, 10).[30]

By the end of Queen Victoria's long reign a profound change had taken place in our way of recording the monarchy for posterity. Indeed, a few conventional images of royalty from early in the present century survive at Buckingham Palace, such as the pair of state portraits *George V* and *Queen*

8 *The Apotheosis of Prince Octavius* by Benjamin West (1738–1820), 1783. Oil on canvas, 239·4 × 153·3 cm *(Silk Tapestry Room)*. The young Prince, who died on 3 May 1783, is seen being greeted in Heaven by his elder brother Alfred who had died on 26 August 1782. On the ground below is a view of Windsor Castle from the south. It was painted for the King and cost the considerable sum of £315. George III had an extremely high opinion of West, who succeeded Reynolds as President of the Royal Academy which had been founded with the King's support in 1768. Both West and Reynolds considered that 'history' painting was the highest form of art. George III was especially distressed at the loss of Octavius, just nine months after the death of Alfred: 'There will be no Heaven if Octavius is not there'. Octavius is included in the Heavenly Host in the stained-glass window of the Resurrection in St George's Chapel, Windsor, on which West was working at the time of Octavius' death

9

10

11

9 *Queen Victoria* by Franz Xaver Winterhalter (1805–73), 1859. Oil on canvas, 241·9 × 157·5 cm *(Marble Hall)*. Westminster is seen in the background, an appealing variation on the usual views of royal palaces in state portraits, and especially fitting for a portrait in Buckingham Palace. It is a pair with that in Fig. 10 and both have been at the Palace since they were painted

10 *The Prince Consort* (detail) by Franz Xaver Winterhalter (1805–73), 1859. Oil on canvas, 241·9 × 158·1 cm *(Marble Hall)*. A pair with that in Fig. 9. Both hung on the Ministers' Staircase until set into the wall of the Marble Hall

11 *Victoria, Duchess of Kent* by Winterhalter, 1849. Oil on canvas, 141·6 × 97·8 cm. This appealing portrait of Queen Victoria's mother hangs next to Winterhalter's state portraits of the daughter and consort. Her husband, Edward, Duke of Kent, fourth son of George III, died in 1820 after a career as a bad governor of Gibraltar and worse debtor. He met his wife, widow of the Prince of Leiningen, whilst living abroad to avoid difficulties and they lived there after their marriage in 1818, only visiting England for the birth (24 May 1819) of Victoria who inherited the crown since Edward's elder bothers all died without legitimate issue

Mary in the Blue Drawing Room by Sir Luke Fildes (Plate III) and Sir William Llewellyn respectively; and as late as the 1940s Sir Gerald Kelly could still regard his grandiose examples of the genre as the most important commission of his career. However, we are now so used to such an enormous range of imagery of the modern monarchy that with the exception of the image on the coinage and postage no one 'official' portrait can ever have widespread familiarity. Except to all but a few institutions, such as the Fishmongers' Company in the City of London which owns Annigoni's celebrated image of the present Queen,[31] the state portrait has now all but lost its meaning.

Most of the information in this article is taken from the outstanding catalogues of the British pictures in the Royal Collection by Sir Oliver Millar: *The Tudor, Stuart and Early Georgian Pictures in the Collection of Her Majesty the Queen*, 2 vols., London, 1963, hereafter referred to as EGP; *The Later Georgian Pictures in the Collection of Her Majesty the Queen*, 2 vols., London, 1969, hereafter LGP; and, most recently, *The Victorian Pictures in the Collection of Her Majesty the Queen*, 2 vols., Cambridge, 1992, hereafter VP.
[1] For a survey of royal portraiture through the ages see Richard Ormond, *The Face of Monarchy: British royalty portrayed*, London, 1977.
[2] See LGP, vol. I, p. xx quoting W. T. Whitley, *Thomas Gainsborough*, London, 1915, p. 177.
[3] See Roy Strong, *Holbein and Henry VIII*, London, 1967.
[4] EGP, vol. I, p. 169, cat. 498, vol. II, plate 189.
[5] EGP, vol. I, p. 188, cat. 568.
[6] Reproduced Ormond, op. cit., plate 108.
[7] EGP, vol. I, p. 144, cat. 345, vol. II, plate 148.
[8] EGP, vol. I, p. 187, cat. 567.
[9] EGP, vol. I, p. 178, cats. 536, 537, vol. II, plates 187, 188.
[10] LGP, vol. I, pp. 93–5, vol. II, plate 1 and Scottish National Portrait Gallery, *Allan Ramsay 1713–1784*, exh. cat. by Alastair Smart, Edinburgh, 1992, pp. 133–5.
[11] See National Portrait Gallery, *Sir Thomas Lawrence 1769–1830*, exh. cat. by Michael Levey, London, 1979, pp. 66–7, cat. 33.
[12] SNPG, Ramsay, op. cit., p. 140, cat. 86.
[13] See 'Horace Walpole's Journals of Visits to Country Seats, &c.' ed. Paget Toynbee in *Walpole Society*, vol. XVI, 1927–8, p. 79 quoted by Millar in EGP, I, P. xii.
[14] For the Dance portrait see EGP, vol. I, p. 23, cat. 723, vol. II, plate 17. The Gainsboroughs are EGP, vol. I, pp. 35–6, cats. 774, 775, vol. II, plates 47, 48.
[15] EGP, vol. II, pp. 58–9, cat. 869, vol. II, plate 16.
[16] EGP, vol. I, p. 22, cat. 720, vol. II, plate 14.
[17] Quoted EGP, vol. I, p. 98.
[18] EGP, vol. I, p. xviii.
[19] EGP, vol. I, p. 130, cat. 1147, vol. II, plate 112. For the Copley, ibid., p. 20, cat. 712, vol. II, plates 129, 130.
[20] EGP, vol. I, p. 128, cat. 1140.
[21] EGP, vol. I, p. 130, cat. 1149, vol. II, plate 116.
[22] EGP, vol. I, p. 50, cat. 834 (Hoppner) and EGP, vol. I, p. 110, cat. 1051, vol. II, plate 131 (Russell).
[23] EGP, vol. I, pp. 5–6, cats. 658–9, vol. II, plates 156, 157.
[24] EGP, vol. I, p. 27 (Dawe) and VP, vol. I, p. 96, cat. 302, vol. II, plate 245.
[25] EGP, vol. I, p. 62, cat. 877, vol. II, plate 229.
[26] EGP, vol. I, p. 116, cat. 1085, vol. II, plate 300.
[27] Quoted by Millar, EGP, vol. I, p. 143, cat. 1186, vol. II, plate 274.
[28] See VP, vol. I, pp. xxviii–XXX. A watercolour of *c.* 1850 by J. Roberts showing the 1844 Room as arranged by the Queen is reproduced VP, vol. I, fig. IX.
[29] VP, vol. I, pp. 293–4, cat. 823, vol. II, plate 730.
[30] VP, vol. I, pp. 296–7, cats. 831–2, vol. II, plates 733, 734.
[31] Ormond, op. cit., plates 1, 167.

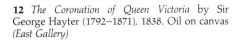

12 *The Coronation of Queen Victoria* by Sir George Hayter (1792–1871), 1838. Oil on canvas *(East Gallery)*

III *King George V* by Sir Luke Fildes (1844–1927), 1911–12. Oil on canvas, 279·4 × 182·9 cm *(Blue Drawing Room)*

13 *Frederick, Duke of York* by Sir Joshua Reynolds (1723–92), completed 1788. Oil on canvas, 240 × 146·7 cm *(East Gallery)*

A place in history

The changing significance of Buckingham Palace

ANDREW SANDERS

Until George IV took the bold decision to build a residence worthy of a
modern king, even provincial Oslo was better provided with a royal
focus. But Buckingham Palace was to enjoy but a brief period as a centre
of cultural life under Queen Victoria

To begin with negatives and might-have beens: it is worth remembering that the site of what is now Buckingham Palace was three times deemed appropriate for equally eminent London monuments. In 1753, when the trustees of the newly-founded British Museum were looking for an available building to house the Museum's collections, the unoccupied Buckingham House was briefly considered. Only the Duke of Buckingham's asking price, some £30,000, acted as an effective deterrent.[1] In 1834 King William IV, who had no love for the new palace with which his late brother had replaced Buckingham House, generously offered to hand over the unfinished building to the homeless Houses of Parliament. Despite the financial consequences of the fire which had ravaged the old Palace of Westminster, Parliament felt obliged to decline the gracious offer and proposed instead to rebuild on its historic site.[2] Finally, amidst the gloom that descended on the Court following Prince Albert's death, it was suggested in 1864 that Buckingham Palace should be sold by the Crown and used instead by the National Gallery.[3] Although the British Museum, the Houses of Parliament and the National Gallery might each have looked splendid as democratic architectural climaxes to the sweep of the Mall, it must be admitted that London would have lacked one of its finest grand gestures if that climax had not been reserved for a royal residence.

Nevertheless, Buckingham Palace will always seem to some observers to lie away from the central axes of London. If by a long and august tradition London has been what German topographers used to call the *Haupt- und Residenzstadt* of Great Britain, for long periods in its history it lacked a worthy *Residenz*. The palaces at Westminster, Whitehall and St James's have passed either into oblivion or have been appropriated to other uses (though St James's still lays official claim to be the seat of the Court). It may be due to the Constitutional tact of the first three Hanoverian sovereigns that they were

1 *Sarah Siddons (1755–1831)* by Thomas Gainsborough (1727–88), 1785. Oil on canvas, 126 × 97 cm. National Gallery. Mrs Siddons, née Kemble, was one of the greatest actresses of all time. She appeared at what was then known as 'The Queen's House' before its transformation by Nash into Buckingham Palace under George IV

2 *Joseph Haydn (1732–1809)* by Thomas Hardy (1757–c.1805), 1791. Oil on canvas, 76·5 × 63·5 cm. Royal College of Music. The composer played at 'The Queen's House' during his visit to London sponsored by the impresario Salomon to conduct the specially commissioned Symphonies (nos. 93–104) which are known as the 'Salomon' or 'London' symphonies

content with the modest suburban pleasures of Kensington and Kew or with the rural splendours of Windsor and Hampton Court, but London always needed its own grandiloquent royal statement to set the seal on its status as a capital city. That statement was never likely to be made by the rambling St James's. To many undiscriminating modern visitors, Buckingham Palace may well seem as much part of the historic London scene as are its royal equivalents at Paris, Vienna, Madrid, Stockholm and Munich, but it is of course no such thing. Unlike new cities such as St Petersburg or Washington, relatively few aspects of the planning of the capital stem from it. Unlike Paris or Vienna, its real parallels as ancient European capitals, relatively little of London's historic sense of itself stems from what remains, unlike Paris or Vienna, a monarchic capital. Until George IV took the bold decision in 1825 to build a residence worthy of a modern king, even provincial Oslo was better provided with a grander royal focus.

Although Buckingham Palace is a nineteenth-century creation, its royal connections date back to 1761 and George III's purchase of the Duke of Buckingham's mansion in order to provide his Queen with a dower house (he paid £2,000 less than the trustees of the British Museum had been asked for seven years earlier). For the next fifty-six years the old-fashioned red-brick palace was to be pointed out to visitors to London as 'The Queen's House' (Plate I). It was noticed as such in H. J. Sarrett's *New Picture of London for 1803–4, or a Guide through this Immense Metropolis on a Plan Hitherto Unattempted*, though it was granted only the same kind of emphasis as the somewhat grander private mansions of the aristocracy such as Burlington and Devonshire Houses. Only its site, 'at the western extremity of St. James' park', and its royal associations seem to have rendered it remarkable in Sarrett's eyes.[4] *The Ambulator; or A Pocket Companion for the Tour of London and its Environs*, which reached its eleventh edition

4 'The King's Palace' (Buckingham Palace), an engraving of about 1831, by Thomas Higham showing the projected East Front by John Nash with the Marble Arch in its original position at the centre. The scheme was much mocked (see Figs. 5, 6)

3 *Dr Samuel Johnson* (1709–84) by James Barry (1741–1806), 1778–80. Oil on canvas, 60·6 × 53 cm. National Portrait Gallery. By far the most compelling portrait of the 'great lexicographer' is this study for a mural in the Royal Society of Arts. Johnson had firm Jacobite sympathies but was graciously received by the Hanoverian George III and allowed to use the King's magnificient octagonal library

in 1811, described the 'Queen's Palace' in a similar vein. The house stood 'in the most favourable situation that St James's Park could furnish', but if its architecture does not seem to have inspired much notice its contents do: 'Here is a fine collection of prints, and a great variety of pictures by the most eminent masters; also many curious *Time Pieces*, his Majesty being deemed very curious in such kinds of machinery.'[5] It was to the Queen's House that Sarah Siddons (Fig. 1) came to act, that Joseph Haydn came to play (Fig. 2) and that Dr Johnson (Fig. 3) came regularly to study in King George III's superb octagonal library. It was, however, grandly domestic rather than palatial. For Rudolph Ackermann, whose celebrated *The Microcosm of London* (1808–1810) found it 'a convenient residence for their Majesties and Princesses', it remained conspicuously lacking in apartments 'sufficiently capacious for the Queen's drawing-rooms' which continued to be held at St James's.[6]

After Queen Charlotte's death in 1818 the house remained unoccupied until her son George IV resolved that it should be converted into what was noted in F. Shoberl's illustrated guidebook *The Public Buildings of London and Westminster Described* as 'a palace befitting the monarch of a great nation'.[7] Shoberl's guidebook (1838), like John Britton's far more discriminating *The Original Picture of London . . . Being a Correct Guide for the Stranger, as well as for the Inhabitant, to the Metropolis of the British Empire* (26th edn. 1828), was, however, obliged to speculate as to what the completed palace might look like. Britton's guide, being

rooted in the earlier years of the century, still gave a fuller account of the demolished Carlton House than it could of a building that was 'not sufficiently advanced to exhibit its decided forms and character'. Nevertheless the 'New Palace' already exhibited 'an imposing and elegant facade towards the park' and seemed to stand fair to be both 'spacious and magnificent'. Internally 'the vestibules, staircases, halls, galleries, audience-rooms, and the king's private apartments' were all to be on a grand scale and 'splendidly adorned with marble, paintings, sculpture and other palatial decorations'.[8] When, however, Britton mentioned the cost of realizing John Nash's designs (estimated at £252,690) he touched on what was already an issue of some public concern.

By the very fact of his intimate association with the extravagant King George IV, Nash was possibly the most unjustly ridiculed of English architects. If one cartoon famously showed him spitted on the point of the spire of his church of All Souls, Langham Place, his works at Buckingham Palace seem to have provoked a particularly acute comic spleen. Nash's Marble Arch which once, like Percier and Fontaine's arc du Carrousel in Paris, announced the presence of a victor-sovereign in the palace behind it (Fig. 4), was held up for especial ridicule. One coloured satirical etching published by T. McLean in June 1829 (Fig. 5) showed John Bull quizzing 'the Arch-itect Wot Builds the Arches – &c – &c – &c – &c' and berating him with the cost of adapting the building to the King's changing demands (*Bull*: 'But the Bill is more than double the Estimate.' *Nash*: Yes that eres *always wrong—we never minds no Estimates*.') Another gesture of Radical complaint, published by S. W. Fores in August 1829, suggested 'An Appropriate Emblem for the Triumphal Arch of the New Palace— Dedicated to the Poor—Pennyless—Priest-Ridden and Paralysed John Bull' (Fig. 6) and showed John Bull knock-kneed, empty-pocketed and in a clown's costume standing on the arch. Behind him, on the pediment of the unfinished Palace's façade, are figures of Lady Conyngham (the King's mistress),

the Duke of Wellington (his Prime Minister) and Robert Peel (his Home Secretary).[9]

If William IV proposed giving the unloved Palace to Parliament (perhaps in recompense to John Bull for George IV's reckless spending), when Queen Victoria came to the throne in May 1837 its destiny as future royal residence seemed at last to be settled. Although the new Queen expressed her regret at leaving 'for *ever* my poor old birthplace' (Kensington) she was determined that Buckingham Palace should be the proper home for a British monarch. Within forty-eight hours of moving in she entertained a large party to dinner and afterwards listened to Sigismond Thalberg (Fig. 9) 'the greatest pianist in the world . . . J'étais en extase'. She held a State Ball at the palace on 10 May 1838 ('I have been dancing till past four o'clock this morning') at which Johann Strauss the Elder (Fig. 7) performed his waltz novelty *Hommage à la Reine d'Angleterre* (the waltz which opens with a quotation from 'Rule Britannia' and ends with an arrangement, in three-quarter time, of 'God Save the Queen'). On 28 June Victoria was the first British sovereign to leave for her Coronation from the Palace.[10]

After her marriage to Prince Albert, Buckingham Palace was to serve the Royal Family, as it has since done, as a combination of a family home, an office and a setting for State ceremonial. Here were held the *bals costumés* which formed part of the entertainments of what rapidly developed into a glittering Court, and which included, in April 1842, the somewhat incongruous ball at which Victoria and Albert appeared costumed as Edward III and Queen Philippa (Plate II). Here the Strauss orchestra were to play again in April 1849, introducing the Alice-Polka in honour of the Queen's six-year-old daughter (see Fig. 7). Despite Prince Albert's complaint to Lord Melbourne in January 1841 that he was 'bored with the sameness of his chess every evening' and the Queen's initial reluctance to accede to the Prince's desire for 'literary and scientific people about the Court',[11] here Felix

I 'The Queen's House', Buckingham House as it then was, in a watercolour for Pyne's *Royal Residences*.
It was here that Sarah Siddons came to act, Joseph Haydn to play, and Dr Johnson to browse
in the King's Octagon Library

Mendelssohn (Fig. 8) was to play for the royal couple in July 1842, January 1844 and in 1847. On this last occasion, shortly before the composer's death, Mendelssohn was to present Victoria and Albert with an arrangement for four hands of one of his *Songs Without Words*. The four royal hands were solemnly to play the piece again in his memory in the November of 1847.

Apart from its musical enterprise, the first part of Queen Victoria's reign was to be remarkable for the radical physical changes in the appearance of Buckingham Palace. In February 1845 the Queen wrote to Sir Robert Peel concerning 'the urgent necessity of doing

5 Satirical cartoon (June 1849) of John Nash (left) interrogated by John Bull. Etching, 23 × 33 cm. London, Guildhall Library, Corporation of London. Note East Front of Buckingham Palace with the Marble Arch

6 Cartoon satirizing the extravagance of Nash's new palace for George IV. Instead of the King on top of Marble Arch, the artist shows John Bull in a clown's costume. On the pediment of Nash's quadrangle front in the background are the King's mistress (Lady Conyngham), his Prime Minister (Wellington) and Home Secretary (Peel)

7 *Johann Strauss the Elder* (1804–49), engraving from the *Illustrated London News*, 1849, recording his performance with his 'band' at Buckingham Palace where they played the 'Alice-Polka' composed in honour of the Queen's six-year-old daughter

8 *Felix Mendelssohn-Bartholdy* (1809–47). Contemporary engraving of the composer who played for Victoria and Albert in 1842, 1844 and 1847. On the last occasion he presented them with an arrangement for four hands of one of his *Songs without Words*: they were to play it in his memory in November of the same year

something to Buckingham Palace' because of its 'total want of accommodation for our little family, which is fast growing up'. She required 'a room, capable of containing a large number of those persons whom the Queen has to invite in the course of the season to balls, concerts etc.' and she saw the future extension of the Palace as an opportunity of rendering its exterior 'such as no longer to be a *disgrace* to the country which it certainly now is'.[12] However much we may deplore the hiding of Nash's original façade behind Blore's worthily boring new east wing (Fig. 10), the Queen was not alone in finding George IV's palace outmoded both in terms of its domestic comforts and its architecture. Peter Cunningham's thoroughly sensible and informative *Hand-Book of London, Past and Present* (1849) complained that the original rebuilding of the palace had been 'clumsy' and a 'mere juggle on the part of the king and his architect— knowing as they did that Parliament would never have granted the funds for an entirely new Palace'. Cunningham heartily approved of the removal of Nash's dome ('like a common slop-basin turned upside down') but, perhaps tactfully, forebore to comment on the precise nature of Blore's incomplete plans for the eastern extension.[13]

Once Blore's façade was complete and the Marble Arch was removed in 1851 a new round of unfavourable criticism began. John Timbs grudgingly remarked in his invaluable source of recherché information about the capital, the *Curiosities of London* (1855), that the style of the palace's east wing was 'German, of the last century'.[14] If *Black's Guide to London and its Environs*

of 1873 could regret that 'an entirely new palace was not built by some architect of skill and taste',[15] Henry Bohn's generally censorious *Pictorial Handbook of London* of 1854 noted of Nash's work that it remained 'a complex medley of the costly and the shabby' which was 'best passed by unnoticed'; of Blore's work Bohn remarked that it 'wisely abandoned all attempt to make it harmonize with what (being at discord in itself) could harmonize with nothing'.[16] The *Handbook*, which is generally scathing about the state of Victorian architecture, uses its sharp criticism of the palace to state a general complaint about modern building: 'Great as our fathers have been in this art [architecture] almost ever since the dark ages, the present century has half elapsed without producing any *proof* that we can erect things capable of standing twenty years without becoming laughing-stocks.' That ridicule was the order of the day is evident enough in George Augustus Sala's fascinating survey of London life *Twice Round the Clock; or the Hours of the Day and Night in London* (1862). Sala found Blore's looming palace façade 'huge in size, clumsy in its proportions, grotesque in decoration, mean in gross, frivolous in detail, infinitely hideous in its general appearance'. Nevertheless, despite such outspoken disparagement, Sala was prepared loyally to rejoice that above the ugly roof of Buckingham Palace there floated 'that grandest and noblest of all banners, the Royal Standard of England' and that wihin the walls of what looks as if it were 'half hospital, half barrack' there dwelt 'our good, and true, and dear Queen'.[17]

Sala's *Twice Round the Clock* also

reminds us that one of the most familiar aspects of modern Palace ceremonial, the eleven-thirty Changing of the Guard, still took place in the early 1860s in the courtyard of St James's Palace. Christopher Robin and Alice would then have gone down to the palace at the far end of the Mall in vain. The only aspect of Blore's dull 'improvements' which has lastingly influenced the way in which most visitors to London perceive the Palace was his introduction of the now famous balcony (a balcony enhanced, as was the façade as a whole, by its recasting by Sir Aston Webb). If the balcony's proportions are relatively modest (at least in relation to those of most other palaces, whether republican or royal) it has, since Queen Victoria watched the last Guards batallion march out of the courtyard on its way to the Crimea in 1854, become an integral part of British life. In 1856 the Queen used the balcony again to watch the return of her victorious army from Russia. Her grandson George V was to make it the focus of national emotion at times of victory, crisis and celebration, and it has continued to function as such in the momentous reigns of George VI and Elizabeth II.

In 1993 when virtually all aspects of the architecture of Buckingham Palace probably stand in higher esteem than at any point in the building's history, it is fitting that

II *Queen Victoria and Prince Albert at the bal costumé of 12 May 1842* by Sir Edwin Landseer (1803–73), finished 1846. Oil on canvas 142·6 × 111·8 cm. Victoria and Albert are dressed as Queen Philippa and Edward III (founder of the Order of the Garter)

9 *Sigismond Thalberg (1812–71),* marble bust by Edward Hodges Baily (1788–1867), 1843. H. 64 cm. Royal College of Music. Thalberg played for Queen Victoria within forty-eight hours of her moving in to Buckingham Palace, and the Queen described him as 'the greatest pianist in the world'

Her Majesty The Queen has determined that parts of the palace should be opened to the general public. Her gracious gesture will ensure that its semi-hidden architectural splendours and its truly royal artistic treasures will find a more generally familiar, if no less established, place in the London scene. Buckingham Palace has been known to a succession of distinguished royal and imperial visitors and to an even longer line of political figures, both British and foreign. Its hospitality, its generous serenity and its riches have impressed foreign heads of state, such as Tsar Nicholas I and the Emperor Napoleon III (Fig. 11), who were accustomed to the most pompous and exhausting of European palaces. It has since received presidents, potentates, premiers and a Pope, all of whom are likely to have recognized the Palace as a fitting symbol of the United Kingdom's international prestige. Perhaps most tantalizing amongst its nineteenth-century non-political visitors was Charles Dickens (Fig. 12) who on 9 March 1870 had an interview with Queen Victoria at the Queen's express request. Dickens, already a sick man, was to die some three months later. The Queen recorded that she had found the greatest of her literary subjects, and one whose works she had read from the time of her accession, 'very agreeable with a pleasant voice and manner'. With due modesty she

> By the very fact of his intimate association with the extravagant King George IV, Nash was possibly the most unjustly ridiculed of English architects

presented Dickens with an autographed copy of her own book about her life in the Highlands. Perhaps posterity's only regret concerning that occasion is that the Queen should not have pressed Dickens for further details of the plot of what was to prove to be the unfinished *The Mystery of Edwin Drood* (though the serialization of the new novel figured in their conversation). If the Queen had learned the enigmatic secret of the end of the novel, Buckingham Palace might briefly have figured conspicuously in the literary as much as it does in the political and artistic annals of the nation.

When the Queen said *'No'*

One hundred years ago the question of opening Buckingham Palace to the public was raised in Parliament

Evidence has come to light at the Public Record Office that there were moves to open Buckingham Palace to the public at the end of the last century. Parliamentary questions in 1898 and 1899 regarding the possible opening arose out of discussion on the role of royal palaces and their finances (*Public Record Office Work 19/58*)

Monday 25 April 1898, question from Mr Hazell:

To ask the First Commissioner of Works, in reference to Buckingham Palace, why it is more difficult to open this palace to the public because it is occasionally occupied by Her Majesty than it is to open Windsor Castle:
And, whether he can state the number of days during the years 1895, 1896, and 1897, respectively, when this palace has not been in use either by Her Majesty, or by the Royal Family, or by distinguished guests, or for any ceremonial purpose; and, if he cannot state the number of days exactly, will he state them approximately.

Mr Hazell received the following answer, which was approved by the Queen:

The Lord Chamberlain, within whose province this lies desires it to be clearly understood that assent cannot be given to the opening to the Public of Buckingham Palace, which is the private residence in London of Her Majesty and of her Family. It must be clearly understood that the internal portions of Buckingham Palace and Windsor Castle are maintained at Her Majesty's expense, and that although The Queen has graciously consented to allow all the Public to visit certain portions of Windsor Castle, where special facilities exist when the Court is not in residence, yet, owing to the position of the State Rooms in Buckingham Palace, and the constant use of the Palace by members of the Royal Family, a similar privilege is altogether out of the question.

The following part of the answer was omitted:

I hope that after what I have said the Honourable member will not think it necessary to press for a reply to the latter half of his question.
N.B. Should he press for a reply, the Lord Chamberlain would add that the Palace is almost in daily use by members of the Royal Family.

Despite this resolute response the subject was raised again the following year—this time with a more European perspective. Mr Samuel Young tabled a question on Friday 14 July 1899 (whether this date influenced the flavour of the proceedings is unclear):

To ask the First Commissioner of Works: whether he is aware that there is a strong desire, not only on the part of the people of London but of all visitors from the provinces, that Buckingham Palace, with its Art treasures should be accessible to the public:
Whether there is any reason why it should be an exception to all the state palaces of Europe and will he take steps to gratify the popular wishes in this matter.

Mr Young received the following reply:

In answer to the Honble. Member's question I have to say that I am not aware that Buckingham Palace is an exception to all the state palaces of Europe. It is, in point of fact, not the case, as nearly every inhabitable Palace in Europe, including that of the President of the French Republic, is closed to the public. I have before stated to the House the objections which there are to the opening of Buckingham Palace. It is unsuitable from the internal arrangement for exhibition, and it is almost certainly occupied by members of Her Majesty's family. The Queen has given every possible facility to the public to view Windsor and the other Royal Palaces; and I am not prepared to ask Her Majesty to make any concession in regard to Buckingham Palace, nor can I hold out any hope that any concession will be made.

DANA ARNOLD

10 Stereoscopic image of the East Front designed by Edward Blore joining the two wings of Nash's Palace (and obscuring Nash's pediment): the Marble Arch was removed in 1851 to take its present pointless position near Speaker's Corner. Note the empty spaces of Green Park in the foreground and absence of the Victoria Memorial

[1] J. Mordaunt Crook, *The British Museum*, London, 1972, pp. 51–52.
[2] J. Mordaunt Crook and M. H. Port, *The History of the King's Works* Vol. VI 1782–1851, London, 1973, p. 285.
[3] *Building News*, 12 June 1863, p. 441; *The Builder*, 25 June 1864, p. 478. Quoted by Geoffrey Tyack, *Sir James Pennethorne and the Making of Victorian London*, Cambridge, 1992, p. 230.
[4] H. J. Sarrett, *Tegg and Castelman's New Picture of London for 1803–4, or A Guide through this Immense Metropolis on a Plan Hitherto Unattempted*, London, 1804, p. 68.
[5] *The Ambulator; or, A Pocket Companion for the Tour of London and its Environs* 11th edn., London, 1811, p. 8.
[6] Rudolph Ackermann, *The Microcosm of London*, 3 vols, London, 1808–1810. Quoted in Fiona St Aubyn, *A Portrait of Georgian London*, London, 1985, p. 52.
[7] F. Shoberl, *The Public Buildings of London and Westminster Described*, London, 1838, p. 87.
[8] John Britton, *The Original Picture of London, Enlarged and Improved: Being a Correct Guide for the Stranger as well as for the Inhabitant, to the Metropolis of the British Empire* 26th edn., London, 1828, pp. 156–7.
[9] Both cartoons are illustrated in Celina Fox (ed.) *London—World City, 1800–1840*, New Haven and London, 1992, pp. 280, 282.
[10] A. C. Benson and Viscount Esher (eds.), *The Letters of Queen Victoria: A Selection from Her Majesty's Correspondence between the Years 1837 and 1861*, 3 vols, London, 1908, Vol. 1, pp. 84–5, 115, 122.
[11] Ibid., vol. I, p. 256.
[12] Ibid., vol. II, pp. 33–34.
[13] Peter Cunningham, *Hand-Book of London, Past and Present*, New Edn., London, 1850, pp. 86–7.
[14] John Timbs, *Curiosities of London: Exhibiting the most Rare and Remarkable Objects of Interest in the Metropolis; With Nearly Fifty Years' Personal Recollections*, London, 1855, p. 567.
[15] *Black's Guide to London and its Environs* 5th edn., Edinburgh, 1873, p. 39.
[16] *The Pictorial Handbook of London, Comprising its Antiquities, Architecture, Arts, Manufacture, Trade, Social, Literary and Scientific Institutions, Exhibitions and Galleries of Art*, London, 1854, pp. 748–9.
[17] George Augustus Sala, *Twice Round the Clock; or the Hours of the Day and Night in London*, London, 1862, pp. 73–74.

11 *The Emperor Napoleon III of France and family*, carte-de-visite, nineteenth century. The emperor was one of many heads of state who visited Buckingham Palace in its new guise under Victoria as a royal palace which was the equal of anything in Europe. Tsar Nicholas I also visited, and the Palace has since seen presidents, potentates and premiers from all over the world—and a Pope

12 *Charles Dickens* (1812–70), carte-de-visite from towards the end of the novelist's life. He had an interview with the Queen on 9 March 1870 at the monarch's express request. The Queen presented Dickens with an autographed copy of her own book about her life in the Scottish Highlands. She found the novelist 'very agreeable with a pleasant voice and manner'

Imperial splendour

Buckingham Palace in 1913

A collection of historic photographs shows the interiors of Buckingham
Palace at the height of its magnificence immediately before the First
World War. Descriptions of the same photographs survive at Windsor
Castle 'compiled chiefly from the notes collected by Her Majesty Queen
Mary . . . by Alexander Hood' in 1914. Extracts from those notes form
the captions to the selected illustrations here.
The photographer, Mr Stanley, was presented with a silver cigarette case
on 2 August 1913 by Queen Mary *via* Hood 'for your kind assistance . . . in
taking the various photographs of Buckingham Palace which have
greatly pleased both Their Majesties'

All the photographs illustrated here are reproduced by courtesy of Marlborough Rare Books

1 (left) **The Royal Closet.** 'On entering the State Apartments from the visitors' Staircase, on the right hand is the Royal Closet, a comparatively small room hung with crimson damask and crimson carpet. The window looks westward on the gardens. Here is a fine mantelpiece of white marble and ormolu with bronze figures, which, together with the Florentine cabinets, chairs and sofas, came from Carlton House. On the mantelpiece a fine clock with a bronze figure of Apollo. The china is Sèvres. (Mirror on door—see reflection of fireplace)'

2 (above) **The White Drawing Room.** 'Through a doorway composed of a massive swinging mirror and a cabinet containing china, entrance is made from the Royal Closet to the White Drawing-room, the first of the fine apartments passed through to the Ball-room on State occasions. The decoration of the walls is white and gold, with pilasters in pairs forming panels or spaces filled by mirrors and mirrored doors. The mantelpieces are of white marble finely carved. The ceiling is richly decorated and profusely gilt. The curtains are of yellow brocade, and the chairs and sofas are covered with silk of the same hue. The Axminster carpet was made 30 years ago at a cost of £1,000.
Piano by Erard in a gilt case elaborately painted with figures, was in the Exhibition of 1851.
North wall—portrait of Queen Alexandra by Hughes.
In panels over doors medallion portraits of Anne Hyde, Duchess of York, Czar Peter of Russia, and Fénélon, Archbishop of Cambray'

3 The Chapel. 'Built by Queen Victoria and consecrated by Archbishop of Canterbury 1843. Square in shape. Iron columns to support roof—from Carlton House where [they] supported screen. Tapestry of Baptism of Christ occupies most of wall above Communion Table. Royal Pew faces it.' *The Queen's Gallery now occupies this site, after its bombing in the Second World War*

4 The Chinese Chippendale Room *(left)*. 'Chippendale mantelpiece and overmantel acquired by King Edward VII from Eltham Golf Club House where it was erected in 1663 by Sir John Shaw to whom the manor was granted by Charles II'

5 Indian Room *(opposite, top)*. 'Oak cases on walls house Edward VII collection of Indian Art, mostly swords, daggers, jewels—all brought from Marlborough House in 1902. A portion of a rare set of Chippendale chairs, made in engraved ivory, probably present from an Indian Prince to George III or IV. Objects catalogued in Catalogue of Indian Arms and Objects of Art presented by the Princes and Nobles of India to HRH The Prince of Wales, KG, KT, KP, GCB, GCSI, etc, on the occasion of his visits to India in 1875–1876'

6 The Tapestry Drawing Room *(opposite, below)*. 'Set of Gobelins tapestries of early Louis XV design.
1—left of fireplace—Bacchus. 2—right of fireplace—Leda. 3—east wall—Neptune. 4—west wall—Ceres'

7 The Queen's Bed and Dressing Room *(over page)*

8 The King's Bedroom *(over page)*. 'Paintings of sea subjects. Late Empire style furniture'

5

6

7

8

George IV: furnishing in the French taste

The place of Dominique Daguerre in the Royal Collection

JOHN WHITEHEAD

George IV developed a passion for all things French, although he
never visited France. Had he done so, his transformation of
Buckingham Palace might have been even more extreme

I Commode with pietra dura plaques, stamped by Martin Carlin. The pietra dura panels were probably made at the Gobelins
workshops in Paris in around 1680 by Gian-Ambrogio Giachetti, an Italian craftsman imported from Florence, and may have
originally decorated one of the great cabinets made for Louis XIV. Many of these were sold off by the Garde-Meuble de la
Couronne in the mid-eighteenth century, and the *marchand-merciers* bought them to dismantle them and re-use the panels on
furniture of more fashionable shape. Daguerre was probably responsible for the creation of this one; at any rate it was
described as a product of the *maison Daguerre & Compagnie* in the catalogue of the baron de Bezenval's sale in 1795. Such an
unusual combination of ebony, pietra dura and bold gilt-bronze plaques seems to recall Louis XIV furniture, albeit on a
smaller scale, and pieces such as this tend to confirm the theory that the French neo-classical style was as much inspired by
the baroque of Louis XIV as by the rediscovery of ancient archaeological sites. In 1782, it appeared in the posthumous sale of
Marie-Joséphine Laguerre, a member of the chorus at the Paris Opera, who supplemented the stipend that institution
provided by exacting enormous prodigalities from an endless string of lovers. By the time of her death, at the age of
twenty-eight, she had already provided rich material for the scurrilous pamphlets which circulated in Paris: 'L'Opéra,
Bacchus et l'Amour, ont perdu au commencement de l'année dernière une de leurs plus fameuses prêtresses . . . [etc]'
(*Green Drawing Room*)

C onsidering the future George IV's passion for the finest French furniture and *objets d'art*, it is surprising to note that he was one of the very few young European royals who, in the latter part of the eighteenth century, did not pay a visit to France.

Marie-Antoinette's brother, the Emperor Joseph II, came to France twice, as did Gustav III of Sweden.[1] The future Tsar Paul I, Catherine the Great's son, and his wife Maria Feodorovna, as well as other princes from Austria and Prussia, also undertook the journey to the capital of European civilization.[2] Many of them travelled under an assumed or subsidiary title, since a state visit would not only have been extremely costly, but would also have restricted their freedom to roam about at will in relative anonymity, and enjoy all the pleasures Paris could provide. Gustav III travelled as comte de Haga, and the Tsarevitch as comte du Nord, which was at least an appropriate geographical reference. One of the main objectives of such visits was the collecting of French works of art, and they all returned home heavily laden with furniture and other objects, as well as with Sèvres porcelain, either purchased from the leading *marchand-merciers* of Paris, or presented to the visitors by Louis XVI and Marie-Antoinette.

Despite being prevented by wars, debt and the state of his father's health from joining his contemporaries (perhaps he should have personally gone after Mrs Fitzherbert when she ran off to Paris in 1784), the Prince of Wales rapidly acquired a taste for all things French, and by the late 1780s was employing the services of Dominique Daguerre, the greatest of all the *marchand-*

merciers, in the decoration of Carlton House.[3]

It would be interesting to know what motivated his excellent choice. Daguerre, as well as supplying a noble clientele born in France and abroad, also sold to the Garde-Meuble de la Couronne, the body within the French royal household which supervised the ordering of all furniture and furnishings. But his role was more complex; the designers, sculptors and gilt-bronze artists he employed were often the same as those working directly for the Garde-Meuble, although his *ébénistes*, notably Weisweiler and Carlin, seem to have worked more or less exclusively for him. Georges Jacob, on the other hand, was not the Garde-Meuble's most regular supplier of seat furniture; his main royal customer was Marie-Antoinette through her own personal Garde-Meuble.

Perhaps Daguerre was consulted on account of his enormous experience, which is reflected in the quality of the work executed by his craftsmen. In 1784, for example, he was given a Japanese lacquer *chaise d'affaire* from the royal collection; he entrusted it to Weisweiler who dismantled it and veneered the panels onto a secretaire for Louis XVI and a writing table for Marie-Antoinette. Since there was not enough lacquer to cover

all the surfaces, he added panels of Japanese lacquer, presumably from his own stock, and of nearly the same date and quality.[4]

In choosing Daguerre, the Prince of Wales was emulating Marie-Antoinette's taste in furniture and objects. Through Bonnefoy Duplan, the *concierge* at the Petit Trianon and head of the Garde-Meuble de la Reine, she ordered small-scale but precious furniture, and objects including Japanese lacquers (of the type of Fig. 2), hardstones and oriental porcelains mounted in delicate gilt-bronzes, of either Etruscan or *chinoiserie* style.[5] It may be no coincidence that the other great English amateur of the period, William Beckford, was also to collect objects of this type.

Sir Francis Watson has plausibly suggested that when Henry Holland, the Prince of Wales's architect, visited Paris in 1785, he must have come across Daguerre.[6] He was already known to the English as a supplier of French furniture, as is shown by a mention in the baronne d'Oberkirch's memoirs. When the baronne visited Daguerre's shop in the rue St-Honoré in 1784, a crowd had gathered there to admire a sideboard made for the Duke of Northumberland.[7] Some of the French artists employed at Carlton House had worked for the comte d'Artois at Bagatelle. Artois, the youngest brother of Louis XVI, was one of Daguerre's important clients.

But it was perhaps the Duke of Dorset, British Ambassador to Paris from 1783–8, who was the Englishman with the best opportunity to admire Daguerre's work for Marie-Antoinette. The marquise de la Tour du Pin, one of her ladies-in-waiting and of Irish origin, informs us in her memoirs that the Duke was a frequent and regular guest at Versailles, and that the Queen often teased them both about the curious British habit of shaking hands, which she apparently had not previously encountered.[8]

Daguerre's precise relationship with Holland remains uncharted, but from 1787 right up until Daguerre's death in London in 1796, Holland filled the houses of many of his most prestigious patrons with furniture

and decorative objects ordered through Daguerre. At first, they came from Paris (Daguerre's partner Lignereux had remained there), but the Revolution soon made it difficult to guarantee supply, and English craftsmen, often of French origin, were employed to manufacture furniture in the French style, sometimes copying pieces recently imported. A typical case is the set of mahogany chairs supplied by Jacob for the Library at Carlton House; examination of the nearly identical chairs at Woburn reveals them to be of English manufacture. In her biography of Henry Holland, Dorothy Stroud has shown that Daguerre was on excellent terms with several English furniture makers, such as Francis Hervé and Nicholas Morel (of Morel & Seddon), and with the architect Charles Heathcote Tatham, whose brother Thomas was a partner of the firm Marsh & Tatham.[9]

Only a small proportion of the French works of art in the Royal Collection today were purchased by George IV directly from Daguerre. They include the set of Jacob chairs (Fig. 3) now in the Music Room at Buckingham Palace.[10] The Lépine clock (Blue Drawing Room) purchased in 1790, is proof that already he was buying from others.[11] Most of his French pieces were bought in the early nineteenth century, often from auctions, such as the Watson-Taylor sale of 1825, years after Daguerre's death. Despite the wide time-span, George IV's taste remained remarkably consistent, and it may be wondered whether he knew he was buying a royal or Daguerre object.

2 Japanese lacquer bowl (one of a pair) with French early neo-classical gilt-bronze mounts. During the eighteenth century, *marchand-merciers* adapted Oriental and European porcelain, lacquer and other exotic and unusual materials into decorative objects designed to appeal to their clientele. Gilt-bronze mounts played a dominant role, encasing the porcelain or lacquer objects, which were frequently cut down to fit. In this case, the seventeenth century Japanese lacquer bowl (which is not of export lacquer, but probably formed part of the private trade which the staff of the Dutch East India Company were allowed) has been mounted with gilt-bronze perhaps as early as the mid-1760's; the heavy mounts are close in style to early neo-classical bronzes on furniture and mounted porcelain of about this period (*Picture Gallery*)

The most important pieces of French furniture in the Royal Collection are unquestionably the pair of marquetry pedestals today in the Picture Gallery at Buckingham Palace. Originally supports for two equation clocks, and delivered in 1762, they formed part of the furnishings of the bedroom created for Louis XV in 1738 in the Appartement Intérieur on the first floor at Versailles. The commode which faced the chimneypiece in this room was made in 1739 by Antoine-Robert Gaudreaus, with gilt-bronze mounts by Jacques Caffieri, to a design by the Slodtz brothers. It is now in the Wallace Collection, having been included in the traditional perks taken at the time of

Louis XV's death by the duc d'Aumont, who held the post of Premier Gentilhomme de la chambre for one year in four. Curiously, the clocks, with their pedestals, remained in the room until the Revolution, and the pedestals on their own were then bought by George IV in 1827. He cannot have known what they were, for Christian Baulez only identified them in 1978.[12]

Also of French royal origin are the two pairs of candelabra (Fig. 4) now in the State Dining Room at Buckingham Palace.[13] François Rémond, who made them for the comte d'Artois, was one of Daguerre's regular *bronziers*, and may have mounted some of the Sèvres vases ordered by Daguerre for that purpose. Indeed, the mounts on the pair of black-ground Sèvres vases (Plate II) in the Picture Gallery recall those, probably by Rémond, on a Japanese lacquer box which Daguerre supplied to Marie-Antoinette.[14] Again, the vases entered George IV's collection late, in 1815, but were placed on the Weisweiler/Daguerre console tables with related mounts (quite possibly by the same *bronzier*), which are shown in Sheraton's

> Like a number of his British contemporaries, George IV continued after the French Revolution to purchase furniture and objects which were no longer in fashion in France

engraving of the Chinese room at Carlton House in 1793.[15]

One piece of furniture with a less than dignified provenance is the Carlin commode (Plate I) with *pietra dura* plaques in the Green Drawing Room at Buckingham Palace, although the plaques themselves are likely to have been originally mounted on a cabinet made for Louis XIV.[16] Marie-Joséphine Laguerre, the commode's original owner, may well have received works of art as gifts from her lovers. Such practices were not uncommon; indeed young ladies of easy virtue often passed on gifts of this type as their New Year presents (*étrennes*) to the

III *Table of the Grand Commanders* (1806) (view of top surface) presented to King George IV by King Louis XVIII in 1817. It is of hard-paste Sèvres porcelain with gilt-bronze mounts. The top is painted with the head of Alexander the Great surrounded by twelve commanders of antiquity in the form of imitation cameo reliefs. It was commissioned by Napoleon in 1806 and finished six years later (it is seen in the Lawrence portrait of George IV in the State Dining Room)

3 *Canapé* stamped by Georges Jacob. From a large suite purchased from Daguerre in the late 1780s for the Drawing Room at Carlton House. The style and carving of these is related to seat furniture being made at about this time for French royal palaces, by Séné and Boulard as well as Jacob. In fact, the *menuisier's* role counted for little, and the extremely fine carving suggests that the same sculptors who worked on, for example, the chairs for the King's Salon des Jeux at Compiègne, could be employed by Daguerre as well as by the Garde-Meuble (*Music Room*)

Paris police officers whose job it was to keep an eye on them. It has even been suggested that the adoption of the rue St Honoré quarter by *les filles* was linked to the fact that the *marchand-merciers'* shops were mostly situated there too, since they apparently shared the same clientele.[17]

French royal taste is reflected in the enormous quantities of Sèvres porcelain bought by George IV, whose appetite for it was nearly as voracious as Louis XVI's. Again, most of the purchases were made after the Revolution, when objects formerly in French royal palaces became available on the open market. It is thus that he was able to capture most of the famous service with a *bleu nouveau* ground and mythological scenes which Louis XVI had ordered in 1782, as well as a number of other royal pieces, including the pair of hard-paste vases decorated with arabesques and mounted with gilt-bronze handles in the shape of rams, which are mentioned in the 1792 inventory of the porcelains in Louis XVI's private rooms at Versailles.[18] Unfortunately, owing to the infuriating habit of the Sèvres factory's sales registers of not describing vases in detail, it is often difficult to discover the names of their original owners. This is sadly the case of the *vase écritoire uni* (Blue Drawing Room), and the *vase royal* and the pair of *vases ferré* (see Plate IV).[19]

Like a number of his British contemporaries, George IV continued after the French Revolution to purchase furniture and objects which were no longer in fashion in France, although Sir Geoffrey de Bellaigue has shown that he also acquired 'modern' decorations from Daguerre's successor Martin-Eloy Lignereux.[20] His nostalgic attitude, if such it was, did not extend to respecting the integrity of the objects; the Vulliamys added and regilded gilt-bronze mounts, replaced clock movements (that in Fig. 5 is an example) and altered furniture to fit in with each new decorative scheme.

If the young Prince of Wales had made it to Versailles (perhaps under the pseudonym of marquis de la Manche?), it is difficult to imagine with what ideas he would have returned. Instead of the Aston Webb façade of Buckingham Palace, we would perhaps be staring today at a faithful copy of Jules Hardouin-Mansart's majestic Garden Front at

4 One of a set of four gilt-bronze candelabra by François Rémond. Supplied in 1783 by Rémond for the comte d'Artois' *cabinet turc* at Versailles. The corn motif was described as *blé de Turquie. Turqueries*, along with *chinoiserie*, formed a popular theme for interior decoration in France at this period; Marie-Antoinette owned two *cabinets turc*, one at Versailles and one at Fontainebleau, for which Riesener made a *bureau à cylindre* and a *tricoteuse* entirely veneered in mother of pearl. Vulliamy added the red marble bases for George IV (*State Dining Room*)

5 A French monumental pedestal clock ('pendule en gaine'), probably originally made by J.-P. Latz (*c.* 1691–1754) in the 1730s (*East Gallery*)

Versailles, with the Bassin d'Apollon replacing Queen Victoria's monument. One hopes, however, that security will be more effective than at Versailles in the eighteenth century; in 1784, a report complained that the Swiss Guards were stealing the gold fringes from the curtains in the Galerie des Glaces, and that their wives used them to trim their petticoats.[21]

[1] See Barbara Scott, 'Gustav III's Love of Paris', APOLLO, vol. XCII, November 1970, pp. 350–7.

[2] See Pierre Ennès, 'The Visit of the Comte and Comtesse du Nord to the Sèvres Manufactory', APOLLO, vol. CXXIX, March 1989, pp. 150–6 and 220–2.

[3] George IV's French purchases have been comprehensively studied by Sir Geoffrey de Bellaigue. See G. de Bellaigue, 'The Furnishings of the Chinese Drawing Room, Carlton House', Burlington Magazine, vol. CIX, September 1967, pp. 518–28; 'George IV and French Furniture', The Connoisseur, June 1977, pp. 116–25; Carlton House, The Past Glories of George IV's Palace, Queen's Gallery, Buckingham Palace, 1991–2.

[4] See Oliver Impey and John Whitehead, 'From Japanese box to French royal furniture', APOLLO, vol. CXXXII, September 1990, pp. 159–65.

[5] Marie-Antoinette's collection of lacquer and other mounted objects was entrusted to Daguerre at the outbreak of the French Revolution. See Alexandre Tuetey, 'Inventaire des Laques Anciennes et des objets de curiosité de Marie-Antoinette' Archives de l'Art Français, 1916, pp. 286–319.

[6] F. J. B. Watson, 'Holland and Daguerre, French Undercurrents in English Neo-Classic Furniture Design', APOLLO, vol. XCVI, October 1972, pp. 282–7.

[7] Suzanne Burkard (ed.), Mémoires de la Baronne d'Oberkirch, Mercure de France, Paris, 1989, p. 306

[8] Comte Christian de Liedekerke Beaufort (ed.), Mémoires de la Marquise de La Tour du Pin, Mercure de France, Paris, 1989, p. 77.

[9] Dorothy Stroud, Henry Holland, His Life and Architecture, A. S. Barnes and Co, New York, 1966.

[10] Geoffrey de Bellaigue, 'George IV and French Furniture', The Connoisseur, June 1977, pp. 119–21.

[11] Adolphe Chapiro, Jean-Antoine Lépine, horloger (1720–1814), Les éditions de l'amateur, Paris, 1988, p. 226 and Fig. 11–11. See also Louis Schreider III, 'Gouverneur Morris: Connoisseur of French Art', APOLLO, vol. XCIII, June 1971, p. 479.

[12] Christian Baulez, 'Notes sur quelques meubles et objets d'art des appartements intérieurs de Louis XVI et de Marie-Antoinette', Revue du Louvre, 5/6 1978, pp. 362–4. François Souchal, Les Slodtz, sculpteurs et décorateurs du Roi (1685–1764), Editions E. de Boccard, Paris, 1967.

[13] Christian Baulez, 'Le Goût Turc', L'Objet d'Art, December 1987, pp. 36 and 39.

[14] See for example, Paris, Drouot Montaigne, Jean-Louis Picard, 24 June 1993, Sale of Importants Tableaux Anciens, Sculptures, Objets d'Art et de très bel Ameublement, lot 61. Entries in Rémond's Journal, transcribed here, indicate that he may have mounted Marie-Antoinette's lacquer box.

[15] For a discussion of the decoration of these vases see Geoffrey de Bellaigue, 'Sèvres Artists and their Sources. II: Engravings', Burlington Magazine, vol. CXXII, November 1980, p. 756 and Fig. 70.

[16] Åke Setterwall, 'Some Louis XVI Furniture decorated with pietre dure reliefs', Burlington Magazine, vol, CI, December 1959, pp. 425–35. Baron Charles Davillier, Une vente d'actrice sous Louis XVI, Mlle. Laguerre, de l'Opéra, Aug. Aubry, Paris, 1870.

[17] John Whitehead, The French Interior in the Eighteenth Century, London, 1992, p. 30.

[18] Archives Nationales, Paris, O¹3356, Inventaire des Cabinets Intérieurs du Roi, 1792, Porcelaines, p. 9.

[19] For the Vase écritoire see Guy Francis Laking, Sèvres Porcelain of Buckingham Palace and Windsor Castle, London, 1907, pp. 91–2 and plate 45. For the others see Sèvres Porcelain from the Royal Collection, Queen's Gallery, Buckingham Palace, 1979–80, pp 53–4.

[20] Geoffrey de Bellaigue, 'Martin-Eloy Lignereux and England', Gazette des Beaux-Arts, vol. LXXI, 1968, pp. 283–94.

[21] See Fernand Evrard, 'Les moeurs à Versailles sous Louis XVI (suite et fin)', Revue de l'Histoire de Versailles et de Seine-et-Oise, July-September 1928, p. 186.

IV Sèvres vase Royal, c. 1768–70 (White Drawing Room). The vase Royal was so named because its cover was in the shape of a royal crown, which is sadly missing in this case. The painted scene is taken from a Boucher painting. This type of vase was known as a vase tourterelle in the eighteenth century because of the doves mounted on either side (a similar vase, with a crown-shaped cover and with a blue ground, exists elsewhere in the Royal Collection). This example has a spray of flowers painted on the back. Similarly, the pair of vases ferré, which flank it, are decorated on the front with scenes of children at play derived from paintings by J.-H. Fragonard, See-Saw and Blind Man's Buff. Such scenes were extremely common in the eighteenth century from about 1720 onward and in this case the engravings (1760) of J.-F. Beauvarlet probably provided the source for the Sèvres manufactory

Clocks in the Royal Collection

From commissioning to collecting

RICHARD GARNIER

1 *(left)* A French mantel clock by Claude Galle in ormolu on a green marble base modelled on Jacques Louis David's painting *Oath of the Horatii* of 1784. The three Horatii brothers are shown on the point of receiving their arms from their father whilst taking a vow of fidelity before fighting the Curatii brothers to establish the supremacy of Rome over Alba. All three Curatii and two of the Horatii were killed in the fight, the frieze on the clock base showing the victorious survivor being greeted by his father, with his two brothers wounded and on the point of death; while running off to the right is their sister who had been betrothed to one of the Curati

Vulliamy replaced the original movement of this clock in 1819 only ten years after it had been bought by George IV in 1809 from Mr Recordon. It was originally placed in the Large Crimson Drawing Room at Carlton House. Louis Recordon is best known today for having been the London agent of the acclaimed French watch and clockmaker, Abraham Louis Breguet, but he was a respected clockmaker in his own right in addition to selling timepieces by other French makers as here.

There was a recurring fashion in the late eighteenth and early nineteenth century for fashioning clocks after famous paintings. The Royal Collection includes a number of clocks in this vein, for example, one modelled on David's *Rape of the Sabine Women* and an earlier clock loosely based on the central group in Poussin's *Rape of Europa (Throne Room)*

I A French large clock of circa 1770, the case signed (Pierre) De La Croix, Fondeur, Cizeleur' and composed of a glazed central section in ormolu flanked by two figures in patinated bronze representing Art and Literature. As the original movement and dial were replaced by Vulliamy in 1851, the identity of the clockmaker is lost, however, the de la Croix family included not only the renowned ébeniste RVLC (Roger van de la Croix) but also a clockmaker. As an alternative clue, Pierre de la Croix when declared bankrupt in 1771 was noted as having amongst his creditors the clockmakers Courvoisier and Gille.

The clock case proper of this clock stands on an early nineteenth-century base of ebony framing four panels of cast and chased ormolu. These panels are in the style of the sixteenth-century School of Fontainebleau and depict the four elements: Earth, Air, Fire and Water personified by the ancient gods and goddesses Cybele (the Phrygian earth mother), Juno, Vulcan and Neptune. Identical panels feature similarly in an ebony pedestal to an earlier eighteenth-century ormolu clockcase by Caffieri, now at Boughton House, Northamptonshire, seemingly bought from Garrard's in 1830 by the 5th Duke of Buccleuch. Such a date would seem to corroborate the tradition that George IV won the de la Croix clock in a wager with Charles X of France (reigned 1820–30). The pedestal bases of both this and the Boughton clock were presumably added in London, perhaps by a personality such as E. H. Baldock who was active in the 1820s as a refashioner of French furniture *(Silk Tapestry Room)*

---

locks and watches have long held great fascination not only as mechanical devices but also as philosophical conceits, and so they have frequently been the preserve of the rich and powerful. As such, they were often used to convey or symbolize messages of intellectual superiority or dynastic permanence. In the case of William III, many of his clocks, such as the Mostyn Tompion, were specifically designed as nationalistic symbols or icons in opposition to Louis XIV of France's 'papist' monarchy and its associated art.

The first domestic clocks date from the early sixteenth century, but it was not until the successful application of the pendulum in the late 1650s that any degree of accuracy

was achieved. It was the English clockmakers who developed the potential of this Dutch invention so that by 1700 English clockmaking led the world. Kings Charles II and William III, along with Queen Anne's Consort, Prince George of Denmark, were particularly enthused by clocks and through their commissioning of important clocks from the leading makers of the day—Knibb, Tompion and Quare—they both furthered advances in horology and established an eminent position for timepieces in the Royal Collection.

Following a lull in interest in the early Georgian era, George III—sometimes called the Scientist King—through his own interest in practising horology (the Royal

The Royal Archive contains George III's handwritten instructions for mounting and unmounting a watch. He was sometimes known as the Scientist King and his contribution to the horological holdings of the Royal Collection remains unsurpassed

---

Archive contains his hand-written instructions for mounting and unmounting a watch) actively commissioned and also collected clocks in some quantity (as was so evident in the exhibition 'George III—Collector and Patron' held at the Queen's Gallery in 1974–5). His contribution to the Royal Collection is unsurpassed, although visitors to Buckingham Palace will see only clocks collected by his son, George IV.

George IV's collecting began when he was Prince of Wales, long before he became Prince Regent or King. His tastes were, by contrast with those of George III, more decorative than technical, but this does not mean that he was insensitive to complicated mechanisms with myriad indications on the dials. He thus bought the triple-dialled astronomical clock by Lepine (Plate II) direct from the maker.

His more normal process of acquisition was through a series of agents of varying social status. The use of courtiers such as Lord Yarmouth to obtain the Latz clock (East Gallery) does not surprise us, whereas the employment of Household Officers as 'scouts' may do. For instance, François Benois, a confectioner, and Louis Weltje, clerk of the kitchen, were both the Prince's agents in buying *objets d'art*.

A word must be said on the role of the Vulliamy family, Royal Clockmakers for three generations from the 1760s. The first Vulliamy, Justin, was an immigrant from Switzerland who came to England with the specific intention of benefiting from the supreme reputation of English clockmaking. Like poachers turned keepers, his son and grandson championed English and almost reviled French clockmaking. Justin's son,

Benjamin, 'repaired' many a royal clock, but he never went so far as his own son, Benjamin Lewis Vulliamy, who replaced wholesale the original movements of French clocks in the Royal Collection, even within ten years of their purchase new, as with the 'very bad' movement of the Horatii clock (Fig. 1). A typical sentiment justifying the replacement of the movement of the Apollo clock (Fig. 2) in 1834 was that 'the works of the clock are good for nothing and the case is very dirty. The case is well worth cleaning and new works'.

II A French astronomical mantel clock by Jean-Antoine Lepine with three dials in a breakfront white marble case with profuse ormolu mounts. This clock was seemingly bought direct from the maker in 1790, along with several others, for which the total bill was £3,250. However, of this sum £2,850 was still owing in 1797. This illustration from George IV's pictorial inventory of clocks.

The central dial showing hours and minutes also has a counterpoised sweep seconds hand. A fourth hand for equation of time indicates the difference between Solar time—as would be registered on a sundial—and Mean time as conventionally used. The left dial is of hard paste porcelain, enamelled by Jean Coteau shows the year, month, day of month and sign of the zodiac; while the right-hand dial, also of hard-paste porcelain and by Coteau, shows the phases of the moon and the weekday. Finally, the arc below the central dial shows the passage of the sun through the day.

This clock was originally in the Royal Closet at Carlton House, where it is described as being in George IV's pictorial inventory. Noted on the inventory sheet is the loan in 1828 of the clock to Windsor, whence it was returned to London. Benjamin Lewis Vulliamy repaired the clock in 1808, but did not replace the movement (*Blue Drawing Room*)

George IV began collecting long before he became Prince Regent or king, although often for reasons more aesthetic than mechanical, but he was not insensitive to complicated mechanisms with myriad indications on the dials. He was also responsible for a scrupulous inventory which often carries his own annotations

3 A French Empire clock by Pierre-Philippe Thomire in ormolu and blued-steel on a red griotte marble base. The dial of the clock, with enamel chapter ring, forms the wheel of a chariot with a quadriga of horses driven by Apollo over an arc in the sky between simulated wisps of clouds. The front of this arc is mounted with four signs of the zodiac.

P.-P. Thomire (1751–1843) was perhaps the foremost Parisian bronzier of his day; he retired in 1823 from when his business was run by his sons as Thomas & Cie. This magnificent clock was bought by George IV in May 1810 from a Mr Boileau. The price is not recorded, but a French auction catalogue of 1829 noted that Thomire's price for this model of clock was 1,500 francs. Almost inevitably, the movement of this clock was replaced by B. L. Vulliamy in 1834 (*State Dining Room*)

Dining in state

Towards a greater simplicity

SUSAN JENKINS

As Buckingham Palace grew, so demands for greater space to dine and entertain multiplied, especially under Queen Victoria. The lavish entertainments of the past have gradually given way to a rather simpler, although still grand, style of dining

Queen Victoria was the first monarch to use Buckingham Palace as the principal royal residence in which to entertain state visitors. She took up residence on 13 July 1837 immediately after her accession, only to discover that the interiors were still being decorated. She soon found that the rooms were insufficiently spacious and complained to Sir Robert Peel in 1845 of the 'total want of accommodation for our little family which is fast growing up' and the need of 'a room capable of containing a large number of those persons whom the Queen has to invite in the course of the season to balls, concerts, etc'.[1]

The Queen's complaints reflect the development of Buckingham House from a quiet retreat for George III and Queen Charlotte to a 'pied à terre' for George IV, soon becoming grander in both design and function than John Nash (1752–1835) had intended or George IV had promised.[2] Requirements for dining and accommodation had moved on from the modest arrangements for George II. He and Queen Charlotte made do with a Parlour measuring 19 × 2.3 m, immediately to the right of the Hall, with a buffet niche painted by Sebastiano Ricci.[3] Queen Victoria, however, who loved dancing and entertaining, needed an *enfilade* of large reception and function rooms in which to entertain.

The extensions to the Palace so desired by the Queen began in 1847 when Edward Blore (1787–1879) was commissioned to build a new East Wing, and continued in 1852 when Sir James Pennethorne (1801–71), the nephew of John Nash, was ordered to build a new Ballroom and State Supper Room. Until these were completed in 1856, the Blue Drawing Room served as the Ballroom, and the State Dining Room was used for dining. The latter had a restricted capacity, and if more than sixty guests were invited, tables were set up in the Picture Gallery (Plate I). After the building of the Ballroom, however, state banquets took place there.

The State Dining Room, therefore, has generally served for smaller functions such as luncheons or dinners rather than state banquets. It was probably not completed until after 1840, when Blore, who had replaced John Nash as architect in August 1831, finished his remodelling of the interiors. The accounts show that workmen were still demanding payment in 1838–40 for work in the new dining room. These payments were for fittings which were being installed, principally picture frames, carpets and sideboards (probably the ten mahogany sideboards which still stand in the State Dining Room). For instance, on 30 September 1838 Spencer demanded £2 12s. for 'Preparing & Gilding Sideboards and Materials', while Faraday provided '8 brass Sideboard backs'; J. Brown 'plate Glass for Sideboards &c (£290)' and Jackson & Sons '4 festoon ornaments for Glass Frames for Dining Room &c. (£38 4s. 1d.)' on 31 December 1839. Only in 1843 was C. Bielefeld paid £3 6s. 6d. for 26 ft of 'papier mache ornaments &c for sideboards'. Most of the gilding work was undertaken by the firm of Ponsonby & Son who charged £42 7s. 7d. for 'Gilders work and Materials' and a further £45 5s. for 'Gilding the Glass Frame/Grand Dining Room &c' on 31 March 1838. They also provided '6 Glass & 1 Picture Frames. State Dining Room' on 31 March 1840.[4] This must reflect the decision to hang the imposing set of full-length royal portraits in the State Dining Room, the whole crowned by Sir Thomas Lawrence's portrait of George IV over the mantelpiece.

Further furnishings were also ordered at this time, as a Saxony carpet and hearth rugs were provided by A. Lapworth at a cost of £144 1s. 9d. Finally, McBean was paid £6 5s. 1d. to 'Asist in making [the] Arch for [the] Sideboard &c.' on 30 September 1838.[5] This must refer to the buffet arch at the end of the State Dining Room, which was swept away in the 1852–5 building programme to make way for the West Gallery, but which can still be seen in a watercolour by Douglas Morison (1814–47) in the Royal Library (Fig. 1).[6]

Descriptions of functions in the State Dining Room show how magnificent it must have looked when it was decorated for dinners. On 5 May 1852, a state ball was held at Buckingham Palace (a common occurrence in the early years of Victoria's reign). So many guests were invited that the Throne Room was used as the second Ballroom for the evening. A newspaper account describes the 'Dining Room with a deep recess at the end within which a buffet was arranged on which the most exquisite specimens of jewelled and ornamental gold plate were most effectively displayed with the aid of a background of dark crimson and numerous lights from golden candelabra.' The tables were arranged around three sides of the apartment and on them; 'The service was entirely of gold plate and some of the most beautiful specimens of artistic skill in the precious metals were displayed.' Only 'single flowers of great beauty and groups of plants in full blossom relieved occasionally the gorgeous magnificence of the golden service'.[7] The Queen and Prince Albert ate supper there between midnight and one o'clock.

From the 1850s it became common to use flowers to decorate the dining table. With the introduction of *dîner à la russe* when the tablecloth and services were not removed (see below) it became more practical to decorate the table with flowers, and a number of books appeared explaining the technique.[8]

A very similar account is given of another ball later that month, on 19 May

---

I Detail of *Banquet in the Picture Gallery, Buckingham Palace, 1853, on the occasion of the Christening of Prince Leopold, 28 June 1853*, watercolour by Louis Haghe. The State Dining Room had a restricted capacity and, if more than sixty guests were invited, tables were set up in the Picture Gallery until the completion of the State Ballroom in 1856. Note the buffet display of plate at the far end, a non-functional show of wealth and status by this period. The watercolour shows the colour scheme and hanging arranged by Prince Albert

tradition of the buffet or sideboard where plate was stacked up to impress and demonstrate power and wealth. But there was no longer any suggestion that the buffet plate was to be used during the meal. Prince Pückler-Muskau commented on a visit to England in the 1820s: 'True hospitality this can hardly be called; it is rather the display of one's own possessions for the purpose of dazzling as many as possible.'[15]

It is important to note that not all meals were as lavish as state ball suppers. Entertaining also took place on a more modest scale, for instance when Victoria and Albert dined with the French Emperor Napoleon III at Buckingham Palace on 19 and 20 April 1855. The Queen described the dinner: 'We dined at a quarter to eight in the usual dining room with all our suites. The Emperor, Albert and all the gentlemen were in uniform... The Emperor, as a matter of course, always leads me and always sits to my right... we two ladies sitting just opposite to each other in the middle.'[16]

Such a dinner usually lasted about one and a half hours, during which about twelve courses were eaten. Sorbets were served before the roast to refresh the palate. A typical dinner included consommé and hot soup, salmon, chicken, lamb, pigeon, salad, ham mousse and hot and cold fowls, with beef and salad on the side table.

After the death of Prince Albert on 14 December 1861 Queen Victoria's enthusiasm for entertaining waned. There were, however, family occasions and state visits when she was required to entertain as before. One of the most troublesome of these was the state visit of the Shah of Persia in June 1873. He stayed at Buckingham Palace where he was entertained to luncheon, dining each evening in private, probably in the Carnarvon Room, which was used as the dining room for guests accommodated in the Belgian Suite. This may have been due to Foreign Office intelligence that 'His Majesty generally dines alone, and when so, prefers to have his meals on the carpet. For that purpose a movable carpet should be kept ready whereupon his servants will put the dishes &c.'[17] Or perhaps it was due to a letter from Lord Odo Russell to Earl Granville describing the Shah's manners on a visit to Berlin: 'nobody ventures to tell the Shah that he should be punctual... that he should not sit down before the Empress can obtain a seat or take Her Majesty by the elbow to make her get up... or raise his voice so as to startle the company or put his fingers into

1852: 'The State rooms... were profusely, and with great taste, decorated with rare plants and beautiful flowers... At the usual hour Her Majesty and His Royal Highness Prince Albert were conducted to supper in the State Dining Room by the Lord Steward, accompanied by the Royal Circle. The tables on which the repast was served displayed some of the most choice specimens of gold plate from the Royal Treasury and the whole apartment presented its usual appearance of gorgeous magnificence.'[9]

The menu for 'Her Majesty's Ball Supper' on 19 May 1852 included a large number of dishes, beginning with soup 'A la Printannier', moving on to 'pâtés de volaille', plover's eggs, macedoine of vegetables, and followed by seventy-two entrées. For dessert there were 'Babas', nougats and *pièces montées*, with a further twelve plates of sandwiches if anyone was still hungry.[10]

It is not surprising to find so many French dishes on the menu. Although the Queen personally favoured simple cooking, it was necessary to conform to the fashion for French food. The Queen also employed Continental chefs, such as Charles Elmé Francatelli and M Ménager, who was Royal Chef at the end of her reign. For important celebrations like the Diamond Jubilee in 1897,

twenty-four extra French chefs were hired to prepare the fourteen-course dinner.[11] In addition, until the 1860s, the French method of serving dinner was favoured (*dîner à la française*). A meal was served in two to three parts with all the dishes removed between services. It was only later when *dîner à la russe* became popular, and dishes were placed in turn on the sideboard and served by waiters, that many guests were able to eat hot food.[12]

On the occasion of another State Ball on 15 June 1853 which was opened by the Queen, dancing with the Hereditary Grand Duke of Mecklenberg-Strelitz, the buffet in the dinner room was laden with 'Vases, jewelled cups, salvers, the shield of Achilles and a great variety of gold plate [with] some magnificent centre pieces, plateaux, epergnes, vases and candelabra'.[13] Many of these pieces were made for George IV by the firm of Rundell Bridge and Rundell and remain in the Royal Collection.[14]

Accounts of the use of the State Dining Room thus emphasize the importance of the spectacular display of plate, both on the buffet and on the tables, particularly at a state ball or banquet given for a visiting foreign ruler. The buffet in the Dining Room was a continuation of the medieval his dishes, or take his food out of his mouth again to look at it, after it has been chewed—or fling it under the table if it does not suit his taste.'[18]

One of the most splendid occasions of Queen Victoria's reign was her Jubilee on 20 June 1887 (Fig. 2). The Queen described it in her Journal: 'Then came the luncheon, an enormous one in the large Dining room which I had not used since '61. The King of Saxony took me in... Had a large family dinner. All the Royalties assembled in the bow room, and we dined in the Supper room, which looked splendid with the buffet covered with the gold plate. The table was a large horseshoe one, with many lights on it. The King of Denmark took me in, and Willy of Greece sat on my other side. The Princes were all in uniform and the Princesses were all beautifully dressed.'[19]

King Edward VII and Queen Alexandra were determined to keep up the high standard of royal dining.[20] They wanted the meals served at Buckingham Palace to be the best in the world. The Coronation Banquet of 9 August 1902 was an opportunity to establish this, with fourteen courses including sturgeon, foie gras, quails and lobster. For the kitchen staff, however, it was a near-disaster. Planned for 26 June, the banquet was postponed due to the king's ill health. One of the staff describes how the jellies were melted down and stored in magnum champagne bottles and the caviare put on ice.[21] Even Edward VII, however, with his love of extravagance, accepted the necessity of economies. When he discovered from his private secretary that the man standing beside the sideboard throughout each meal was the wine-taster who received £600 but had no other duties, he was promptly dismissed.[22]

George V was not as personally interested in the quality of his table as his father, and left Queen Mary to deal with the kitchen arrangements. His indifference coincided with the onset of war and the effect of rationing on the royal table. The monarchy took rationing seriously, restricting meals to three courses and banning the consumption of wine. Queen Mary, who kept a menu book in which she issued instructions to the kitchens, suggested instead that 'water boiled with a little sugar' should be served in the dining room.[23] The servants, who appreciated the selection of fine wines available to them, were understandably distressed at this suggestion.

After the War, the number of courses served at the royal table remained limited to four or five, even for a state banquet. At the wedding of Princess (now Queen) Elizabeth, in November 1947, the wedding breakfast was a relatively simple meal, with half the traditional number of courses, including Filet de sole Mountbatten, Perdreau en casserole and Bombe glacée Princesse Elizabeth. This

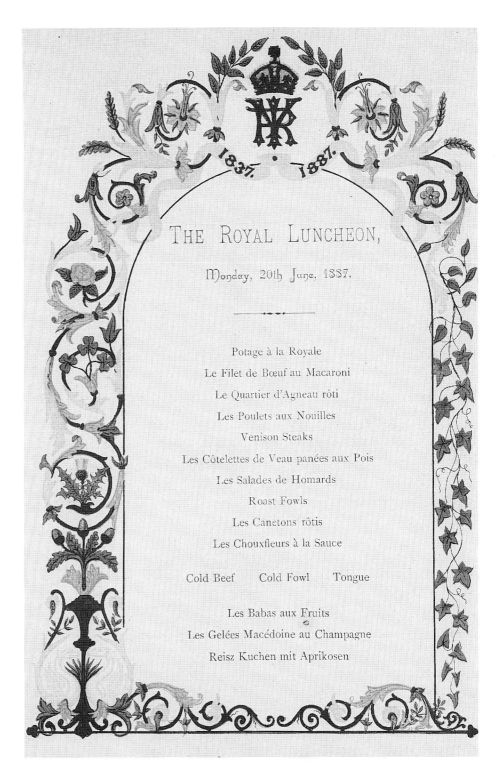

2 Menu for Queen Victoria's Jubilee luncheon, 20 June 1887, which took place in the State Dining Room which the Queen had not used since 1861 (the year of Prince Albert's death)

modern simplicity is also reflected in the state banquets for Queen Beatrix and Prince Claus of the Netherlands in November 1982 (Fig. 3) and King Fahd of Saudi Arabia in March 1987 (Fig. 4). The menus on both occasions consisted of only five courses.

Although the number of courses served at the royal table may have halved, in other ways dining at Buckingham Palace has changed little since the reign of Queen Victoria. In particular, the protocol and splendour surrounding state dinners have survived. Formal dinners have always been tightly regulated. For instance, at a large dinner for Queen Victoria in 1838, the royal family assembled in the Throne Room at 7.45 p.m. (sometimes the White Drawing Room was used instead). Simultaneously the guests assembled in the Green Drawing Room. They were usually introduced to the royal family in the Throne Room or the Picture Gallery and were then paired off for the procession to the dining room, preceded by

[99]

the Lord Chamberlain and the Lord Steward walking backwards.[24]

The pairings for the procession could cause problems. Sir Robert Chester, Queen Victoria's Master of Ceremonies, commented in his notebook in 1837 that the foreign ministers caused a particular problem in 'finding the precedence at the dinners'.[25] For certain favoured individuals, however, protocol was occasionally waived. Baron Stockmar, Prince Albert's adviser, for instance, occupied 'an exceptional position ... he was not expected to wear the official court uniform when the Queen dined; and he assuredly would not, with his thin legs, have cut a very happy figure in the official knee-breeches'.[26]

Similarly, Harold Nicholson describes a dinner which he attended at Buckingham Palace on 17 March 1937. He arrived at 8.20 p.m. to find 'upon each fourth step stands a footman dressed in scarlet and gold epaulettes and powdered about the hair'. At 8.45 p.m. the King and Queen entered the Drawing Room to meet the guests and the Duchess of Rutland and Mr Baldwin preceded the company to dinner. As the procession approached the dining room the Grenadier Guards played 'God Save the King'. As ever the dining room was impressive: 'The dining table is one mass of gold candelabra and scarlet tulips. Behind us the whole of the Windsor (gold) plate is massed in tiers'. Nicholson was less impressed by the food, however, commenting: 'The dinner has been unwisely selected since we have soup, fish, quail, ham, chicken, ice and savoury. The wine on the other hand is excellent and the port superb. When we have finished our savoury the King rises and we all resume our procession back to the drawing room.'[27]

On the other hand, protocol was relaxed when the royal family dined in private. Such meals, which were not court functions, did not require the attendance of Royal Household officials such as ladies-in-waiting. In July 1939, for instance, George VI was host to a private ball which was not attended by the Royal Household or any official guests. The King and Queen did not withdraw in state at supper but sat at their table in the Ball Supper Room. In addition, a private lunch or dinner allowed the chefs to provide dishes which were personal favourites. George V, for instance, was served curry for lunch every day and his private menus reflect his taste for Irish stew, cottage pie and roast beef.

Even fewer courses were offered at private meals. The menu for a private lunch party for twelve guests at Buckingham Palace given by Queen Elizabeth II on 30 July 1992 had only three courses. Such meals are taken occasionally in the State Dining Room, depending on the number of guests. More frequently, the Chinese Lunch

---

Menu

Crème Solferino

———

Coquilles St. Jacques Mornay

———

Faisan Farci Souvaroff
Endives Braisées
Haricots Verts
Pommes Cretan

———

Salade

———

Bombe Glacée Canadienne

Les Vins

Fine Old Amontillaldo
Trierer St. Maximiner Kreuzberg Spätlese 1979
Nuits St. Georges Les Pruliers 1969

Music Programme

March	COLONEL BOGEY	*Alford*
Selection	PERCHANCE TO DREAM	*Novello*
Polka	THE LITTLE SWISS POLKA	*Siebert*
Waltz Selection	FLIGHTS OF FANCY	*arr. Winter*
Interlude	COUNTRY GARDENS	*Grainger*
Selection	MARY POPPINS	*Sherman*
Waltz	WESTMINSTER WALTZ	*Farnon*
Selection	H.M.S. PINAFORE	*Sullivan*
Serenade	NEAPOLITAN SERENADE	*Winkler*
Interlude	THE PRINCESS OF WALES	*Davies/Jones*
Interlude	THE SWING O'THE KILT	*Ewing*
March	PASSING OF THE REGIMENTS	*Winter*

Major D.N. TAYLOR,
Director of Music,
Welsh Guards

Pipe Programme

March	THE CRAGS OF TUMBLEDOWN MOUNTAIN
Strathspey	THE ROES AMONG THE HEATHER
Reel	THOMPSON'S DIRK
March	ROY COVE

3 Menu for state banquet in honour of Queen Beatrix and Prince Claus of the Netherlands, November 1982, reflecting the relative simplicity of modern times

---

Room on the first floor, is used, furnished with exotic furniture ordered by George IV for Brighton Pavilion.

Inevitably, the organization of so many different functions required an efficient household system. The Royal Household had basically evolved from the medieval model which successive monarchs had attempted to reform and slim down. George IV was no exception when he laid down a set of 'Rules for the Household' in 1822, which described the responsibilities of individual members.[28] Menus were to be decided by the Master Cook, in discussion with the Clerk Comptroller of the Kitchen. Responsibility for laying and serving at table was to lie with the Principal Table Decker, an officer of the Ewry. Food was to be carried to the table by the Footmen and Stewards Room men and drink was to be supplied by the Officers of the Wine and Beer Cellar who were 'constantly in person [to] attend our service ... and daily wait at our sideboard'. Finally, the Silver Pantry was to disburse the silver and gold plate.

By Queen Victoria's reign, however, the system of household management was not working efficiently. Baron Stockmar in his 'Observations on the present state of the Royal Household' in January 1841, noted that 'more than two thirds of all the male and female servants are left without a master in

the house ... they may commit any excess or irregularity' and 'In the time of George III the Lord Steward had the custody ... of the whole palace ... In George IV and William IV's reign it was held that the whole of the ground floor including halls, dining room etc were in his charge ... In the present reign the Lord Steward has surrendered to the Lord Chamberlain the Grand Hall and other rooms on the ground floor but whether the kitchens, sculleries, pantries remain under his charge is a question which no one could perhaps reply to'.[29] As a result of Stockmar's criticisms, Prince Albert wrote firmly to Sir Robert Peel in November 1841: '[The Household] is clumsy in its original construction and works so ill that as long as its wheels are not mended there can neither be order nor regularity, comfort, security nor outward dignity in the Queen's Palace'.[30] The Prince's reforms, which govern the running of the modern Household, were implemented soon after, involving the appointment of the Master of the Household as the Lord Chamberlain's deputy. An account of 1847, describes a reformed and efficient Household service, explaining how food was served to the State Dining Room. Each meal was supervised by the Clerk of the Kitchen who 'always attends during Her Majesty's dinner walking around the room to see that the other servants do their bidding. He also carves ... when required, gives orders for the removal of the first course and superintends the arrangement of the second on the royal table.' His assistants carved the joints on the side tables. The three table deckers and their assistant laid the cloth and were in charge of the napery. They also washed all the decanters and glasses and looked after the pickles and bread. The food was supplied by the kitchen staff, who were the Chief Cook and the three Master Cooks, the two Roasting Cooks, two Yeomen of the Kitchen, two Yeomen Confectioners and three Yeomen in charge of the plate.[31] By the end of Queen Victoria's reign, the number of chefs had risen to eighteen, according to Gabriel Tschumi, one of the twentieth-century kitchen staff.[32] These included eight Master Cooks, two Pastry Cooks, two Roast Cooks and two Larder Cooks. No doubt this was to cater for the large number of meals provided each month. An entry in the ledger for June 1853, for instance, shows that a total of 14,282 meals were supplied in that month of which only 526 were served at the royal table.[33]

The kitchen staff thus had one of the most important roles to play in the smooth running of the dining operation at Buckingham Palace. Inevitably, their task was a difficult one and standards had to be high. Queen Victoria's chef, M Ménager, was a perfectionist, believing that 'A chef is an

> In private, George V liked to indulge his taste for daily curry, for Irish stew, cottage pie and roast beef. A vegetarian professor who dined with the King worked out a menu of seven courses which the King regarded with a pained expression while his guest helped himself liberally to the mixture

artist . . . His triumph is a momentary one. To achieve that short triumph he must expend all his skill and experience'.[34] Inventive chefs regularly created new dishes for occasions such as royal wedding breakfasts. They relied on the footmen serving the dishes, however, to report on whether they were well received.

Developments in cooking methods have obviously made a great difference to the quality of food on the royal table. One disillusioned chef deplored the effect of modern labour-saving methods such as deep-freezing meat. He commented gloomily: 'It is strange to think how little the fourteen course meals served at Buckingham Palace at the end of the last century have in common with those which are served to members of the Royal Family today'.[35] Concessions have also had to be made to modern food fads. A vegetarian professor, dining with George V, 'worked out a menu of seven courses . . . King George, I believe,

4 Menu for state banquet in honour of King Fahd of Saudi Arabia in March 1987. It is usual to find at least one German wine on the list, while the selection of music is designed to appeal to a wide range of taste

looked on with a pained expression as his guest helped himself liberally to the mixture'.[36]

Thus, despite some inevitable differences in the pattern of dining at Buckingham Palace, the structure and formality, if not the number of courses, of state banquets is today remarkably similar to those of Queen Victoria's reign. Dinners are still held in the State Dining Room, the Ballroom or, more rarely, the State Supper Room, which are laid out in the same way as they have been for over a century. Clearly royal guests today could have no reason to comment, as did François de la Rochefoucauld, visiting the Duke of Grafton in 1784 that: 'Dinner is one of the most wearisome of English experiences, lasting, as it does, for four or five hours. The first two are spent eating.'[37]

[1] H. Clifford Smith: Buckingham Palace, London, 1931, p. 4.
[2] For a history of the building of Buckingham Palace see: H. M. Colvin ed., The History of the King's Works, vols. V and VI, London, 1976, 1973, p. 133–8 and 263–93.
[3] See J. Harris, G. de Bellaigue and O. Millar, Buckingham Palace, London, pp. 23 and 98.
[4] Public Record Office: LC9/373 f. 131 ff.
[5] PRO LC9/373 f. 132.
[6] Royal Library, Windsor, catalogue number R.L.19898. Signed and dated Douglas Morison/1843. One of a series of watercolours commissioned by Queen Victoria of the interiors of Buckingham Palace. My thanks to Martin Clayton, Assistant Curator of the Print Room for this information.
[7] PRO LC5/252 5 May 1852.
[8] See B. Howe, 'Decorating the Victorian Dinner Table', Country Life, 7 January 1960.
[9] PRO LC5/252 19 May 1852.
[10] Royal Archive Ledger May 1852. My thanks to Lady Sheila de Bellaigue for access to this information.
[11] See J. Burnett, Plenty and Want, London, 1966, p. 169.
[12] Ibid, p. 178.
[13] PRO LC5/252 15 June 1853.
[14] See Carlton House: The Past Glories of George IV's Palace, exhibition catalogue, The Queen's Gallery, Buckingham Palace, 1991–2, Cat. no. 73ff.
[15] Prince Pückler-Muskau, Tour in England, Ireland and France in the Years 1826, 1827, 1828 and 1829 in a series of Letters by a German Prince (translated by S. Austin), Zurich, 1940, p. 34.
[16] Leaves from a Journal, with an introduction by R. Mortimer, London, 1961, p. 52.
[17] V. Watson, A Queen at Home, London, 1942, p. 221.
[18] Idem.
[19] Ed. G. Buckle, The Letters of Queen Victoria, vol. I, 1886–90, London, 1930, p. 32. My thanks to Lady Sheila de Bellaigue for drawing this to my attention.
[20] J. Burnett, Plenty and Want, London, 1966, p. 166.
[21] G. Tschumi, Royal Chef. Recollections of Life in Royal Households from Queen Victoria to Queen Mary, London, 1954, p. 91.
[22] M. D. Peacocke, The Story of Buckingham Palace. The Royal Home through Seven Reigns, London, 1951, p. 177.
[23] G. Tschumi, op. cit., p. 133.
[24] See B. Hoey, Invitation to the Palace. How Royalty Entertains, London, 1989, p. 18.
[25] PRO LC5/9 f. 214 22 July 1837.
[26] P. Emden, Behind the Throne, London, 1934.
[27] Quoted in D. Edgar, Palace, Bath, 1984, p. 73.
[28] PRO LS3/194.
[29] C. Woodham-Smith, Queen Victoria, her Life and Times, vol. I, 1819–61, London, 1972, p. 263.
[30] C. Woodham-Smith, op. cit. p. 264.
[31] Anon, Sketches of Her Majesty's Household, published by William Strange, Paternoster Rd., 1847, p. 53–91.
[32] G. Tschumi, op. cit., p. 32.
[33] Royal Archive, Windsor Ledger June 1853. My thanks to Lady Sheila de Bellaigue for access to this information.
[34] G. Tschumi, op. cit., p. 66.
[35] Ibid., p. 208.
[36] Ibid., p. 133.
[37] A. Palmer, Moveable Feasts, London, 1952, p. 21–3.

Fashion in the gallery

The Picture Gallery's changing hang

CHARLES NOBLE

The history of the Picture Gallery reflects the changing taste of successive monarchs as surely as the works of art on view

Few who saw Alan Bennett's play *A Question of Attribution* will forget the imaginary encounter between The Queen and her Surveyor of Pictures, Anthony Blunt. The setting was the Picture Gallery at Buckingham Palace. This mythical private meeting, however, masks the essentially public nature of the gallery. Until James Pennethorne added the State Ballroom in 1854, the largest banquets were held in the Picture Gallery (see also colour illustration, p. 97); today, parties and receptions still take place here.

1993 is the first time that the general public will be able to tour the State Apartments, but schemes to permit visitors to enter Buckingham Palace date back as early as 1762. At that time George III apparently considered allowing the nobility and gentry in to Buckingham House to view the newly-purchased Consul Smith collection, although nothing seems to have come of it.[1] However, the Picture Gallery as we now know it was not conceived until the reign of George IV, following his decision to make Buckingham Palace his principal residence. It was intended to house his collection of predominantly Dutch and Flemish seventeenth-century paintings from Carlton House. It is a sad irony that he did not live to see the paintings displayed in the Palace Picture Gallery, particularly as he had put so much thought and care into its design.

The Picture Gallery forms the backbone of the first floor State Apartments on the garden front. It is 47 m long and is in the tradition of galleries of nineteenth-century aristocratic London houses. Flanked by other state rooms, by necessity it had to be top-lit and an individual picture lighting scheme, only fully superseded in 1914, was designed by John Nash. He devised a tripartite ceiling, the sides of which were punctuated by a series of square glazed domed compartments, formed by pendant arches, which directed the light down onto the pictures (Plate I). He may well have recalled the novel lighting scheme in the gallery which he had designed for Benjamin West's

1 *Banquet in the Picture Gallery, Buckingham Palace on the occasion of the Christening of Prince Leopold, 28 June 1853* by Louis Haghe (1806–85) (see colour detail, p. 97). Until the construction of the Ballroom in 1854, large banquets were held here. The hanging of the pictures seen here was the work of Prince Albert in 1851

house, where light was similarly excluded from the centre of the room.[2]

For all its novelty, the scheme had its detractors. One contemporary observer objected that 'the sub-divisions in the ceiling make the room narrow'.[3] More importantly, the King's Surveyor of Pictures, William Seguier, reported that Nash's scheme failed to light the paintings adequately.[4] The fault was subsequently remedied by Nash's successor, Edward Blore, who introduced raised skylights into the central section of the ceiling (visible already in the 1843 watercolour illustrated in Plate I).

It is not known exactly when George IV's paintings were first hung in the Picture Gallery. As Buckingham Palace did not become habitable, in normal royal terms, until early in the reign of Queen Victoria, it is most likely then. Indeed, it is conceivable that the gallery was hung in time for the young Queen's first ball on 10 May 1838. It was certainly ready by 31 July 1839, for Queen Victoria recorded in her *Journal* a discussion with Lord Melbourne 'of the beautiful pictures in the gallery here . ... of their being all Dutch, which we agreed was a low style; our preferring the Italian Masters'.[5]

The paintings in the State Apartments were presumably hung by Seguier, who compiled a printed catalogue of them in 1841. Together with Mrs Jameson's account of her visit in 1844 and a watercolour of 1843 (see Plate I),[6] a good idea of this early arrangement in the Picture Gallery can be gained. The paintings were hung tight-packed in three and, in some places, four tiers. The hanging scheme was traditional, with the cabinet pictures in the lowest tier, at eye-level, and the larger pictures in the two top tiers. The pictures were mostly in deep Regency frames, fitted on the top rail with

picture labels. These would have allowed the spectator to refer to the catalogue, which recorded that all but eighteen of the pictures were of the seventeenth-century Dutch and Flemish schools. The majority of the rest of the paintings were nineteenth-century British. This hanging of Old and Modern Masters together had been discussed by Queen Victoria with Lord Melbourne in early 1839 and was, he considered, 'a very good way'.[7] His advice no doubt resulted in the hanging of paintings with contemporary themes by such British artists as Sir William Allan and Sir David Wilkie, such as the latter's *The entrance of George IV at Holyroodhouse*. References to the Old Masters can be found in the inclusion of Zoffany's *The Tribuna of the Uffizi* together with no fewer than three works by Reynolds.[8]

The influence of Prince Albert, whom Queen Victoria had married in 1840, can perhaps be detected in the hanging of their two recently acquired Old Master paintings: the large *Pythagoras and his pupils* and *The triumph over Paracelsus*, both then attributed to Rubens.[9] The latter came from the collection of Professor d'Alton of Bonn, whose lectures the Prince had attended in 1837. From then on the high-minded, serious and well-educated Prince Albert would guide the Queen in all artistic matters. He was, for

example, instrumental in commissioning two marble sculptures from Rome for the gallery to add to George IV's dominating *Mars and Venus* by Canova at the south end.[10]

In 1851 Prince Albert's further influence was demonstrated by his rehanging of the gallery, which is shown in the background of

> 'Even in Buckingham Palace there was yesterday a thick fog consisting chiefly of coal smoke. Pictures, gold frames, and embroidered work, must suffer very severely under it'

an 1853 watercolour by Louis Haghe of a banquet there (Fig. 1).[11] The Surveyor of Pictures, Thomas Uwins, prepared a catalogue which records the rearrangement.[12] Prince Albert's scholarly intentions can doubtless be traced in the inclusion of a lengthy appendix with biographical details of each painter together with a provenance for every picture. Uwins wrote that 'It is a

catalogue raisonné and I have made it so unlike all other such things that have ever yet been done, that it has cost me no small labour'.[13] The paintings recorded in Uwins's catalogue are essentially the same as those in the 1841 catgalogue but with the removal of all those by British artists except Reynolds. The arrangement of pictures appears, so far as it is possible to judge from the watercolour, more individual and less structured. However, a sense of uniformity has been attained through their being placed in identical gilded composition frames made by William Thomas (Fig. 2).[14]

The replacing of the frames may have been the result of the Prince's passion for order, as well as his desire to bring the Picture Gallery into line with the decorations elsewhere in the Palace. Queen Victoria noted with pride in her *Journal* for 4 February 1851: 'We went over the new wing . . . & walked through the Gallery, which has been fresh painted, dove colour, and all the pictures have been framed & re-hung which makes them look beautiful'.[15] Although they had not changed the paintings, the Queen and Prince had stamped their taste on the gallery, as Haghe's watercolour demonstrates (see colour illustration on p. 97). The walls were painted lilac, a colour already used in the Queen's Sitting Room.[16] The

The sepulchral state of the Palace left by Queen Victoria was to give way to the glittering Court of Edward VII, and Gruner's painted marble walls yielded to C. H. Bessant's white and gold decorative scheme. Electricity gradually replaced gas, and the chandeliers in the gallery were duly converted. Many of the pictures were cleaned and repaired by F. H. Haines.[23] The King himself took an active part in their rehanging, 'enjoying', as Cust related, 'nothing so much in the intervals of leisure as sitting in a roomful of workmen and giving directions in person'. Cust recorded the King's quick eye for what was right and what pleased, but admitted in matters of artistic taste he was guided by others. With the characteristic

An Edwardian watercolour shows the paintings hung in a manner wholly characteristic of later Victorian collections, almost filling the walls from frieze to dado

ceiling is picked out in terracotta and blue in accordance with Gruner's cinquecento-style decorative scheme elsewhere in the State Apartments.[17]

With the death of the Prince Consort in 1861, Queen Victoria lost not only her guide and mentor, but also some of her enthusiasm for the arts. For example, accounts from the mid-1860s show a reduced expenditure on picture frames, cleaning and gilding at Buckingham Palace. The widowed Queen also spent less of her time in London. Sir J. C. Robinson, who was appointed Surveyor in 1881 on the retirement of Richard Redgrave, reported immediately on the state of the pictures in the gallery: '. . . The entire Collection, I think, not having received any systematic examination for many years'.[18]

The new Surveyor was chiefly concerned with the effects of atmospheric pollution. As early as 1839 the Queen had talked to Melbourne about smoke in the rooms, and by 1858 the visiting Prussian von Moltke could write: 'Even in Buckingham Palace there was yesterday a thick fog consisting chiefly of coal smoke. Pictures, gold frames, and embroidered work, must suffer

very severely under it.[19] Robinson was eventually allowed to glaze the smaller pictures,[20] but in 1898 his proposal to clean, rearrange and relight the pictures was met with a mixed response. After taking advice, the Queen allowed some cleaning tests but would not allow rehanging as 'The pictures at Windsor Castle and Buckingham Palace were settled by the Prince Consort, and the Queen desires that there shall be no change'.[21]

Queen Victoria's lack of confidence in Robinson and his failure to ameliorate the conditions in the gallery is in sharp contrast to the confidence placed in Lionel Cust by Edward VII, who succeeded his mother in 1901. Cust replaced Robinson on 5 March that year, and inaction was replaced by activity. The new King set about modernizing and re-decorating Buckingham Palace, his principal residence, with enthusiasm.[22] Cust relates in his memoirs that those paintings in the gallery that hung on a level with the gas-lit chandeliers were, when taken down, 'found in parts to be coated with a thin dark film of dirt in some cases amounting to opaque black.'

rolling of his 'rs' and his Germanic accent, the King would say, 'I do not know much about Arrt but I think I know something about Arr-r-angement.'[24]

Perhaps with hindsight, Cust bemoaned his lack of freedom in rehanging the Picture Gallery. In his words, '. . . There were more pictures of outstanding merit than could be shown to advantage on the walls,' and he wished to disperse some of them. The King, however, had filled his private apartments with selected Victorian pictures and others from his collection at Marlborough House and he felt that if pictures were dispersed around the Palace he would never see them.[25] It is likely that the King also wished for magnificence of effect. An Edwardian watercolour (Fig. 3) shows the paintings hung in a manner wholly characteristic of later Victorian collections, almost filling the walls from frieze to dado.[26] Cust's 1909 catalogue of pictures in the Palace indeed records that the number of paintings in the gallery had increased to 207. Among these, he had introduced a few Italian paintings, a trend that was to be re-established after 1945.

Cust was not succeeded until 1928, and had a second chance to rehang the Picture Gallery in the reign of George V. By this time Nash and Blore's interior was considered too old-fashioned and too dark. Early in 1914 George V asked for a small committee to submit proposals on the redecoration and relighting of the gallery.[27] The general appearance of the Picture Gallery today dates back to the King's decisions at that time.

It was decided to rebuild the ceiling, lowering it two feet, and to introduce an Adam-style frieze around the entire gallery. Nash's ceiling and the chandeliers were dismantled, and an arched glazed ceiling was substituted. The longitudinal support beams hid the lighting. The frieze squared the arches at either end and the central doorcases were redesigned. This necessitated the removal both of the surmounting coats of arms and of William Croggon's tall flanking scagliola figures. The latter were replaced by wooden panelling with attached Grinling Gibbons style carvings.[28] The parquet floor (see Fig. 3), echoing the forms of the Nash ceiling, was also replaced. Figured olive-green silk damask was chosen for the wall covering because, as Sir Derek Keppel noted, the King disliked gold walls, 'and both Their Majesties favour green'.[29]

3 *The Picture Gallery, looking south.* Anonymous, British School, early twentieth century. This style of hanging shows that under Edward VII the walls were crowded in a manner characteristic of later Victorian collections

The reduced wall height gave Cust and Sir Charles Holroyd the opportunity to plan a new hang. Haines meanwhile cleaned and attended to the paintings, which were rehung on chains. On 22 March 1915 Keppel reported that 'Their Majesties were delighted with the Picture Gallery yesterday and expressed their approval'. A comparison of photographs of the gallery before (Fig. 4) and after alterations (Fig. 5) shows that although the top line of the pictures has been lowered to the height of the door frames, the paintings were still densely hung.[30] What is noticeable is the introduction of a strict symmetry to the picture hang. The paintings in each quarter of the room were arranged symmetrically around two large important paintings hung over each central fireplace.[31] Otherwise the larger paintings remained at the top level. However, at the south end the cabinet pictures were treated differently, being hung in 'drops', perhaps echoing the carvings on the door frames. Such formality can be seen in

photographs of other rooms in the Palace in this period, a reaction against the cluttered Edwardian interior.

It was not until after the Second World War that further changes to the picture hang resulted in the arrangement we see today. In keeping with the times, the number of paintings was much reduced and the hang restricted to two tiers. Many of the Dutch and Flemish cabinet pictures were rehung to great effect in the privacy of the side-lit Royal Closet. Large paintings such as the Van Dycks of *Charles I with M de St Antoine* and *Charles I and Henrietta Maria with their two eldest children* were introduced into the Picture Gallery.[33] Italian paintings, both from the settecento, that had formerly hung at Buckingham House, and from earlier periods, were brought in to create diversity. Above all, the finest pictures were given ample space and were hung at a more favourable viewing height.

Conservation and framing were not left out of this overhaul. The inadequate nineteenth-century Picture Gallery frames were steadily consigned to storage in favour of more suitable original frames. Sir Oliver Millar, on his retirement as Surveyor, reviewed this re-framing:

Early eighteenth-century gilded frames, such as

would have been made for the pictures in the eighteenth century, have been successful because they will look well in any part of the collection; but putting dark frames, which are in theory so appropriate, on a number of small Dutch pictures and on such masterpieces as the Vermeer, the Hals and Rembrandt's *Shipbuilder and his wife* and *Lady with a fan* was a less happy move because the frames . . . have never been suitable for the richly articulated and heavily gilded interiors at Windsor and Buckingham Palace.[34]

A long-term conservation programme has brought to life many of George IV's great Dutch and Flemish paintings.[34]

The appearance of the gallery itself has also changed. The walls are no longer olive green, but are covered with a warm pink flock wallpaper which, with the additions of carpets, give the room a softer, less forbidding air. Those who visit it may find it worth recalling that it is one of the last survivors of the great private picture galleries that grew up in London after the French Revolution. Much has happened since 1844 when that indispensable chronicler of these great collections, Mrs Jameson, visited it. It was full then of George IV's Dutch and Flemish pictures, and she described it as 'cer-

4 Photograph of the Picture Gallery, looking north, *c.* 1913. Compare with the redesigned and re-hung Gallery in Fig. 6

5 Photograph of the Picture Gallery, looking south, *c.* 1915. The ceiling was altered and the wall height reduced, the doors changed and an Adam-style frieze introduced after George V aked for proposals on relighting and redecorating the Gallery early in 1914

---

tainly the finest gallery of this class of works in England'. The pictures, however, will still surely astonish and captivate the late twentieth-century visitor.

The author wishes to thank especially Gwyneth Campling and Eva Zielinska Millar. Anyone working on the history of the Royal Collection of Pictures will be greatly indebted to the research of Sir Oliver Millar, whose encouragement and advice is here gratefully acknowledged.

[1] Information from Frances Vivian, quoted in John Harris, Geoffrey de Bellaigue, Oliver Millar, *Buckingham Palace*, 1968, p. 243. Consul Joseph Smith's collection is the subject of the exhibition at The Queen's Gallery, Buckingham Palace, 'A King's Purchase' (1993).
[2] Similar domed compartments on pendant arches may still be seen in the Belgian Suite Corridor, see *Buckingham Palace*, 1968, op. cit., illustrated p. 82. Architecturally, the pendant arches had their antecedents in Soane's ceiling for the Chancery Court at Westminster, and Nash had used similar domes in the gallery of his own house in Regent Street; see Celina Fox (ed.), *London World City, 1800–1840*, 1992, exh. cat. no. 57 (ill. p. 258); John Summerson, *The Life and Work of John Nash Architect*, 1980, ill. 39C. For the lighting scheme in Benjamin West's gallery, see Giles Waterfield (ed.), *Palaces of Art, Art Galleries in Britain 1790–1990*, 1991, exh. cat., no. A 19.
[3] Howard Colvin (ed.), *The History of the King's Works* (J. M. Crook and M. H. Port), vol. VI (1973), p. 266, fn. 6.
[4] *Report of the Select Committee appointed to enquire into Matters connected with Windsor Castle and Buckingham Palace*, printed 1831.
[5] Windsor, Royal Archives (WRA), *Queen Victoria's Journal*, quoted in Lord Esher (ed.), *The Girlhood of Queen Victoria*, 1912, vol. II, p. 223. The pictures were reported to be 'on removal' to Buckingham Palace in March 1836; *Athenaeum*, 5 March 1836, quoted by Oliver Millar in *Dutch Pictures from the Royal Collection*, 1971, Queen's Gallery exh. cat., p. 32, fn. 51. Also significant is Melbourne's earlier reference to Zoffany's *The Tribuna of the Uffizi* in the Picture Gallery, recorded in *Queen Victoria's Journal*, 18 March 1839, WRA.
[6] Mrs Jameson, *A Companion to the Most Celebrated Private Galleries of Art in London*, 1844, pp. 2–73. The preface to her account of Queen Victoria's gallery has a familiar ring to it: 'Visitors are admitted only by an order from the Lord Chamberlain, and during the absence of Her Majesty from the Palace.' The Queen recorded in her *Journal* for 27 March 1843: 'We looked at a very pretty drawing that Mr Morison is making of the Gallery for me', WRA.
[7] *Queen Victoria's Journal*, 10 January 1839, WRA.
[8] His self-portrait, *The death of Dido* and *Cymon and Iphigenia* elsewhere in this issue, (see pp. 00–00).
[9] The former is stated to have come from the collection of Philip IV of Spain; the latter, now thought to be from Rubens' studio, was then identified as *The family of Olden Barneveld*.

[10] Emil Wolff's *Naiad* and C. Steinhauser's *Siren*. The Queen recorded in her *Journal*, 19 October 1841: 'We went to look in the Gallery at Wolfe's beautiful statue of a Water Nymph . . . Albert ordered it last year, & it is really quite beautiful'. Both are signed, dated and inscribed Rome 1841.

[11] In the Royal Collection (RL 19917).

[12] Seguier survived until 1843, and the sick A. W. Callcott who replaced him only held the post until his death late in 1844. Uwins was appointed in 1845 and died in 1857.

[13] Letter to Miss Minshull, 13 December 1852, quoted in Mrs Uwins, *A Memoir of Thomas Uwins, R.A.*, 1858, vol. I, p. 140. In a letter to Colonel Biddulph, 21 August 1852, Uwins records 'the very difficult arrangements consequent on the newly framing and hanging the pictures last year', WRA, PP Vic, Add. 46.

[14] William Thomas, 39 London Street, Fitzroy Square, London. PRO L.C.11/134, quoted in E. Joy, 'The Royal Victorian Furniture-Makers, 1837–87', *Burlington Magazine*, vol. CXI, 1969, p. 682. In the estimate the work is specified to be completed in three months. Thomas charged the large sum of £1,053 for 185 gilt frames. However, deductions reduced the sum he received to £919. Six frames were not supplied because the pictures had been removed from the gallery, and a credit of £100 was given for 'old Frames'. This may represent the value of the replaced Regency frames, whose gilding would have been re-covered.

[15] *Queen Victoria's Journal*, WRA. The East Wing of the Palace had been completed by Blore in 1850.

[16] See James Roberts 1848 watercolour, ill. p. 29 and cover, Theresa-Mary Morton, *Royal Residences of the Victorian Era: Watercolours of Interior Views from the Royal Library, Windsor Castle*, 1991, exh. cat. It can perhaps be assumed that this lilac, later used at Frogmore House, is the same as the Queen's 'dove colour'.

[17] Professor Ludwig Grüner was an artistic adviser to the Royal couple from 1843 until his appointment in

1856 as Director of the Print Collection, Dresden. He commanded large fees for the re-decoration of the interiors of Buckingham Palace in 1854–6; see E. Joy, 'The Royal Victorian Furniture-Makers', op. cit., pp. 681–2. The Grand Staircase (1848) is illustrated in *Royal Residences*, 1991, op. cit., p. 27, and the Ballroom in *Buckingham Palace*, 1968, op. cit., pp. 8–9.

[18] PRO, L.C.1/386, II, 93; quoted in Oliver Millar, *The Queen's Pictures*, 1977, p. 199.

[19] *Queen Victoria's Journal*, 19 & 20 January 1839, WRA; von Moltke's letter to his wife, 26 January 1858, in *Moltke's Letters to His Wife and Other Relatives*, 1896, vol. II, p. 89. Moltke had been appointed ADC to Prince Frederick William of Prussia, and was in London in 1858 for the latter's marriage to Victoria, Princess Royal.

[20] Lord Chamberlain's Office (LCO) Annual Reports, 1882–6; it should be noted that such glazing had been initiated as early as 1859.

[21] Millar, *The Queen's Pictures*, op. cit., p. 199. The Queen had, however, agreed in 1888 to the fitting up of the Silk Tapestry Room, adjoining the south end of the gallery, as the Wilkie Room. Two large paintings by Frith and Leighton made way for at least five pictures by Wilkie. This in some way countered the Prince Consort's decision in 1851 to remove nineteenth-century British paintings from the gallery; LCO Annual Report 1888.

[22] Parliament voted £50,000 for the renovation of Windsor Castle and Buckingham Palace; LCO Annual Report 1901.

[23] Sir Lionel Cust, *King Edward VII and his Court*, 1930, p. 29. Messrs F. & F. H. Haines had received a Tradesmen's Warrant in 1882 as Picture Cleaners in Ordinary to the Queen.

[24] Cust, *King Edward VII and his Court*, op. cit., pp. 34–5.

[25] Cust, *King Edward VII and his Court*, op. cit., p. 45.

[26] By an anonymous British artist in the Royal Collection at Buckingham Palace; RL 24592. The paintings are hung much in the same manner as before, but are arranged symmetrically about four large paintings, e.g.

on the right, Mytens *Charles I and Henrietta Maria departing for the chase*, purchased in 1894.

[27] LCO Records 252/1914. The committee, at George V's suggestion, was made up of Colonel Sir Douglas Dawson, Comptroller, LCO; The Hon. Sir Derek Keppel, Master of the Household; Sir Charles Holroyd, Director, National Gallery; Lionel Earle, permanent secretary, HM Office of Works; Lionel Cust, and Frank H. Baines, Principal Architect i/c Royal Palaces, HM Office of Works. The committee had the remit to consider the arrangement of the lighting, treatment of the walls, provision of a new parquet floor and the rehanging of the pictures. The work was to be carried out by HM Office of Works.

[28] Presumably a Queen Mary touch.

[29] The silk damask was woven by Warners. Queen Mary had produced for the committee a sample of green silk from Welbeck.

[30] The 1920 catalogue of paintings in the Picture Gallery records 181 paintings.

[31] On the right wall in the foreground of Fig. 6 Rubens' *Landscape with St George* hangs over the glazed Rembrandt *The shipbuilder and his wife*.

[32] Both paintings had hung together in Buckingham House in the reign of George III. The latter during recent restoration was reduced to its original size.

[33] Sir Oliver Millar in *The Queen's Pictures: Royal Collectors Through The Centuries*, 1991, exh. cat., p. 21.

[34] At the opening of The Queen's Gallery, Buckingham Palace, in 1962, Benedict Nicolson noted of the newly-cleaned pictures: 'So unobtrusive is the restoration, so free from idiosyncracies, that no-one could say which restorer has been responsible for which picture' (quoted in Millar, *The Queen's Pictures*, op. cit., p. 216). It is worth pointing out, however, that in the case of the Picture Gallery the sensitive cleaning and restoration of the paintings was the work of, principally, Horace Buttery, Sebastian Isepp, Roy Vallance, John Brealey, Herbert Lank and Viola Pemberton-Pigott.

The Picture Gallery today

Focus on paintings

CHRISTOPHER LLOYD

The Surveyor of The Queen's Pictures shares his thoughts
about hanging this great collection today to maximum effect and
explains his strategy for this 'focal point'

The Picture Gallery in Buckingham Palace is a focal point in the display of paintings in the Royal Collection. Elsewhere in the Palace—the Grand Staircase, the State Dining Room, the Marble Hall and the Bow Room—paintings form part of special installations illustrating aspects of royal iconography. The Picture Gallery, however, fulfils the traditional purpose of a Long Gallery in a grand house as part of a series of State Rooms. In this respect it is comparable with similar contemporary spaces in Bridgewater House and Cleveland (now Lancaster) House across Green Park in neighbouring St James's.[1]

The proportions of the Picture Gallery in Buckingham Palace allow for a representative selection of paintings and, although the emphasis has changed over the years, the present display is a microcosm of the history of royal collecting. By including neighbouring areas such as the Silk Tapestry Room, the East Gallery and the Cross Gallery as an extension of the main Picture Gallery, the achievements of the principal royal collectors of paintings are honoured, namely, Charles I, Frederick, Prince of Wales, George III, George IV, and Queen Victoria together with Prince Albert.

The largest paintings in the Picture Gallery were commissioned by Charles I from Sir Anthony Van Dyck. *Charles I and Henrietta Maria with their two eldest Children, Prince Charles (later Charles II) and Princess Mary* (Plate I), known as 'The Greate Peece', was the artist's first commission for the king following his appointment as court painter in 1632. The success of this appointment is readily apparent in the mastery of Van Dyck's design combining the trappings of formal state portraiture with a distinctly informal grouping of the figures. Van Dyck's fluid composition with a view of Westminster visible in the background is an advance on the anonymous group *The Family of Henry VIII* (c. 1545, Hampton Court). It set new standards for this type of portrait, and is echoed, for instance, by Franz Xaver Winterhalter in *The Family of Queen Victoria* (1846) now hanging close by in the East Gallery.

Originally 'The Greate Peece' hung at one end of the Long Gallery at Whitehall Palace. Today in the Picture Gallery at Buckingham Palace the painting can only be hung on the east wall where, on the opposite side, it is balanced by *Charles I with Monsieur de St Antoine* dating from 1633. This commanding image, in which Van Dyck not only emphasizes the King's status but also pays homage to Titian and Rubens, was originally placed on the end wall of the Gallery in St James's Palace.

Other works by Van Dyck on view are less grand, but are, nonetheless, important in so far as they represent a less highly regarded category of his work. Both *The Mystic Marriage of St Catherine* (c. 1630) and *Christ healing the paralytic man* (c. 1619) were acquired by George IV and given places of honour in Carlton House. George IV was always keen to align himself with Charles I whom he rightly regarded as his greatest predecessor in royal connoisseurship. An outstanding example of this sense of allegiance is the *Landscape with St George and the Dragon* by Rubens. This painting, as indicated by the landscape, which shows a number of London buildings, was begun in 1629/30 in England, but finished in Antwerp where it was bought from the artist by Endymion Porter for Charles I in 1635. After the Civil War the picture is recorded in France, but returned to England with the Orléans Collection in 1798, eventually being acquired by George IV for display in Carlton House.[2]

Frederick, Prince of Wales (1707–51), the son of George II, also admired Flemish painting as represented by Rubens and Van Dyck, but his taste included Jan Brueghel the Elder and David Teniers the Younger. Works by Teniers were eagerly sought after by eighteenth-century collectors who appreciated the painter's diversity of subject-matter and wide-ranging style. The many facets of his art seem to match the multifarious activities he carried out as court artist in Brussels to Archduke Leopold-Wilhelm, a position which he held from 1651. There are three works by Teniers in the Picture Gallery. *The stolen kiss* (c. 1640) was acquired by Frederick, Prince of Wales, and the others, *Two fishermen on the seashore* (c. 1660) and *Peasants outside a country house* (1645), belonged to his grandson, George IV, whose taste was in many ways complementary.

Frederick, Prince of Wales, also admired Italian and French painting of the seventeenth century. His interest in these areas is represented by the *Cleopatra* (c. 1630) by Guido Reni (Plate III) and by the three works by Gaspard Dughet that are in similar specially made frames and which demonstrate the care with which the Prince of Wales presented his collection. Of these *Jonah and the Whale* (c. 1653–4) (Fig. 1) is the most significant, being Dughet's only sea-piece on canvas. It is a composition that was engraved and influenced the course of eighteenth-century painting in Britain, particularly the concept of the 'sublime'. The Prince of Wales lived at Leicester House where in 1749 he was visited by the antiquarian, George Vertue, who opined that 'no prince since King Charles the First took so much pleasure nor observations on works of art or artists'.

To a certain extent George III, Frederick, Prince of Wales's own son, emulated his father in his love of the arts. Although George III was more interested in books and aspects of the applied arts, he did take immense trouble over the arrangement of the paintings in Buckingham House, which he bought for Queen Charlotte in 1762. A plan of the distribution of the pictures room by room was made in 1774 after the house had been remodelled, principally by Sir William Chambers.[3] This shows how the

I *Charles I and Henrietta Maria with their two eldest Children, Prince Charles (later Charles II) and Princess Mary ('The Greate Peece'),* by Sir Anthony van Dyck (1599–1641), 1632. Oil on canvas, 298·1 × 250·8 cm

acquired by George IV. This is certainly the case with the artists he particularly admired such as Rembrandt, Rubens (*The farm at Laeken, c.* 1617–18), Cuyp (Plate II), Claude Lorrain (Plate V), and Jan Steen (*Interior of a tavern with cardplayers and a violin player*).

Queen Victoria was also enthusiastic about art, but exercised far more restraint in this matter than her uncle. The Queen was more purposeful in her collecting, more controlled in her spending, and more fastidious in her taste, in which she was nearly always guided by Prince Albert until his death in 1861. Two paintings in the East gallery are highly typical of Queen Victoria's interest in art. *The Coronation of Queen Victoria 28 June 1838* by Sir George Hayter illustrates her desire for artists to commemorate events from her reign. It was, however, the ubiquitous F. X. Winterhalter who finally usurped the British painters attached to the Court. *The Family of Queen Victoria* (1846) by this artist was likened by the Queen to works by Paolo Veronese, which is not an uninteresting comment and reflects the art-historical

1 *Jonah and the Whale*, by Gaspar Dughet (1615–75), *c.* 1653–4. Oil on canvas, 114 × 159 cm

king successfully incorporated paintings from other palaces in order to enrich the visual effect, including the two huge works by Van Dyck mentioned above and the Cartoons by Raphael now on loan to the Victoria and Albert Museum. It also shows how George III himself augmented the collection. The purchase in 1762 of the collections formed in Venice by Consul Joseph Smith introduced a number of eighteenth-century Venetian works into the Royal Collection, notably the group of forty or so paintings by Canaletto.[4]

The emphasis in the Picture Gallery, however, is on works by Luca Carlevaris and Francesco Zuccarelli, although it should not be forgotten that Smith owned a number of paintings by Northern European artists, including Vermeer, whose *A lady at the virginals with a gentleman* (Plate IV) (usually on view) was in the eighteenth century attributed to Frans van Mieris.

George III also commissioned several works, mainly from his Principal Painter, Benjamin West, who executed numerous portraits of the king and his family, as well as whole decorative schemes of historical and religious subjects for rooms in Buckingham House and Windsor Castle. The pictures in the Warm Room in Buckingham House, dating from between 1769 and 1773, proved to be of the greatest significance for the development of history painting in Britain. The subjects were taken from different his-

torical periods and extolled the virtues of valour and magnanimity. The largest paintings were on the side walls of the Warm Room (*The Departure of Regulus* and *The Oath of Hannibal*) and are both now in the Cross Gallery. The most important pictures, however, were grouped around the fireplace. There *The Death of Epaminondas* and *The Death of Chevalier Bayard* were hung on either side of *The Death of Wolfe* in which West depicted a far more recent historical event in contemporary dress and thereby challenged the ground rules for history painting. In West, George III found a painter with the perfect qualifications for illustrating his ideals of public morality and national pride: in George III, West found a patron who required the services of an artist prepared to translate these ideals into visual terms.[5]

George IV, on the other hand, did not easily identify with the ideals espoused by his father. Of all the royal collectors whose activities are represented in the Picture Gallery it is George IV who has pride of place and this is right in so far as in essence he created it. Like his grandfather, Frederick, Prince of Wales, George IV supported contemporary British artists, but in accordance with the taste of his time he was a passionate collector of seventeenth-century Dutch, Flemish and French paintings. He did not worry too much about the cost and he relied on friends to find pictures or recommend purchases. Yet, there is always an underlying sense of quality both for the painting and frequently for its frame that is wholly George IV's own. Some of the greatest paintings in the Picture Gallery were

> Of all the royal collectors whose activities are represented in the Picture Gallery it is George IV who has pride of place which is right in so far as, in essence, he created it

dimension in her approach that emerged under the tutelage of Prince Albert. According to Queen Victoria, Lord Palmerston remarked that this was simply 'the finest modern picture he ever saw'.

[1] See A. Jameson, *Companion to the Most Celebrated Private Galleries of Art in London*, London, 1844.
[2] *Carlton House, The Past Glories of George IV's Palace*, exh. cat., The Queen's Gallery, Buckingham Palace, 1991–2.
[3] F. Russell, 'King George III's picture hang at Buckingham House', *Burlington Magazine*, CXXIX (1987), pp. 523–531.
[4] *A King's Purchase. King George III and the Collection of Consul Smith*, exh. cat., The Queen's Gallery, Buckingham Palace, 1993.
[5] See L. Colley, *Britons. Forging the Nation 1707–1837*, New Haven and London, 1992, Chapters 4 and 5.

II *The Passage Boat*, (detail) by Aelbert Cuyp (1620–1691), *c.* 1650. Oil on canvas, 124·4 × 144·2 cm. A passage-boat approaches a landing-stage, heralded by a drummer on board. The river is almost certainly the Merwede at Dordrecht, where Cuyp had a house. The costumes suggest the likely date. George IV bought this masterpiece from the Baring collection in 1814 and hung it in the Audience Room at Carlton House

III *Cleopatra*, by Guido Reni (1575–1642), *c.* 1630.
Oil on canvas, 113·7 × 94·9 cm

IV *A lady at the virginals with a gentleman* (above) by Jan Vermeer (1632–75), *c.* 1660.
Oil on canvas, 73·3 × 64·5 cm. This great and rare masterpiece was bought from the collection of
Consul Smith in the eighteenth century, attributed to Frans van Mieris

V *The Rape of Europa* (overleaf) (detail) by Claude Gellée, called Lorrain (1600–82), 1667.
Oil on canvas, 134·6 × 101·6 cm

[113]

Zuccarelli in the Royal Collection

George III knew what he liked

GEORGE KNOX

The huge paintings by Francesco Zuccarelli in Buckingham Palace will come as a surprise to most visitors, who might have anticipated views by Canaletto, but they offer an insight into the taste of George III for contemporary Italian art

Visitors to Buckingham Palace with an interest in Italian painting, and more specifically Venetian painting of the eighteenth century, may be a little surprised to encounter, instead of an array of Canaletti, large canvases by Francesco Zuccarelli. Zuccarelli (1702–88) was born and died in Tuscany. When he arrived in Venice *c.* 1730–32 he was already fully-trained in the art of landscape painting, and was prepared to assume the mantle of Marco Ricci, who had died in 1729, and whose art was likewise founded upon Italian rather than Venetian traditions. His success at first seems to have been moderate, but by the early 1740s he was well-established in the circle of Consul Smith, and in 1746 he collaborated in a series of canvases with Smith's protégé, Antonio Visentini, eight of which are in the Royal Collection (Levey 1964, nos. 689–676).

Apart from these, of the thirty canvases by Zuccarelli in the Royal Collection, it seems that all but three belong to the early 1740s and belonged to Consul Smith. Among them are the two chimney-pieces in the Picture Gallery (Figs. 1, 2) which are part of a set of six pictures dateable to the year 1743 (Michael Levey, *The Later Italian Pictures in the Collection of Her Majesty the Queen*, London, 1964, nos. 683, 684).

The abundance and quality of the Consul Smith collection, acquired by the King in 1762, and above all the celebrity of the paintings by Canaletto in that collection, have overshadowed the interest of the Hannoverians in other Venetian paintings which came to England in the course of the eighteenth century.

The first such Royal commission went to Sebastiano Ricci to paint the semi-dome of the apse of Chelsea Hospital, which Jeffrey

The pictures illustrated here are by Francesco Zuccarelli (1702–88)

1 *River landscape with two seated women embracing*, 1743. Oil on canvas, 244·8 × 129·5 cm. Part of the same set as that in Fig 2 (*Picture Gallery*)

Daniels has suggested to be a memorial to Queen Anne, who died in August 1714. This was perhaps followed by a commission to Antonio Pellegrini, possibly inspired by Caroline, Princess of Wales, and her Chamberlain, Sir Andrew Fountaine, to paint a series of mythological figures which are still at Hampton Court. There is some indication that they were painted on Pellegrini's second visit to England in 1719 to decorate the small Banqueting House in the gardens of the palace (Levey 1964, nos. 561–574).

Next, though not a Royal commission, one should perhaps recall the great ceiling painted for Buckingham House by Antonio Bellucci in 1721–22, for which the artist was paid the very considerable sum of £500 by the Duchess of Buckingham. It celebrated the virtues of her deceased husband and lasted until the remodelling of Buckingham Palace for George III by Sir William Chambers in the 1760s, when it was replaced by a ceiling by the Florentine Giovanni Battista Cipriani, also no longer extant.

Next on the scene was Jacopo Amigoni, who worked in London for a decade in the 1730s. As a portrait painter he was warmly patronized by Queen Caroline, and one may recall in particular the portrait of the Queen which she presented to Dr Mead, and which is now in the National Portrait Gallery, and the portrait of Frederick, Prince of Wales, which after

2 *Landscape with two young children offering fruit to a woman*, 1743 (detail). Oil on canvas, 233·7 × 140 cm. This is one of a set of six pictures bought by George III with the collection of Consul Smith who probably commissioned them from the artist in Venice (*Picture Gallery*)

various vicissitudes is now back in the Royal Collection.

Some little flurry was caused in London art circles in 1751 by the arrival of a fine large painting by Giambattista Tiepolo, *St James of Compostela*, which had been commissioned by the Spanish Ambassador to the court of St James, Don Riccardo Wall. It was much admired by Frederick, Prince of Wales, but sadly it led to no other English commissions for Tiepolo, who is also virtually unrepresented in the Consul Smith collection. The ambassador took the painting back to Spain with him. It is now one of the great ornaments of the Budapest Museum of Fine Arts.

This brings us to the time of Zuccarelli's arrival in England. He arrived in 1752 and stayed for ten years. In February 1762 he held a sale of pictures in London 'by reason of his returning to Italy', where he stayed for three years, becoming a member of the Venetian Academy of Painting in 1763. From 1765 until 1771 he was again resident in London, becoming a founder-member of the Royal Academy in 1768.

The notion of ideal landscape painting in this country, then and now, is dominated by the classical landscapes of Claude and Poussin, somewhat superseded in due course by the later glories of Constable and Turner. In this magnificent panorama Francesco Zuccarelli is forgotten, though his success in this field exceeded that of either of his contemporaries, Richard Wilson and Thomas Gainsborough. In fact it appears that Wilson became aware of the possibilities of landscape painting as a consequence of meeting Zuccarelli in Venice in 1751, when Wilson painted his portrait in exchange for a picture, and described him as 'a famous painter of this place'. And while Gainsborough's debt to Dutch landscape is well understood, it would be interesting to speculate about his reaction to Zuccarelli's success in London in the 1750s and 1760s.

There is still no proper account of Zuccarelli's career as a whole or of the nature of his artistic achievement. His work is actually founded upon the classical landscape painters of the seventeenth century and their followers in the early eighteenth century, but he clearly introduced 'additional elements' a Rococo elegance and a charming sentiment into his often monumental canvases which made them ideal decorations for ambitious English interiors of the 1750s and 1760s. Of this genre the great picture in the Silk Tapestry Room is typical (Plate I). Signed and dated 'Francesco Zuccarelli/ Londra 1768', it is said to have been commissioned by King George III (Levey 1964, no. 693). Sir Michael Levey writes: 'Whatever the exact circumstances of the present picture's origin, it is tempting to connect it with the founding of the Royal Academy in 1768 and Zuccarelli's founder-membership.'

The Finding of Moses is a typical exercise in the manner of Claude, with a small group of figures in the centre foreground carrying the story. Claude's Tiber is changed into the Nile by the addition of a sphinx on the left, pyramids in the distance and two palm-trees on the right—but apart from these details it might equally well be an ideal view of the Thames at Richmond. There can be little doubt that this was the kind of contemporary painting that George III most enjoyed, and he is on record as having purchased two smaller canvases by Zuccarelli in 1771 (Levey 1964, 691 and 692).

After the launching of the Royal Academy in 1768 Zuccarelli returned briefly to Venice, serving as president of the Venetian Academy of Painting in 1772. In 1773 he returned to Florence, where he remained for the rest of his life.

I River landscape with the *Finding of Moses* (detail), 1768. Oil on canvas, 227·3 × 386 cm. Note the artist's transformation of a European landscape by the addition of such details as a pyramid (*Silk Tapestry Room*)

A taste for history

Reynolds, West, George III, and George IV

MARTIN POSTLE

George III loved pictures by West—George IV hated West.
George III hated Reynolds—yet George IV bought over twenty
pictures by Reynolds and also had miniatures specially made to
record them . . .

1 *The oath of Hannibal* by Benjamin West (1738–1820), signed and dated 1770. Oil on canvas, 229·1 × 304·1 cm (*Cross Gallery*). One of a series commissioned by George III intended to celebrate qualities of leadership and loyalty

'We are all extremely afflicted for the loss of the Prince of Whales [*sic*] who certainly would have been a great Patron to Painters . . .' wrote the twenty-seven year old Joshua Reynolds, on hearing of the death of Prince Frederick in March 1751.[1] The letter, written from Italy (although it might—suggested its publisher in 1796—have been sent from Greenland), contains Reynolds's first recorded opinions concerning the prospect of royal patronage. In the event Reynolds had to wait until January 1759 to obtain his first commission, when the twenty-one-year-old Prince George sat for the portrait (now at Windsor Castle).[2] Less than two years later, in September 1761, George III—as he had become—was married in the Chapel Royal. Reynolds, presumably in the hope of a further commission, made an oil sketch of the event.[3] However, neither the portrait of 'Prince' George, nor the painting of the royal wedding, entered the Royal Collection until

after the King's death. Indeed, none of the twenty-three works by Reynolds in the Royal Collection today was purchased by the painter's contemporary, George III.[4] Reynolds's presence in the Royal Collection was almost entirely owing to the patronage of George IV, who—in addition to collecting Reynolds's portraits—acquired two rather less well-known history paintings by the artist, *Cimon and Iphigenia* and *The death of Dido* (Fig. 2). It is ironic, therefore, that George IV was also responsible for divesting the Royal Collection of the bulk of the paintings which had formed the cornerstone of his father's own taste—the history paintings of Reynolds's rival, Benjamin West.

Benjamin West arrived in England from Italy in August 1763, although it was not until five years later, in 1768, that he first attracted the patronage of George III. The occasion was the inspection by the King of West's history painting, *Agrippina landing at Brundisium with the ashes of Germanicus* (Yale University Art Gallery, New Haven), which the artist had recently painted for the Archbishop of York, Robert Hay Drummond.[5] The painting's subject had been suggested by Drummond, who may also have assisted the King in the choice of *The departure of Regulus from Rome* (Fig. 3, Plate I), which he promptly commissioned from West.[6] On receiving West's oil sketch for the painting, George III decided that the finished picture should hang in the (ground-floor) Warm Room in the King's new residence, Buckingham House. As it transpired, the choice of location was to be crucial in terms of West's future Royal patronage. *The departure of Regulus* was painted on a canvas designed to fit into one of seven panelled recesses in the room.[7] Once it had been completed to George III's satisfaction in 1769, the King commissioned West to fill the remaining six panels with history paintings on related themes. These West executed between 1770 and 1773, at a total cost of £2,100.[8] In 1770, West painted *The oath of Hannibal* (Fig. 1) as a pendant to *The departure of Regulus*.[9] It was exhibited the following year at the Royal Academy, alongside West's seminal modern history painting, *The death of Wolfe* (first version in Canada). Although West's biographer John Galt later stated that the King had initially decided not to purchase *The death of Wolfe* owing to West's controversial use of contemporary costume, he nevertheless asked him to paint him a version as the third painting for the Warm Room (Fig. 4).[10] Indeed, West's theme—heroic death—formed the subject for the next two paintings for Buckingham House, *The death of Chevalier Bayard* and *The death of Epaminondas*, of 1772 and 1773 respectively.[11] West's final pictures, also of

1773, were the smallest, and were designed as pendants to fill the remaining vacant panels. The subjects, apparently chosen by West, were *The family of the King of Armenia before Cyrus* and *Segestes and his daughter before Germanicus* (Fig. 6).[12] As it has been observed, West's choice of subject matter in the above pictures took up the theme also present in the *Oath of Hannibal*, of duty and loyalty among families of royal lineage. Aware of George III's general interest in such matters, West must also have known of the Hanoverian belief that the King's family was descended from the daughter of the German chieftain, Segestes.[13]

At the very time that George III's attention was first being drawn to West, preparations were in hand for the formation of the Royal Academy (founded in 1768). West, who was closely involved with the scheme (and who, according to his biographer, often discussed with George III 'the means of promoting the fine arts') was dispatched to ask Joshua Reynolds take up the Presidency of the new Academy.[14] Reynolds did not—as one might have expected—accept immediately, but chose to consult his close friends, Edmund Burke and Samuel Johnson. 'This hesitation,' recalled the diarist Joseph Farington, 'was mentioned by Sir Wm. Chambers to the King, who from that time entertained a prejudice against Reynolds, for both Johnson & Burke were then disliked by the King, the latter particu-

2 *The death of Dido* by Sir Joshua Reynolds (1723–92), 1781. Oil on canvas, 147·3 × 239·4 cm. George IV bought this original in 1821, having already commissioned a copy of it in miniature by Henry Bone

larly on political accounts.'[15] Whether George III had any particular reason to dislike Reynolds prior to the foundation of the Royal Academy is uncertain. Afterwards, he certainly had very little time for him: to be precise, he allowed Reynolds around two hours on 21 and 26 May, 1779, when he sat for the official portrait now in the Royal Academy.[16] George III disliked Reynolds, the company he kept, and his paintings, telling the portraitist William Beechey that they were 'coarse and unfinished'. 'This feeling,' stated Beechey, 'was probably, in some degree, occasioned by the habit of looking at pictures closely, which, as his Majesty was very near sighted, he always indulged in when practicable.'[17] Reynolds was, in return, unimpressed by George III. And when he was made to suffer the indignity of applying for the post of Painter in Ordinary to the King in 1784, Reynolds told Boswell, 'If I had known what a shabby and miserable place it is, I would not have asked for it. Besides, as things have turned out, I think a certain person is not worth speaking to, or speaking of . . .'[18]

By this date, Reynolds could afford to ignore the King, as he had attracted the

patronage of the Prince of Wales, later George IV. Although non-committal about politics, by the mid-1780s Reynolds's principal source of patronage came from the Whig circles of the Duchess of Devonshire and the young Prince. Unlike George III, who maintained a distant, autocratic, attitude towards the Royal Academy, Prince George took an active interest in the Royal Academy's social calendar—as well as commissioning several portraits of himself and his friends from Reynolds.[19] 'The Prince,' noted Reynolds after the Academy Dinner of 1785, 'behaved with great propriety; we were all mightily pleased with him.[20]

By the late 1780s, as Reynolds assiduously courted the Prince of Wales at Carlton House, West was embarked upon a series of hugely ambitious historical projects for the King at Windsor, including a series on 'Revealed Religion' for the Royal Chapel, designs for a ceiling in the Queen's Lodge, cartoons for glass paintings in St George's Chapel, as well as eight scenes from the life of Edward III for the Presence Chamber, which he completed, with the help of studio assistants, between 1786 and 1789. In addition to the individual sums charged for these commissions West had, since 1780, received an annual Royal pension of £1,000. On the surface, West's prospects at this time could not have looked rosier, especially on his succession to the Presidency of the Royal

3 *The departure of Regulus* by Benjamin West (1738–1820), signed and dated 1769. Oil on canvas, 229·9 × 304·8 cm. The American painter Charles Willson Peale, who was in London 1767–69, is supposed to have posed for the central figure of Regulus (disguised by a beard)

I Detail of *The departure of Regulus* (Fig. 3) (*opposite*)

4 *The Death of Wolfe* by Benjamin West (1738–1824), 1771. Oil on canvas, 153·7 × 245·1 cm. This version in the Royal Collection is larger than that exhibited at the Royal Academy in 1771, a shape dictated by George III's desire to set it into the panelling of his 'Warm Room' (? on the ground floor) of Buckingham House

Academy in 1792, following the death of Reynolds. Paradoxically, however, it was from this time onwards that West began to lose his grip on Royal patronage. In 1789 he received his last commission from George III at Windsor; and although work continued throughout the 1790s, by August 1801 he was requested to stop work altogether on his paintings for the Royal Chapel. In December 1810, as George III entered his final period of mental illness, West's pension was finally cut off—despite pleas to the Prince Regent to restore it.

As Allen Staley has observed, West's demise was brought about by a combination of circumstances, including the Royal distrust of West's democratic principles, the intriguing of James Wyatt, and King George's mental decline.[21] West's increasing alienation from George III was matched by the correspondingly steady growth in appreciation of Reynolds's art by the Prince Regent.

After Reynolds's death in February 1792, the late President of the RA was viewed retrospectively as the founding father of the British School of art, by virtue of his Presidency of the Royal Academy, his *Discourses on Art*, his subject pictures, and his portraits, which were considered by acolytes

5 *Sir Michael* by Sir Joshua Reynolds (after Guido Reni), painted in Italy *c.* 1750. It was given with other pictures by Reynolds to the Prince of Wales (later George IV) by Lady Thomond, the artist's niece

disfigured by bitumen (George IV's picture restorer refused to clean it for fear of stripping away the painting's glazes) an idea of its original appearance can be gained through Henry Bone's enamel copy made for the Prince of Wales in 1806.[25] Indeed, Lady Thomond's decision to present him with paintings by Reynolds was probably prompted by the collection of miniatures by Bone after Reynolds, which the Prince had already assembled the previous decade. ('Were I a rich man', said Bone, 'I wd. rather work for the Prince for nothing than for many other for money'.[26]) The Prince's collection included two self-portraits, as well as the five subject pictures: *Cupid and Psyche, The death of Dido, Cimon and Iphigenia, Venus,* and *Hope nursing Love.*[27] The Prince's admiration for such works was confirmed by his purchase, at Lady Thomond's posthumous sale in 1821, of the original painting of *The death of Dido* (Fig. 2), which today hangs in Buckingham Palace.[28]

George III died in February 1820. On hearing the news West said, 'I have lost the best friend I ever had in my life.'[29] Less than six weeks later, already plagued with illness, West died. The following year an exhibition of his paintings was mounted by the artist's sons in imposing galleries, designed by John Nash, in the gardens of his former house.[30] The exhibition, although initially popular, gradually ceased to draw the public. In 1826 Benjamin and Raphael West unsuccessfully petitioned the United States Government to purchase the paintings, as the basis of an American National Gallery.[31] Three years later they offered them up for auction in London. The sale received a great deal of pre-publicity, the *Morning Post,* announcing that 'agents from America and from various parts of Europe have arrived in London expressly to procure some of the larger works for foreign galleries'.[32] Among the pictures on sale were the nineteen large religious paintings, which West had painted (for George III) for the Royal Chapel at Windsor, as well as all the artist's designs for St George's Chapel. Although Crown property, neither George III nor George IV had attempted to take possession of any of these works. Indeed, George IV's only acknowledgement of their existence was his presentation of one of the Royal Chapel pictures—*The Last Supper*—to the National Gallery in 1828.[33] Advertising the sale, the auctioneer George Robins singled out the Windsor paintings for special attention:

Our present Monarch was graciously pleased to restore to Mr West's family these precious gems; they include the sublime composition, *Moses receiving the Laws, The Universal Deluge,* and *The Crucifixion of our Saviour.* The remaining ones are all appropriate for altarpieces.[34]

The sale proved a financial disaster for West's sons and the King's pictures were sold

as specimens of 'confined history painting'. At the same time, West's own Presidency of the Academy came under increasing fire, until in December 1805 James Wyatt temporarily ousted him from the chair. The same year plans were put in hand by the Academy to erect a monument to Reynolds in St Paul's. George III, eager to assert his authority within the Academy, refused to sanction the scheme, stating that he wished it to be recorded in the Minutes that 'His Majesty wd. not suffer the money of the Academy to be squandered for purposes of vain parade and Ostentation'.[22] In order to raise funds, Reynolds's niece, Lady Thomond, suggested a subscription, adding, 'It

was probable that the Prince of Wales who always expressed much regard for Sir Joshua, would subscribe.'[23]

The Prince of Wales already owned at least six portraits which he had commissioned directly from Reynolds. His continuing regard for the artist was to be reflected during the following years by the acquisition of another fourteen works, including four presented to him by Lady Thomond (Fig. 5).[24] The most interesting of Lady Thomond's gifts was *Cimon and Iphigenia,* which was received at Carlton House in 1814, the year after its exhibition at the British Institution's Reynolds retrospective. Although today the painting is

for a fraction of the price paid for them.[35] In addition to relinquishing the royal claim to these works, George IV also broke up West's series of paintings from the life of Edward III in the Presence Chamber at Windsor, the seven historical pictures in the Warm Room at Buckingham Palace, and demolished the Queen's Lodge at Windsor which had ceiling designs after West.[36] During the 1840s and '50s West's glass paintings at St George's Chapel were dismantled and destroyed, the last window being removed in 1864.[37] Today, only one religious history painting by West, *St Peter denying Christ*, remains in the Royal Collection.[38] Like Reynolds's paintings which survive in the Royal Collection today, it cost George III himself nothing, for West had given it to the King as a present in 1779.

6 *Segestes and his daughter before Germanicus* (detail) by Benjamin West (1738–1820), signed and dated 1773. Oil on canvas, 104·1 × 136·5 cm. George III liked this subject because of his interesting belief that the Hanoverian royal family was descended from the daughter of Segestes

[1] F. W. Hilles, *Letters of Sir Joshua Reynolds*, Cambridge, 1929, p. 10. The letter was first published by John Williams (alias 'Anthony Pasquin') in *An Authentic History of the Professors of Painting, . . . involving Original Letters from Sir Joshua Reynolds, which prove him to have been illiterate*, London, 1796, pp. 63ff.
[2] Oliver Millar, *The Later Pictures in the Collection of Her Majesty The Queen*, London, 1969, cat. 1011, p. 99. In 1756 Reynolds had made a copy of a portrait of George II by Sir Godfrey Kneller. See A. Graves and W. V. Cronin, *A History of the Works of Sir Joshua Reynolds, P.R.A.*, 4 vols., London, 1899–1901, vol. 1, p. 355.
[3] See Oliver Millar, *The Later Georgian Pictures in the Collection of Her Majesty The Queen*, 2 vols., London, 1969, vol. 1, cat. 1012, p. 100.
[4] See Millar, op. cit., vol. I, cats. 1008–1031, pp. 98–107.
[5] See Helmut von Erffa and Allen Staley, *The Paintings of Benjamin West*, New Haven and London, 1986, cat. 33, pp. 179–80.
[6] For discussion of the commissioning of this work, and Drummond's role in the choice of subject see von Erffa and Staley, op. cit., cat. 10, p. 168.
[7] 'When Mr. West had made a sketch for the Regulus, and submitted it to His Majesty, after some conversation, as to the dimensions, the King fixed on an advantageous part of the walls in one of the principal apartments, and directed that the picture should be painted of a size sufficient to fill the whole space'. John Galt, *The Life, Studies, and Works of Benjamin West, Esq.*, 2 Parts, London, 1820, Part 2, p. 33.
[8] Idem, p. 207.
[9] See von Erffa and Staley, op. cit., cat. 17, pp. 170–1.
[10] See Galt, op. cit., pp. 46–50. von Erffa and Staley, op. cit., cat. 94, p. 214.
[11] Ibid., cats. 77 and 5, p. 203 and pp. 165–66 and Galt, op. cit., pp. 50–1.
[12] Von Erffa and Staley, op. cit., cats. 2 and 32, p. 164 and pp. 178–79.
[13] See Galt, op. cit., p. 51, and von Erffa and Staley, op. cit., p. 179.
[14] Galt, op. cit., pp. 33–4.
[15] Kenneth Garlick and Angus Macintyre, eds., *The Diary of Joseph Farington*, New Haven and London, 1979, volume IV, p. 2469.
[16] See Reynolds's sitter-book for 1779, Royal Academy of Arts. Joseph Farington recalled: 'The King sat only *once* for the Portrait of His Majesty now in the Royal Academy. Sir Joshua prepared a Head so as to be able to complete it at one sitting.—The King was never well inclined to Sir Joshua.' K. Cave, ed., *The Diary of Joseph Farington*, 1982, vol. III, p. 2605.
[17] Edmond Malone, *The Literary Works of Sir Joshua Reynolds . . . to which is prefixed a Memoir of the Author . . . by Henry William Beechey*, 2 vols., London, 1835, p. 171.
[18] Reynolds to James Boswell, 2 September, 1784, in Frederick W. Hilles, *Portraits by Sir Joshua Reynolds*, London, 1952, p. 152.
[19] For The Prince of Wales's portrait commissions see Millar, op. cit., 1969, vol. 1, cats. 1010, 1017, 1018, 1025, 1026.
[20] Frederick W. Hilles, *Letters of Sir Joshua Reynolds*, Cambridge, 1929, pp. 124–5.
[21] See von Erffa and Staley, op. cit., pp. 97–8.
[22] Cave, ed., op. cit., vol. VII, p. 2581.
[23] Ibid., p. 2754.
[24] See Millar, op. cit., 1969, vol. 1, cats. 1008, 1011, 1030 and 1031.
[25] For Reynolds's original painting see Millar, op. cit., 1969, vol. 1, cat. 1030, p. 106; and C. R. Leslie and Tom Taylor, *Life and Times of Sir Joshua Reynolds*, 2 vols., London, 1865, vol. 2, pp. 536–7. For Bone's enamel copy see Richard Walker, *The Eighteenth and Early Nineteenth Century Miniatures in the Collection of Her Majesty The Queen*, Cambridge, 1992, cat. 792, pp. 308–9.
[26] Cave, ed., op. cit., vol. X, p. 3831.
[27] See Walker, op. cit., cats. 789, 790, 792, 795 and 796. In Walker's catalogue (no. 795) *Venus* is called *Nymph and Cupid*, although this is the title given by Reynolds to a different picture exhibited at the Royal Academy in 1784 (177). *Venus* was originally exhibited at the Academy in 1785 (126).
[28] See Millar, op. cit., 1969, vol. 1, cat. 1029, p. 106. George IV, who bought the painting through the agency of Sir Charles Long, paid £735 for it.
[29] William T. Whitley, *Art in England, 1800–1820*, Cambridge, 1928, p. 306.
[30] See von Erffa and Staley, op. cit., 1986, p. 150 (illus.).
[31] Ibid., p. 151.
[32] *Morning Post*, 20 May, 1829. Quoted in William T. Whitley, *Art in England, 1821–1837*, Cambridge, 1930, p. 168.
[33] Von Erffa and Staley, op. cit., cat. 344, p. 352.
[34] T. Whitley, op. cit., p. 168.
[35] According to West's own accounts a total of £21,705 was paid by the Crown for the paintings made for the Royal Chapel, and the designs and cartoons for St George's Chapel, Windsor. Aside from the sum of £1,302 paid out by Raphael West—who bought back three pictures—the rest of the works in the sale realized, altogether, only £2,262. See Galt, 1820, pp. 207–15. See also von Erffa and Staley, op. cit., 1986, *passim*, for the amounts paid for West's pictures at auction in 1829.
[36] See von Erffa and Staley, op. cit., pp. 90–93, p. 192 and p. 410; H. M. Colvin, *The History of the King's Works*, vol. VI, 1782–1851, London, 1973, pp. 267 ff, p. 374, p. 380 and p. 390.
[37] For a full account of West's designs for St George's Chapel see Jerry D. Meyer, 'Benjamin West's Window Designs for St. George's Chapel, Windsor', *American Art Journal*, XI, 1979, pp. 53–65.
[38] Von Erffa and Staley, op. cit., cat. 351, pp. 357–8.

Forming the taste of a prince

Richard Cosway and George IV's early collecting

STEPHEN LLOYD

The Prince of Wales, later George IV, needed advising on all matters of
taste and fashion, art and collecting, and most importantly on image making.
The fashionable painter Richard Cosway was ready to help

Little attention has been given until now to the early development of King George IV's visual taste, which in its maturity was especially marked by a love of rich decoration and ornate French furniture, as well as seventeenth-century Dutch and Flemish paintings.[1] The Prince of Wales's prolonged involvement in the construction and continual redecoration of Carlton House from 1783 until its demolition in 1827, was his first great statement of patronage. Less is known about how the Prince's taste emerged to create that palace with its remarkable interiors, from which so many of the contents survive today at Buckingham Palace. A key question to be answered is who was advising the Prince in the crucial decades of the 1780s and 1790s? In the period after 1800 the Prince, in his love of paintings from the Low Countries, was advised by various dealers and in particular by Lord Yarmouth (later the 3rd Marquess of Hertford). The major purchase was the collection of the banker Sir Thomas Baring.

In 1780 the Prince of Wales was about to turn eighteen and just beginning to establish his own personality and style away from the stifling atmosphere of his father and mother's Court at Buckingham House. Probably as a sign of his new-found independence he sat for his portrait miniature to Richard Cosway, who was one of the finest exponents of the genre in London. In his choice of artist the Prince was likely to have been influenced by the fact that Cosway had been studiously ignored by King George III and Queen Charlotte, in favour of the German-born miniaturist Jeremiah Meyer. Almost immediately the alliance between the profligate and flamboyant Prince of Wales and the notoriously vain and

1 *George, Prince of Wales*, by William Sharp after Richard Cosway, 1790. Line engraving, 24·2 × 16·5 cm, Courtauld Institute of Art, University of London. This fine print is based on an untraced portrait miniature showing one of Cosway's fashionable images of the flamboyant Prince, seen here dressed in the garter robes

foppish Cosway was successful. The artist created a fashionable image of his patron, permutations of which in portrait miniatures, drawings, prints and oils were to be promoted over the next twenty-eight years of their relationship (Fig. 1).

Indeed throughout this period Cosway remained the Prince's favourite artist, from 1785 being entitled to sign his portrait drawings and miniatures with the long and elegant title, *Primarius Pictor Serenissimi Walliae Principis*. In the 1770s the artist had already exploited his dandified fashion sense as a *macaroni*, but royal patronage fuelled his highly extrovert nature, leading to his drawing the remarkable *Self-portrait with busts of Michelangelo and Rubens* (Fig. 2). Here Cosway envisages himself as the serious artist paying homage to the ancient masters, but appearing as a courtier in a fusion of late Elizabethan and Van Dyckian fancy dress. The physical act of painting is left to the putto who knowingly traces the Hogarthian s-curve of ideal beauty on to the artist's palette.

It can be argued that the Prince was attracted to Cosway, who was more than twenty years older than his patron, not only by the merit of his portrait miniatures and fashion-conscious image, but also his rounded artistic personality and experience as a connoisseur. The Prince needed advising on all matters of taste and fashion, art and collecting, and most importantly on image-making. Cosway was an Academician, an accomplished oil painter, and also an established collector and *virtuoso*. In January 1781 he married the artist and musician, Maria Hadfield, who had recently arrived from her native Florence. Their salon was to become one of the most fashionable in London during the 1780s.[2] This socially adroit but privately unhappy marriage transformed Cosway's social status during the following decade. The artist's ostentatious lifestyle, in particular when living at Schomberg House on Pall Mall (still in existence) between 1784 and 1791, can be seen as an essential foil to that of the Prince who was based at nearby Carlton House (which was roughly where Waterloo Place is today).

While principally active as a portraitist, Cosway also acted as an adviser and artistic factotum to his patron. He was the highly paid 'principal painter' and decorator at Carlton House, and he held particular responsibilities as Surveyor of the Prince's burgeoning first collection of paintings. In 1795 Cosway 'ascertained' a large bill for the cleaning of the Prince's pictures, which had been submitted for checking by George Simpson.[3]

Apart from military scenes and family portraits, this first collection comprised mainly works by Italian sixteenth- and seventeenth-century masters. However, there were also a few later French, Flemish

2 *Self-portrait with busts of Michelangelo and Rubens* by Richard Cosway (1742–1821), *c.* 1790. Pen and ink on paper laid on card, 24.2 × 13.8 cm, Fondazione Cosway, Lodi. The artist, who was notorious for his vanity and ostentatious dress, represents himself in the guise of a seventeenth century courtier and *virtuoso*, while paying homage to the old masters in a temple dedicated to art

and Dutch paintings present. Works from the latter three schools laid the foundations for the second collection of pictures, which was essentially formed after 1806, much of which can be seen at Buckingham Palace today. But the first collection very much reflected the influence of Richard Cosway's taste, and was dominated by the Italian Old Master tradition. It also reflected a notable passion for the work of Rubens and his Flemish pupils, together with some Dutch and French pictures.[4]

3 *The Princess begging Don Quixote to restore her to the throne*, Gobelins Tapestry, Don Quixote series, 3·5 × 3·1 m, The Royal Collection, Buckingham Palace. One of four tapestries presented by Richard Cosway to the Prince of Wales in 1789, for the decoration of Carlton House. The artist had been given them by Louis XVI in 1787 in gratitude for Cosway's gift of four tapestry cartoons attributed to Giulio Romano

return for the artist's presentation to the Louvre—during his visit to Paris in 1786—of four huge tapestry cartoons of the *Fructus belli* series, then attributed to Giulio Romano. The gift to the Prince was remarked upon by the London press: 'The Tapestry, so sumptuous as to be princely, Mr. *Cosway* has therefore very properly presented to the PRINCE'. Another contemporary, the writer William Combe, noted that 'they form one of the principal embellishments of Carlton House'.[7] There they would have joined Sir Joshua Reynolds' portrait of Louis-Philippe, duc d'Orléans, also known as Philippe-Egalité

Cosway's greatest contribution occurred with the gift of four Gobelins tapestries from the Don Quixote series

(see Fig. 4). Orléans was a notoriously decadent friend of the Prince of Wales during the 1780s and a patron of Cosway on his Parisian visit, and his anglomania was matched by the francophile nature of the Prince and his *primarius pictor*.

Eventually the Prince tired of Cosway's increasingly eccentric behaviour, and their relationship ceased in 1808, by which time the Prince had found new artistic projects and advisers. But throughout the 1780s and 1790s Cosway should be regarded as one of the key figures in forming George's IV's visual taste, and he was the dominant influence on his patron's first collection of Old Master paintings.

[1] See *George IV and the Arts of France*, exh. cat., The Queen's Gallery, Buckingham Palace, London, 1966; Oliver Millar, *The Queen's Pictures*, London, 1977, pp. 129–62; and *Carlton House: The Past Glories of George IV's Palace*, exh. cat., The Queen's Gallery, Buckingham Palace, London, 1991–2.
[2] Stephen Lloyd, 'The accomplished Maria Cosway: Anglo-Italian artist, musician, salon hostess and educationalist (1759–1838)', *The Journal of Anglo-Italian Studies*, vol. 2, 1992, pp. 108–39.
[3] Oliver Millar, 'George IV when Prince of Wales: his debts to artists and craftsmen', Documents for the History of Collecting: 2, *The Burlington Magazine*, vol. CXXVIII, August 1986, pp. 589–91. A number of these paintings were sold at Christie's on 29 June 1814, cf. Christopher White, *Dutch Pictures in the Collection of Her Majesty the Queen*, Cambridge, 1982, pp. 333–6.
[4] Stephen Lloyd, 'Richard Cosway, RA: The artist as collector, connoisseur and virtuoso', APOLLO, vol. CXXXIII, June 1991, pp. 398–405, esp. nn. 9–11 and 16.
[5] See Millar op. cit. at n. 3 above, p. 387; Windsor, Royal Archives, MSS Geo. 26460 and 26792; and see Lloyd op. cit., at note 4 above, p. 495 n. 16.
[6] See Lloyd op. cit., at n. 4 above, pp. 400–1 and 405 n. 12.
[7] See Lloyd op. cit., at n. 4 above, pp. 399–400, 402 and 405 n. 7; *The World*, 12 April 1789, p. 3; Throgmorton Trust, Combe MSS, II, fol. 174r.

In addition to offering advice, Cosway also sold a number of pictures directly to the Prince, including a portrait of *Frederick, Prince of Wales, with his hunt* by Charles Philips for twenty guineas in 1784; an unidentified picture by Watteau for ten guineas in 1792; *The duet* by Carel de Moor for fifteen guineas at Baron Nagel's sale in 1795; a picture from the Chalons sale for seven guineas, also in 1795; and *The Funeral of Louis XIV* for fifteen guineas in 1796 or 1799. This last was then considered to be by Van der Meulen, but is now attributed to Pierre-Denis Martin.[5] It is also likely that Cosway placed pictures from his own collection on approval for purchase with his patron. One work the Prince may well have rejected was *The Mass of St Giles* from around 1500 by the eponymous Master, which is now in the National Gallery, London.[6]

Cosway's greatest contribution, however, to the Prince of Wales's collection and to his evolving taste in French decorative arts occurred in 1789 with the artist's spectacular gift of four Gobelins tapestries from the Don Quixote series (Fig. 3). Cosway had been presented with these—which were normally reserved for foreign royalty and ambassadors—by Louis XVI in 1787, in

4 *His most Serene Highness Louis Philip Joseph Duke of Orléans* by George Hadfield after Richard Cosway, 1788. Stipple engraving, 33·7 × 24·1 cm.

The guards at the Palace

Unchanging in splendour

PHILIP MANSEL

1 Guard Room in a photograph of 1913, showing the interior to have been plainer than it is today (when Gobelins tapestries are on view). The central sculpture is *Queen Victoria* by John Gibson (   ) 1847, which originally was partly coloured

The Guard Rooms at the entrance to the State Apartments in Hampton Court and Windsor are spacious chambers lined with swords and halberds. The Guard Room on the first floor of Buckingham Palace is a white and gold vestibule, with one window, decorated with a relief by Pitts of *War and Peace*. Its diminutive size is due to the fact that it was installed by Nash for the sake of tradition rather than use. Photographs of the interior in 1913 show it as an even starker interior than it is today, although the same fine British nineteenth-century sculptures can be seen (Figs. 1, 2)

The reason for the contrast in guard rooms is that, in 1837, when Queen Victoria moved to Buckingham Palace, many of the outer departments of the Court stayed at St James's Palace, the residence of her uncle, William IV, and his predecessors. The traditional internal palace guards of Gentlemen-at-Arms and Yeomen of the Guard, dating from 1509 and 1485 respectively, hitherto on daily duty in St James's Palace, stayed there—and they are still there, with greatly reduced duties, today. Now composed of officers and non-commissioned officers who have received the appointment as a reward for 'long or meritorious service', they come to Buckingham Palace only on formal occasions, such as a state visit or a garden party. With impressive adaptability, the Gentlemen-at-Arms help guide members of the royal family through the crowd at a garden party—although they sometimes find it 'difficult to deal with thrusters'.

Of the other units in the present Household Division, originally created to guard the monarch, the Household Cavalry guards the official entrance to Buckingham Palace, at Horse Guards in Whitehall. The location is a reminder of their role at Whitehall when it was the palace of their creator Charles II. 'The Queen's Guard' guarding Buckingham Palace is drawn from one of the five regiments of foot guards, the Grenadier Guards founded in 1656, the Coldstream Guards (1660), the Scots Guards (1660), the Irish Guards (1900) and the Welsh Guards (1915). They have been guarding the exterior of the Palace, without a break (even between 1818 and 1837 when it was not a royal residence)[1] since George III moved to 'the Queen's House' in 1762.

When Queen Victoria moved to Buckingham Palace on 13 July 1837, one of the first changes was to increase the guard on duty to roughly forty-five, a figure which has changed little to this day. Since 1972 the foot guards have 'gone tactical' and, from their Guard Room on the left of the Palace, in front of the entrance to The Queen's Gallery, patrol the grounds at night

with loaded weapons. However, the police now have overall responsibility for palace security. The principal role of The Queen's Guard is ceremonial.[2]

The scarlet uniforms present a welcome note of colour against the grey stone of the facade. The changing of the Guard is one of London's main tourist attractions, and since 1963 has been performed whether the monarch is in residence at the Palace or not. Every other day a new detachment of guards, accompanied by a band, arrives from Wellington Barracks in Birdcage Walk, and relieves the detachment on duty. Osbert Sitwell, in 1913 a young officer in the Grenadier Guards stationed in Wellington Barracks, wrote that it took weeks of practice to perfect the 'stately ceremonial crawl' used. On one occasion the band tried an adventurous tune from Richard Strauss's *Elektra*. A scarlet-coated page swiftly emerged from the Palace, bearing the following note from King George V: 'His Majesty does not know what the Band has just played but it is never to be played again.'[3]

The history of the guards at Buckingham Palace has been relatively untroubled. In 1848, at the time of the Chartist demonstrations, artillery was stationed

2 Guard Room in 1913 showing opposite apsidal end, with *Prince Albert* by Emil Wolff in the centre, a replica of the original now at Osborne

in the royal stables. Guards have gone into Khaki during the World Wars. Otherwise, as the Duke of Edinburgh, Colonel of the Grenadier Guards and Senior Colonel in the Household Division, has written, 'Guard duties, although demanding, have fortunately never been vital.'

The last survivor of the great guards parades which used to feast the eye in Paris, Berlin and St Petersburg takes place every year on the sovereign's birthday, as it has done since 1729, on Horse Guards Parade. Elizabeth II has just as sharp an eye for details of drill and dress as any of her predecessors. However, a state visit provides the clearest demonstration of the ceremonial duties of the different guard units at Buckingham Palace, which have changed relatively little since the nineteenth century.

On the first day of a state visit the Household Cavalry provides both an escort to the Palace and also—a reminder of their original role, under Charles II, as noble

bodyguards—a 'staircase party' of eight, lining the staircase to the State Apartments inside the Palace. Foot guards are on duty along the route and outside the Palace, and mount a Guard of Honour of approximately one hundred, excluding the band, in the quadrangle. Detachments of Yeomen of the Guard and Gentlemen-at-Arms are stationed in the Grand Hall. At the state banquet an orchestra from a guards regiment plays. The Yeomen of the Guard are on duty in the State Rooms, and a detachment of Household Cavalry in the Grand Hall. This is the role for which, after the function of guarding, guards were originally created: to add splendour to the monarch's palace—and to impress foreign visitors.

Philip Mansel is author of *Pillars of Monarchy: an Outline of the Political and Social History of Royal Guards 1400–1984*. (Quartet 1984). His latest book is *Charles-Joseph de Ligne, Le Charmeur de l'Europe* (Stock 1992). He is currently working on a history of Istanbul under the Ottomans.

[1] See e.g. Lt. Gen. Sir F. W. Hamilton, *The Origins and History of the First or Grenadier Guards*, 3 vols., 1874–7, vol. III, p. 108.
[2] Philip Mansel, *Pillars of Monarchy: an Outline of the Political and Social History of Royal Guards 1400–1984*, 1984, pp. 59, 67.
[3] Osbert Sitwell, *Great Morning*, 1948, pp. 147–8.
[4] Mansel, p. 132.

The arch at Constitution Hill

A new axis for London

DANA ARNOLD

Few realize that the Constitution Arch was originally designed to
align with the Hyde Park Screen, to form an entrance into
Buckingham Palace through the garden in one direction and into
Hyde Park in the other

George IV's contribution to the urban development of London has been greatly underestimated. His vision of the city as a modern metropolis to rival any of its European counterparts began with the development of the Regent's Park and Regent Street, and while these projects were well under way his attention turned to the parks in the south-west corner of London. On 22 April 1823 the Treasury requested the Commissioners of Woods to report on the state of Hyde, St James's and Green Parks and to supply some proposals for improvement. These were submitted with estimates on 28 September 1825. Surprisingly, the architect was not John Nash but the young and relatively inexperienced Decimus Burton (1800–81). Despite his youthfulness Burton had clearly established himself as a competent practitioner: Charles Arbuthnot, the Chief Commissioner of Woods had chosen him on the basis that his 'plans for the other improvements of the parks [i.e. Regent's] have met with so much approbation'.[1]

It was to be a large-scale, costly project involving work on every aspect of the parks, from drainage to layout and planting. Arbuthnot's choice of Burton added weight to his argument that all the work should come under the aegis of one of the two agencies charged with the maintenance of crown land and property, namely the Office of Works and the Commissioners of Woods and Forests. Arbuthnot argued that Burton could only be employed through the Office of Woods;[2] it was therefore logical that all the work should be carried out by them.

This was agreed in September 1824.[3] This financial arrangement may in itself appear pragmatic and sensible—indeed it was, but it shifted an important project of George IV's out of the limelight. Most of George IV's building and development schemes came under the aegis of the Office of Works[4] and John Nash enjoyed the lion's share of the work here. But the work in Hyde, St James's and Green Parks was out of the Office of Works' sphere of influence, and this work took on increasing significance and importance as the monarch's ideas for the development of London into a royal metropolis evolved.

1 Perspective of the Hyde Park Screen and the Entrance to Buckingham Palace Gardens. RIBA drawings collection XOS/D/5. Unsigned, undated, watercolour, 24 × 40·5 cm. This shows the original alignment of the two arches and the gates to Constitution Hill to the east of the royal entrance to the palace gardens through the centre of the arch. The figure sculpture on the Green Park arch was not executed, nor were the sculptural embellishments above the side arches on the Hyde Park screen or the group above the central archway. This may well have been a presentation drawing (?perhaps for exhibition) produced after the altered design for the Green Park Arch (Fig. 4) was approved to give a fuller idea of the scheme and the sculptural embellishments (see colour detail, Plate I)

The fashionable new London lacked one essential ingredient of any urban plan—a focal point and, more specifically, a royal focal point. The absence of a substantial royal palace in the capital was largely a result of historical circumstance. The culmination of the Regent's Park and Street development was Carlton House which had been George IV's residence well before he ascended the throne. Regent Street led, in a rather roundabout way, from the Park to Carlton House, so providing a dominant north-south axis for the city and a starting point for further axial roads. But, despite his extravagant renovation projects, Carlton House did not meet George IV's requirements for a royal residence, and in any case it had severe structural problems.[5] As early as November 1818, when Queen Charlotte died, he was tempted by the prospect of a move to Buckingham House and its potentially grander accommodation.

In August 1822 John Nash submitted plans to the Surveyor General for the con-

version of Buckingham House, but the work did not begin until June 1825. George IV took a very active role in all his architectural projects, and so it is unlikely that he was not aware of the convergence of the development of Buckingham House and the development of Hyde, St James's and Green Parks. Green Park would now be the King's own back garden whereas St James's Park would be the foreground to the main Palace entrance. But the park developments were placed in the hands of Decimus Burton. The evidence suggests that the overall plan for this area was developing in the King's mind in the early 1820s and the initial plans for both parks and Palace were fixed by 1825. His new residence was to be on the edge of London, which would allow him a freer hand in the development of axial roads and open spaces and so would avoid the problems he and Nash had faced in the Regent Street development. Indeed this move westwards and the realignment of the focal point of London that it implied detracted from many

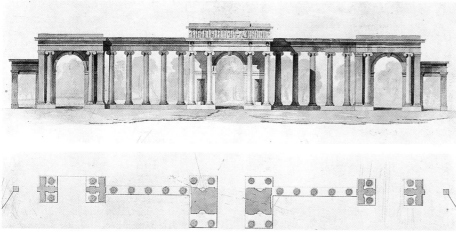

ingham Palace in June of that year; perhaps Burton was responding to this in his annotation.

Burton originally intended that the gateway into Green Park and the Hyde Park screen (Figs. 2, 3) should be a homogeneous pair, and he had worked on the designs together. To ensure uniformity and to produce a coherent, monumental space Burton virtually repeated the central arch of the Hyde Park screen in his design for the Green Park entrance. In doing so he achieved a mirror image of a single arch flanked on either side by two Ionic columns with a heavy entablature surmounted by a plinth. The composition was further pulled together by the addition of a continuous Ionic frieze around the top of both arches. This was the height of Greek Revival fashion: a replica of the panathenaic procession from the Elgin Marbles by J. Henning Jr. This subtle symmetry complemented the axiality of the design both in terms of the line from Buckingham Palace and to the east-west, as travellers from the west, instead of going through toll gates, now passed between two triumphal arches lying parallel to the road.[10]

Once work had begun at Buckingham Palace, it appears that George IV decided to aggrandize the entrance to his new gardens. A drawing by Burton dated November 1825 (Fig. 4) shows a design for a larger triumphal arch into the Palace gardens which received royal approval in January 1826. The change in scale is curious as the two entrances were always meant to be aligned and the original, approved designs for each show homogeneity of scale and style. The second and executed design for the arch breaks with this and overpowers the Hyde Park screen, as can be seen in a painting by James Holland (Fig. 5). The order was changed to the grander Corinthian and the sculptural decoration was extended to include emblamatic figures placed around the entablature[11] and military ensignia. These can be seen in an unsigned, undated watercolour (Fig. 1, Plate I) which shows the intended alignment and the richer sculptural embellishment of both the Green Park arch and Hyde Park screen. Both arches were intended to be surmounted by monuments—a quadriga and Britannia

of the metropolitan improvements that the King had already implemented and that Nash was overseeing.

Perhaps with an eye to France, the monarch wanted triumphal arches as entrances. Nash's own Marble Arch was to stand as an entrance to the railed forecourt in front of the Palace (see illustrations elsewhere). Meanwhile, a second triumphal entrance into the gardens of the Palace was being designed by Decimus Burton.

George IV's choice of Hyde Park Corner as the site of a monumental entrance into his gardens was prodigious.[6] The site had traditionally been seen as the most important gateway into London from the West, and the idea of creating a monumental entrance had been around for at least fifty years.[7] George IV's plans for Hyde Park

Corner changed the orientation and purpose of such an entrance by providing not only a way into the King's gardens but also an entry to Hyde Park itself. The gardens and the Park were to be aligned on a new axis.[8]

This axis appears to have been determined fairly early on. It is laid out in an undated drawing[9] probably related to the Commissioner of Woods' proposals and which can be dated between 1823–5, showing a plan of the Hyde Park screen and an entrance lodge at Constitution Hill. Burton's design for this dated July 1825 (Fig. 1, Plate I) received royal assent in August that year. It includes the following pencil note added by Burton on the east side of the arch: 'It is here proposed to place the gates to Constitution Hill—if the king's commands are that the centre shall be the royal entrance.' Work had begun at Buck-

---

2 Plan and elevation for the Entrance into Green Park at Hyde Park Corner dated 20 July 1825, by Decimus Burton (1800–81). Victoria and Albert Museum E 2334–1910 A 149a, pen, tinted, scale 1:10". 45 × 64·8 cm. This was the original design approved by George IV to be put into execution with the exception that the windows should not be diminished at the top so avoiding any hint of an Egyptian revival style. The arch mirrors the central arch of the Hyde Park Screen which was to be placed directly opposite.

3 Plan and elevation (here condensed) for the entrance to Hyde Park at Hyde Park Corner dated 20 July 1825, by Decimus Burton. V & A, D 1299–1907, pen, tinted, scale 1:14. 45 × 66 cm

I Detail of watercolour illustrated in Fig. 1

PORTERS·LODGE
FOR THE
PUBLIC·GATE

PORTERS·LODGE
FOR THE
ROYAL·GATE

funding for the development of Hyde Park Corner, despite strong representations to the Treasury for extra funds to complete the sculptural decoration.[15]

The fortunes of the Green Park arch plummeted further after the death of George IV in 1830. Work was not resumed by his successor as William IV loathed the new Palace and died before ever having to live there. The popularity of both arch and Burton was at such a low ebb that in September 1846 the arch was used as a plinth for a giant equestrian monument to the Duke of Wellington.[16] Although this was removed, since it looked as ridiculous as Burton had predicted (see caption to Fig. 4), later in the century the orientation of the arch was changed. It was moved off its axis with the Hyde Park Screen and the triumphal royal route from Palace to park disappeared.

[1] Public Record Office Cres 8:16 p. 3.
[2] This was not strictly the case as Burton was engaged by the Office of Works in 1825 as superintending architect for the Parliamentary Mews at Westminster, although the Commissioners of Woods and Forests had employed him to prepare the original plans. PRO Work 12/63/7 f. 5.
[3] PRO Cres 8:14 p. 472.
[4] For a fuller account of these see J. M. Crook & M. H. Port, History of the King's Works, vol. vi (1973), 1782–1851.
[5] PRO Work 19/3 fs. 219, 220.
[6] It was directly opposite the Duke of Wellington's London home, Apsley House. There had been talk of erecting a monumental entrance for many years. Wellington mentions in a letter to Thomas Croker that a statue had been proposed to be placed in front of his house by the Duke of Rutland to commemorate his victory at Waterloo. Croker Papers, ed. L. J. Lennings (11885), iii, p. 124. Rutland certainly got his way when the arch was used as a plinth for such a statue (see below).
[7] Designs had been produced as early as 1770 by Robert Adam.
[8] This change in axis did not go without comment. The Mechanics Magazine of 18 August 1827, p. 654, was most critical of the change as it robbed London of its best opportunity for a monumental entrance to the city.
[9] PRO Cres 2:637.
[10] The Mechanics Magazine (as above) praised the quality of the design of Hyde Park Screen which it likened to the Propylaea on the Athenian Acropolis.
[11] Designs for female figures representing History and Astronomy by J. Henning Jr. exist in the Victoria and Albert Museum, E 2338–E2340–1910.
[12] This is mentioned by The Mechanics Magazine (as above).
[13] Burton's work at Hyde Park Corner exceeded its estimate as the foundations for the screen proved more expensive because of the discovery of underground watertanks on the site. This is described in PRO Cres 8:16. Burton also insisted on the highest quality workmanship which caused some of his craftsmen to exceed their estimates.
[14] Burton's design for the Athenaeum Club was enjoying an enthusiastic reception. This, together with his competent handling of large projects and Arbuthnot's praise of Burton to the Commissioners, must have irked Nash who was very much under scrutiny.
[15] A statement of work remaining is given in PRO 8:16. Burton wrote to Milne on 17 November 1829 (PRO Cres 8:17 p. 349) pointing out that all the other works were completed and the accounts paid but the sculptural decoration was still to be finished. Burton wished the design to be finished as he felt it looked unsightly. He had even suggested a reduced decorative scheme. The Treasury replied to the Commissioner of Woods on 19 January 1830 that no more work could be sanctioned until the work at Buckingham Palace had ceased. Both projects were receiving funds from the Land Revenues Account.
[16] For a fuller discussion of the later history of the arch see J. Physick, The Wellington Monument, 1970.

Triumphans over the Green Park arch (see Plate I) and an equestrian statue of George III over the Screen.[12] There were also plans to alter the line of Knightsbridge to make it more on a level with Grosvenor Place. A drawing which can be dated some time after the second design for the entrance to the gardens—it shows the ground plan of this and refers to the arch quite clearly as the entrance to the Palace gardens (Fig. 6)— shows the plans to raise the level of the road in order to improve the appearance of this increasingly important area.

The development of Buckingham Palace and Hyde Park Corner had been divided up between the Office of Woods and the Office of Works. But it was essentially one project. Despite this, Nash's evidence in the *Report from the Select Committee on the Office of Works 1828* implies that he had no idea about the nature of the works at Hyde Park Corner. He stated that the arch was never contemplated as an entrance to the Palace gardens and went on to claim he did not know who had ordered the arch. When asked, 'Will the position of the cistern [designed to hold water from the Serpentine]

4 Plan and front and side elevation of the design for the Green Park entrance at Hyde Park Corner dated November 1825, by Decimus Burton. Victoria and Albert Museum E 2334–1910, pen and wash 1:10″ scale. 50·8 × 38 cm. This design was approved by the King, superseding that in Fig. 1, and was eventually executed. The design is much grander and the scale larger than the original, so disrupting the intended harmony with the Hyde Park Screen

prevent a straight road being made from the arch to the palace?' Nash replied, 'There is no entrance to the palace on that side nor ever was, it was never intended there should be an entrance there.'

It is not surprising that Nash felt so aggrieved. Not only had the focal point of London changed, moving attention away from much of his work on the metropolitan improvements, but Burton was proving himself to be reliable[13] and a leading light in the Greek Revival movement.[14]

The question of the cistern and the approach to the Palace through the gardens remained unresolved. More significantly, the excessive spending on the Palace project resulted in a moritorium on any further

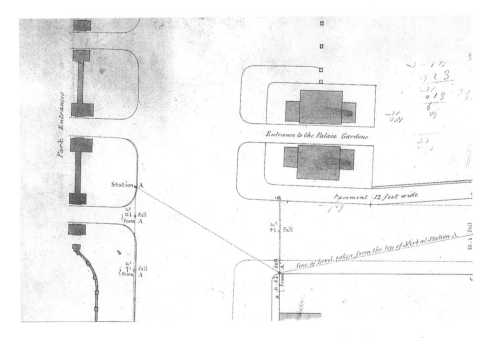

5 Photograph of a oil painting by James Holland showing Hyde Park Corner in 1827. Victoria and Albert Museum: not accessioned (in box no. A149a). The inscription on this photograph bears testimony to the later fate of the arch: 'The Royal Entrance to Buckingham Palace by Constitution Hill and the Facade Entrance at Hyde Park as shown by this photograph accord with the Architect's designs approved by the King Nov 1825. They remain unfinished 1875. But yet more to be regretted, a colossal equestrian statue has taken the place of the Quadriga with Britannia Triumphans, the surmount approved in the original design. Lord Morpeth as First Commissioner of Woods unhappily permitted the Stature to be put up on sufferance Sept 1846, contrary to the wishes of the sculptor, and the earnest and repeated protests of the Architect—

The sculptor had designed the statue to stand on a pedestal of proper proportions & not on the summit of a massive building where its appearance is very unsatisfactory and where at the height of 70 feet the high finish if the work is entirely thrown away— The Architect feels and deplores that the Arch is degraded by such an unsuitable Surmount. Artists and men of taste universally condemn and even cast ridicule on the existing conjunction.'

6 Detail of a drawing showing sections of road heights at Hyde Park Corner and junction of Grosvenor Place. PRO MPE 796, undated, pen and ink by E. J. Wards, 16 Upper Eaton Street, Pimlico. This detail shows the original alignment of the two arches and shows the intention to reduce the drop in the road heights to create a more level and so homogeneous area. Grosvenor Place was to be raised to the level of the plinth of the Arch into Buckingham Palace gardens and the pavement down Knightsbridge was also to be raised.

Buckingham Palace Gardens today

A surviving oasis

DANA ARNOLD

1 *The Garden Front of Buckingham Palace*, in a photograph of 1913 *(courtesy Marlborough Rare Books)*

George IV's vision of his new palace included its landscape setting. The work on the improvements of the Royal Parks which surrounded the palace, Hyde, Green and St James's, was already underway. But the new royal residence needed a suitable private garden. When the work on Buckingham House began in 1825, William Townsend Aiton, the head gardener at Kew gardens, was appointed to superintend the laying out of the grounds.[1] The new gardens were not solely Aiton's responsibility as John Nash also had a considerable input into the more ambitious aspects of the design.[2] The gardens were never completed according to the designs of Aiton and Nash but their executed work provided the blueprint.

The two main alterations made to the formal gardens of Buckingham House were the creation of a lake and the building of a large mound to screen the palace from the road and the royal stables. The use of water in the new gardens was influenced by English landscape design theory which had developed over the preceding century through the work of Capability Brown and Humphrey Repton. The large lake a traditional ingredient in such layouts, was created out of two existing small pools which were joined together and enlarged. It was finished in 1828 and was known as the fish pond. The absence of fountains also follows the English landscape tradition and distinguishes the gardens from the fountain-strewn examples of European royal palaces. The lake was fed by a reservoir tank which stood very near Decimus Burton's triumphal arch which was originally to be the entrance into the gardens (see pp. 129–31).[3] This was filled via an underground conduit from the Serpentine which was also the water supply for the palace.

By 1854 the water had become quite impure and Lord Palmerston suggested that the lake should be drained and turned into a flowerbed which would have destroyed much of the original character of the landscape. Fortunately fish were introduced instead. In 1863, with the death from cholera in 1861 of Prince Albert in mind, the water was inspected and declared 'of excellent qualities for dietic purposes'.[4] Despite the lake's being lined with concrete in 1869, the long hot summer of 1883 caused it once again to become stagnant and less than fragrant.

The earth excavated during the creation of the lake was used to make the mound to the south of the garden, which was originally some twenty-five feet high. This was very unpopular with the public and in 1838 the mound was lowered and the plantings further to the south of it altered.[5] Prince Albert added several gravelled paths on the top of it in 1840 and four years later the Pavilion was added by Ludwig Grüner, who later designed the mausoleum for the Prince Consort.[6] Both the paths and the mausoleum have now disappeared. The most notable features which remain from this period are the huge herbaceous border and the grey border, a silver wedding present from Lord and Lady Astor of Hever.

Since the death of Prince Albert in 1861 few changes to the gardens have taken place as Queen Victoria wished to keep the grounds largely untouched. The most notable exception is the cascade which was added by George VI and Queen Elizabeth, who also revived the Garden Parties (originally called breakfasts though they took place in the afternoon) begun by Queen Victoria. The eighteenth-century summer house, which was originally in the Admiralty gardens, was also added this century and placed near the enormous fifteen-foot-high Waterloo Vase. The gardens are now a walled oasis in the middle of London which provides a home for a great variety of wild birds including, of course, flamingoes.

I The Garden Front today. Note the absence of the decorative sculptures from the top of the central section and its flanking loggias and the changes which have taken place in the area of the Queen's Gallery at the right

2 *The Garden Entrance* in a photograph of 1913 (*courtesy Marlborough Rare Books*). In the notes of Queen Mary, 'Private entrance to Palace used by Royal Family.' 2 tapestry panels on wall. 4 (*sic*) huge elephant tusks. There are also displays of spears of the kind familiar in households of the imperial period. This entrance retains part of the private entrance to the wing added for George IV when Prince of Wales

[1] Aiton states this in a letter to Stephenson 22 Feb 1832 Public Record Office Work 19/4 folio 650.
[2] Ibid. Aiton states that he supervised the general formation of the lawns, turfing and forming various rough surfaces of the grounds and plantations of the new gardens; but the excavations of the making of the lake and raising the mass of the mound adjoining the king's mews on the southern side of the water was done entirely under the management of Nash.
[3] The lake had been placed there by John Nash so blocking the processional route from the arch to the palace. In his evidence to the 1828 Parliamentary Committee Nash had denied any knowledge that the arch was intended as an entrance into the palace gardens.
[4] See Peter Coats *The Gardens of Buckingham Palace*, London 1978, for this and further information about the gardens.
[5] Public Record Office PRO Work 19 104 folio 60.
[6] Details of the Pavilion can be found in Ludwig Grüner, *Her Majesty's Pavilion at Buckingham Palace Garden*, London, 1846.

BUCKINGHAM PALACE

Contributors

Brian Allen is Director of the Paul Mellon Centre for Studies in British Art. He writes mainly on eighteenth-century British painting, has published a book on Francis Hayman and is currently working on a catalogue raisonné of Hogarth's paintings and drawings.

Colin Amery is architecture correspondent of the Financial Times. He sits on the building committee of the National Gallery and is a trustee of the Prince of Wales's Institute of Architecture.

Dana Arnold is Education Secretary of the Georgian Group. She was previously a lecturer in Architectural History at the University of London. She has published widely on eighteenth- and early nineteenth-century architectural subjects and is currently writing a booklet on 'The Georgian House: Form and Function'.

Richard Garnier is Head of the Antique Clock Department at Garrard. From 1975–90 he was Head of Clocks and Watches at Christie's, London, and has written extensively on the subject for numerous encyclopedias of decorative arts and antiques. He contributes regularly on the subject of architecture, as well as clocks and watches, to *Country Life* and *The Antique Collector.*

John Harris is an architectural historian and now devotes much of his time to the International Confederation of Architectural Museums, of which he is now perpetual President. He is currently Consultant to the Heinz Architectural Center of the Carnegie Museum of Art, Pittsburgh. He has recently prepared the exhibition 'A Palladian House and Garden: the Making of Lord Burlington's Chiswick House' to be held in Montreal and Pittsburgh, and in London in 1995.

Gervase Jackson-Stops OBE worked at the Victoria and Albert Museum before joining the National Trust in 1971. He has been the Trust's Architectural Adviser since 1975, and was curator of the exhibition 'The Treasure Houses of Britain: Five Hundred Years of Private Patronage and Art Collecting' held at the National Gallery of Art, Washington DC, in 1985–6. His publications include *The English Country House – A Grand Tour* (1987) and *The Country House in Perspective* (1990), and he has since written the catalogue for the exhibition 'An English Arcadia: Designs for Gardens and Garden Buildings in the Care of the National Trust', 1992–3. He is also a regular contributor to *Country Life* and other periodicals on art and architectural history. He is a member of the Export Review Committee.

Susan Jenkins, after studying at Cambridge and the Courtauld, worked in the Prints and Drawings Department of the V&A. She is now Assistant Curator for Historic Royal Palaces, based at Hampton Court with responsibility for Hampton Court, the Tower of London, Kensington Palace, the Banqueting House, Whitehall, and Kew Palace. Her present job has involved work on the Tudor kitchens at Hampton Court and the restoration of the fire-damaged wing.

Christopher Lloyd is the Surveyor of the Queen's Pictures. He has written extensively on the work of Camille Pissarro, including a cata-

logue of the artist's drawings at the Ashmolean Museum where for twenty years he was Assistant Keeper in the Department of Western Art. He is the author of *Pissarro* (Skira, 1981) and contributed to the catalogue of the 1992–3 Alfred Sisley exhibition. Recently he wrote and presented the Channel 4 TV series 'A Journey Through The Queen's Pictures'. His book on the early Italian paintings in the Art Institute of Chicago is forthcoming.

Stephen Lloyd is an Assistant Keeper at the Scottish National Portrait Gallery in Edinburgh. He is currently completing a doctoral thesis on Richard Cosway for Oxford University and preparing an exhibition on the Cosways for the Fondazione Cosway, Lodi, in 1994.

Philip Mansel is the author of *Pillars of Monarchy: An Outline of the Political and Social History of the Royal Guards* (Quartet, London, 1984). His latest book is *Charles-Joseph de Ligne: Le charmeur de l'Europe* (Stock, London, 1992). He is currently working on a history of Constantinople under the Ottoman Empire.

Charles Noble MVO studied Art History at Cambridge and has worked for the Royal household since 1979. He was appointed Assistant to the Surveyor of the Queen's Pictures in 1985, and awarded the MVO in 1990. He has contributed an article on Laurits Tuxen's work for the British Court to the catalogue exhibition devoted to Tuxen at Frederiksborg in 1990, and is currently working on the catalogue of the Edwardian and later paintings in the Royal Collection.

Martin Postle writes on the subject of eighteenth- and nineteenth-century British art. In 1991 he organized the exhibition 'The Artist's Model from Lely to Etty' at Kenwood and the University of Nottingham Art Gallery. He is currently organizing a sequel exhibition and has recently completed a book on Joshua Reynolds's subject paintings for Cambridge University Press. Dr Postle is Director of the London Centre of the University of Delaware.

Alan Powers is a freelance writer and artist, and is the Librarian of the Prince of Wales's Institute of Architecture.

John Martin Robinson is a partner in Historic Buildings Consultants and is the author of a number of books on architecture including *The Wyatts, Royal Residences, Country Houses of the North West* and (jointly with Somerset Herald) *The Oxford Guide to Heraldry*. He has advised on the restoration of several historic buildings including Spencer House, The London Oratory, Arundel Castle and Abbot Hall, Kendal.

Andrew Sanders is Reader in Modern English Literature at Birkbeck College, University of London. At present he is completing a history of English Literature for Oxford University Press.

John Whitehead has been an antiques dealer specializing in French eighteenth-century works of art since 1980. He is the author of *The French Interior in the Eighteenth Century* published by Laurence King, London, in 1992.

Published by APOLLO Magazine Ltd

29 Chesham Place
London SW1X 8HB

Tel: 071-235 1676   Fax: 071-235 1673 (*Editorial*)
Tel: 071-235 1998   Fax: 071-235 1689 (*Advertising*)

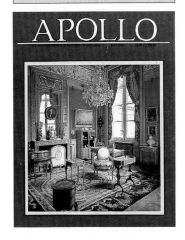

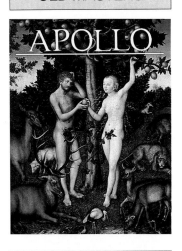
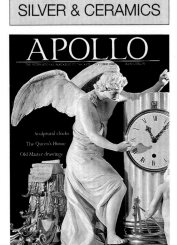
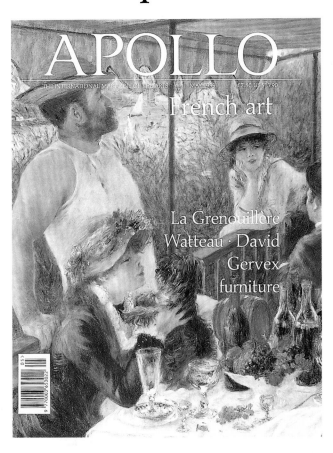
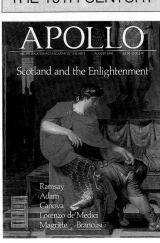
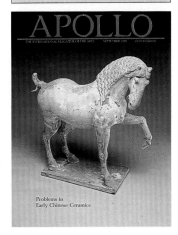

BY APPOINTMENT TO HER MAJESTY
THE QUEEN

BY APPOINTMENT TO HRH
THE DUKE OF EDINBURGH

BY APPOINTMENT TO HER MAJESTY
QUEEN ELIZABETH THE QUEEN MOTHER

BY APPOINTMENT TO HRH
THE PRINCE OF WALES

The Royal Warrant of Appointment dates back to the twelfth century, when Henry II first granted his royal patronage to the Weavers Company: since then, the list of companies who hold this privilege has grown to 880, including firms supplying goods ranging from clothes and food to technology and machinery. It is universally considered a badge of distinction, reflecting the consistent high quality of goods supplied and the integrity of the company itself The Royal Warrant may be granted by four members of the Royal Family, HM The Queen, HRH The Duke of Edinburgh, HM The Queen Mother, and HRH The Prince of Wales, and only to tradesmen, manufacturers and retailers – professional and financial services have always been ineligible for the Warrant.

Requirements for eligibility for a Royal Warrant have always been stringent, and rigorously applied. After an unbroken three-year period of substantial supply of goods to the Royal Household, the company may apply to The Royal Household Tradesmens Warrants Committee, which meets once a year to consider new applications, and which may then make a recommendation to Her Majesty. If the Royal Warrant of Appointment is granted as a result, the individual Grantee to whom the Warrant is issued on behalf of the firm is responsible for ensuring that the rules which apply to the use of the Royal Arms are observed, and is then able to use the Royal Arms in specific and prescribed circumstances. The Warrant cannot be transferred, and holders are required to comply with a strict code of confidentiality with regard to the Royal Famiy and the goods they receive from the company.

Clothes and Sports Goods

BURBERRY'S LTD.   18-22 HAYMARKET, LONDON SW1Y 4DQ   071-930 3343
Manufacturers and retailers of weatherproofs and clothing.
By appointment to HM The Queen and HRH The Prince of Wales.

COOPERS OF MARBLE ARCH LTD.   72-74 EDGWARE ROAD, MARBLE ARCH, LONDON W2 2FA   Fax 071-706 0572 071-402 8635
Gentlemans Outfitters.
By appointment to HM The Queen.

FARLOW'S OF PALL MALL   5 PALL MALL, LONDON SW14 SNP   071-839 2423
Suppliers of fishing tackle, shooting accessories and country clothing.
By appointment to HRH The Prince of Wales.

HARDY AMIES LTD.   14 SAVILE ROW, LONDON W1X 2JN   071-734 2436
Haute Couture and Ready to Wear.
By appointment to HM The Queen.

HENRY POOLE & CO.   15 SAVILE ROW, LONDON W1X 1AE   Fax 071-287 2161 071-734 5985
Bespoke (custom) tailors, shirtmakers and tiemakers since 1806.
By appointment to HM The Queen.

Food

LYONS CAKES LTD.   FISH DAM LANE, CARLTON, BARNSLEY, SOUTH YORKSHIRE S71 3HQ   Fax 0226 291003 0226 286191
Cake manufacturers.
By appointment to HM The Queen.

PINNEYS OF SCOTLAND   BRYDEKIRK, ANNAN, DUMFRIESSHIRE DG12 5LP   Fax 0576300 466 0576300 401
Purveyors of quality Scottish smoked salmon
By appointment to HM The Queen and HRH the Prince of Wales.

RUSSELL HUME LTD.   SIMS FOOD PARK, SHERBOURNE DRIVE, TILBROOK, MILTON KEYNES MK7 8BQ   Fax 0908 271978 0908 375155
Butchers
By appointment to HM The Queen, HM The Queen Mother, and HRH The Prince of Wales.

R. TWINING & CO. LTD.   SOUTHWAY, ANDOVER, HAMPSHIRE SP10 5AQ   Fax 0264 337177 0264 334477
Tea and coffee suppliers.
By appointment to HM The Queen, HM The Queen Mother, and HRH The Prince of Wales.

Interior Decorators and Furnishers

G.P. & J. BAKER LTD.   P. O. BOX 30, WEST END ROAD, HIGH WYCOMBE, BUCKINGHAMSHIRE HP11 2QD   0494 471155
Producers and distributors of furnishing fabrics and wallcoverings.
By appointment to HM The Queen.

ALBERT E. CHAPMAN   17 CROUCH HILL, LONDON N4 4AP   Fax 071-263 1033 071-272 2536
Upholstery, re-upholstery, specialist curtain makers and soft furnishers.
By appointment to HM The Queen.

COPE & TIMMINS LTD.   ANGEL ROAD WORKS, ANGEL ROAD, EDMONTON, LONDON N18 3AY   Fax 081-884 2322 081-803 6481
Manufacturers and distributors of curtain tracks, poles, and window furnishing and upholstery accessories. Supplier of barrier ropes and standards for the Palace opening.
By appointment to HM The Queen.

KOSSET CARPETS LTD.   TOFTSHAW LANE, BRADFORD, WEST YORKSHIRE BD4 6QU   Fax 0274 685161 0274 681881
Manufacturers of Kosset and Crossley Carpets
By appointment to HM The Queen.

HUGH MACKAY CARPETS   P. O. BOX 1, DURHAM CITY DH1 2RX   Fax 091-384 0530 091-386 4444
Designers and Manufacturers of Axminster, Wilton and Tufted Carpets.
By appointment to HM The Queen.

WILTON ROYAL CARPETS   ROMSEY INDUSTRIAL ESTATE, GREATBRIDGE ROAD, ROMSEY, HANTS SO51 OHR Fax 0794 523376 0794 515011
Manufacturers of woven Wilton, woven Axminster and tufted carpets. Bespoke and stock qualities available.
By appointment to HM The Queen.

Jewellers and Silversmiths

COLLINGWOOD & CO. LTD.   171 NEW BOND STREET, LONDON W1Y 9PB   Fax 071-629 5418 071-734 2656
The oldest royal jewellers
By appointment to HM the Queen, HM The Queen Mother and HRH The Prince of Wales.

MAPPIN & WEBB   170 REGENT STREET, LONDON W1R 6BQ   071-734 3801
Silversmiths
By appointment to Hm The Queen and HRH the Prince of Wales.

Luxury Gifts

H. BRONNLEY & CO. LTD.   BRACKLEY WORKS, BRACKLEY, NORTHANTS NN13 5AU   Fax 0280 703912 0280 702291
Manufacturers of high quality, luxury perfumes and toiletries since 1883.
By appointment to HM The Queen, HM The Queen Mother, and HRH The Prince of Wales.

THOMAS GOODE & CO. LTD.   19 SOUTH AUDLEY STREET, MAYFAIR, LONDON W1Y 6BN   Fax 071-629 4230 071-499 2823
The finest china and glass shop in the world.
By appointment to HM The Queen, HM The Queen Mother and HRH The Prince of Wales.

HALCYON DAYS   14 BROOK STREET, LONDON W1Y 1AA   Fax 071-409 7901 071-629 8811
Suppliers of objets d'art: enamels, antiques, porcelain.
By appointment to HM The Queen, HM The Queen Mother, and HRH The Prince of Wales.

METAMEC CLOCKS   SOUTH GREEN, DEREHAM, NORFOLK NR19 1PP   Fax 0362 693022 0362 692121
The largest UK manufacturer and distributor of high quality clocks.
By appointment to HM The Queen and HM The Queen Mother.

MINTON   MINTON HOUSE, LONDON ROAD, STOKE-ON-TRENT, STAFFORDSHIRE ST4 7QD   Fax: 0782 416962 0782 744766
China manufacturers, Minton Ltd.
By appointment to HM The Queen.

ROYAL ALBERT   MINTON HOUSE, LONDON ROAD, STOKE-ON-TRENT, STAFFORDSHIRE ST4 7QD   Fax: 0782 416962 0782 744766
Manufacturers of Paragon Fine Bone China, Royal Albert Ltd.
By appointment to HM The Queen, and HM The Queen Mother.

ROYAL CROWN DERBY   OSMASTON STREET, DERBY DE3 8JZ   Fax 0332 291162 0332 47051
Manufacturers of Fine Bone China, the Royal Crown Derby Porcelain Company Limited.
By appointment to HM The Queen Mother.

ROYAL DOULTON   MINTON HOUSE, LONDON ROAD, STOKE-ON-TRENT, STAFFORDSHIRE ST4 7QD   Fax: 0782 416962 0782 744766
Manufacturers of Fine Bone China.
By appointment to HM The Queen, and HRH The Prince of Wales.

Restorers, Conservators and Shippers of Art

CARVERS & GILDERS   9 CHARTERHOUSE WORKS, ELTRINGHAM STREET, LONDON SW18 1TD   Fax 081-874 0470 081-870 7047
Designers and restorers of traditional and contemporary woodcarving, giltwood mirrors and furniture. Specialists in the laying of gold leaf.
By appointment to HM The Queen.

MOMART PLC   199-205 RICHMOND ROAD, LONDON E8 3NJ   Fax 081- 533 0122 081-986 3624
Transporter of fine arts.
By appointment to HM The Queen.

Specialist Services

AUTOGLYM   WORKS ROAD, LETCHWORTH, HERTFORDSHIRE SG6 1LU   Fax 0462 677712 0462 677766
Specialised car polishes, shampoos and car valeting equipment.
By appointment to HRH The Prince of Wales.

BENSON & HEDGES LTD.   13 OLD BOND STREET, LONDON W1X 4QP   Fax 071-491 2276 071-493 1825
Tobacconists
By appointment to HM The Queen.

BUTLER (1843) LTD.   COUNTY HOUSE, BAYSHILL ROAD, CHELTENHAM, GLOUCESTERSHIRE GL50 3BA   Fax 0242 234111 0242 222999
Suppliers of fuel oils.
By appointment to HRH The Prince of Wales.

CANNON HYGIENE LTD.   MIDDLEGATE, WHITE LUND, MORECOMBE, LANCASHIRE LA3 3BJ   Fax 0524 64393 0524 60894
Suppliers of Hygiene Services.
By appointment to HM The Queen

CHARRINGTONS   CHARRINGTON HOUSE, BISHOP'S STORTFORD, HERTFORDSHIRE. CM23 2EW   Fax 0279 755244 0279 755111
Supplier of heating oils.
By appointment to HM The Queen

CHARRINGTONS SOLID FUEL   12 STATION ROAD, ST IVES, HUNTINGDON, CAMBRIDGESHIRE PE17 4BH   Fax 0480 464986 0480 464049
Retail distribution of solid fuel and ancillary products.
By appointment to HM The Queen.

ELECTROLUX   101 OAKLEY ROAD, LUTON, BEDFORDSHIRE LU4 9QQ   Fax 0582 588867 0582 491234
Suppliers of suction cleaners and floor polishers.
By appointment to HM The Queen.

JOHN FYFE LTD.   FYFE HOUSE, WESTHILL INDUSTRIAL ESTATE, WESTHILL, SKENE, ABERDEEN, SCOTLAND AB32 6TQ   Fax 0224 744500 0224 74444
Granite, ready mixed concrete, brick, paving, architectural masonry block, coated stone, sand and gravel, road surfacing.
By appointment to HM The Queen.

G.B. KENT & SONS PLC.   LONDON ROAD, ASPLEY, HEMEL HEMPSTEAD, HERTFORDSHIRE. HP3 9SA   Fax 0442 231672 0442 232 623
Personal care and brush, comb manufacturers
By appointment to HM The Queen

OFFICE CLEANING SERVICES LTD.   FREDERICK HOUSE, BREWER STREET, MAIDSTONE, KENT ME14 1RY   0622 671414
Office, window and special cleaning contractors.
By appointment to HM The Queen

PILGRIM PAYNE & CO. LTD.   290-294 LATIMER ROAD, LONDON W10 6QU   Fax 081-964 0598 081-960 5656
Specialist cleaners of curtains, carpets and upholstery
By appointment to HM The Queen

PEDIGREE PETFOODS   NATIONAL OFFICE, WALTHAM-ON-THE-WOLDS MELTON MOWBRAY, LEICS LE14 4RS   Fax 0664 415232 0664 410000
Prepared petfood provided to the Royal Family.
By appointment to HM The Queen.

PITMAN-MOORE LTD.   BREAKSPEAR ROAD SOUTH, HAREFIELD, UXBRIDGE, MIDDLESEX UB9 6LS   Fax 0895 626481 0895 626277
Veterinary pharmaceuticals
By appointment to HM The Queen.

JOHN PLAYER & SONS (IMPERIAL TOBACCO LTD)   PO BOX 61, WEST PDO, NOTTINGHAM NG7 5QQ   Fax 0602 864553 0602 242888
Tobacco Manufacturers
By appointment to HM The Queen Mother

T. ROGERS & CO. (PACKERS) LTD.   P. O. BOX 8, 1A BROUGHTON STREET, LONDON SW8 3QL   Fax 071-627 3318 071-622 9151
Packers and transporters of works of art.
By appointment to HM The Queen.

SKY PHOTOGRAPHIC SERVICES LTD.   RAMILLIES HOUSE, RAMILLIES STREET, LONDON W1V 2EL   Fax 071-434 0828 071-434 2266
Photographic Services.
By appointment to HM the Queen.

SLEEPEEZEE LTD.   61 MORDEN ROAD, MERTON, LONDON SW19 3XP   Fax 081-542 0547 081-540 9171
Makers of top quality beds incorporating "Beautyrest", the worlds best selling pocketed spring system.
By appointment to HM The Queen and HRH The Prince of Wales.

WADDINGTONS PLAYING CARD CO. LTD.   CASTLE GATE, DULTON, LEEDS, WEST YORKSHIRE LS26 8HG   Fax 0532 822958 0532 826195
Suppliers of playing cards.
By appointment to HM The Queen.

Quality in an age of change.

English Classics

Burberrys
OF LONDON

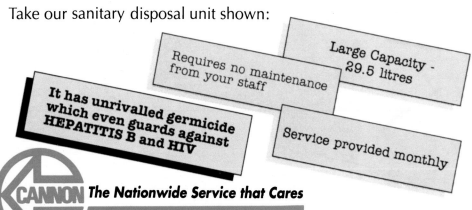

There's only one feature of a Jaguar that hasn't changed in twenty five years.

It was back in 1968 that the press and VIP car section of Jaguar Cars first tried Autoglym.

They were so impressed with the ease of use and outstanding effect, Autoglym was immediately chosen for all their specially prepared cars, which now includes the latest edition of the world acclaimed XJS range.

Naturally, over the years Autoglym products have not stood still. Today, other manufacturers and thousands of specialist finishers around the world, follow Jaguar's shining example.

You'll find a complete range of Autoglym car care products at all discerning car accessory shops.

So even if your car hasn't quite the same graceful curves as a Jaguar, it can still have the same perfect shine.

BY APPOINTMENT TO
H.M. QUEEN ELIZABETH THE QUEEN MOTHER
SUPPLIER OF CAR CARE PRODUCTS
AUTOGLYM, LETCHWORTH, ENGLAND

BY APPOINTMENT TO
H.R.H. THE PRINCE OF WALES
SUPPLIER OF CAR CARE PRODUCTS
AUTOGLYM, LETCHWORTH, ENGLAND

The Shine.

THE ONLY 5 STAR RATING
AWARDED BY AUTO EXPRESS
IN RECENT TEST.

AUTO GLYM

AUTOGLYM, WORKS ROAD, LETCHWORTH, HERTS SG6 1LU. TEL: 0462 677766 FAX: 0462 677712

BY APPOINTMENT TO HM QUEEN ELIZABETH II
SUPPLIERS OF WALLPAPERS PAINTS & FABRICS
ARTHUR SANDERSON AND SONS LTD LONDON

Sanderson

LONDON · PARIS · NEW YORK

Glade from the Sanderson Archives
Telephone: 071 636 7800

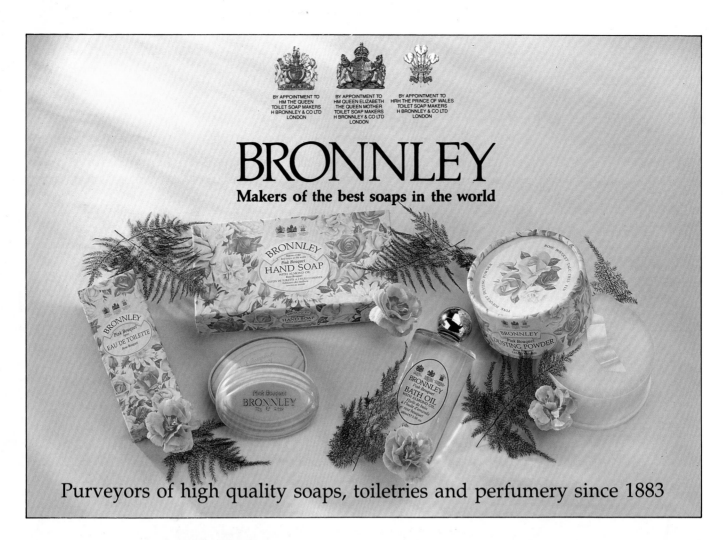